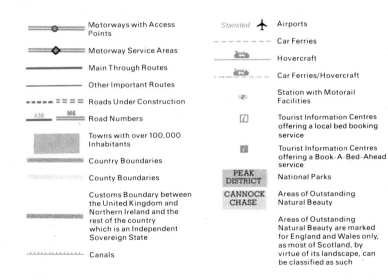

| | | |
|---|---|---|
| Motorways with Access Points | *Stansted* ✈ | Airports |
| Motorway Service Areas | | Car Ferries |
| Main Through Routes | | Hovercraft |
| Other Important Routes | | Car Ferries/Hovercraft |
| Roads Under Construction | ⇌ | Station with Motorail Facilities |
| A38 M6 Road Numbers | 𝑖 | Tourist Information Centres offering a local bed booking service |
| Towns with over 100,000 Inhabitants | 𝒊 | Tourist Information Centres offering a Book-A-Bed-Ahead service |
| Country Boundaries | | |
| County Boundaries | PEAK DISTRICT | National Parks |
| Customs Boundary between the United Kingdom and Northern Ireland and the rest of the country which is an Independent Sovereign State | CANNOCK CHASE | Areas of Outstanding Natural Beauty |
| | | Areas of Outstanding Natural Beauty are marked for England and Wales only, as most of Scotland, by virtue of its landscape, can be classified as such |
| Canals | | |

**Scale      1:1,175,000**

0   5   10        20        30        40        50   Statute Miles

0  5  10    20    30    40    50    60    70    80   Kilometres

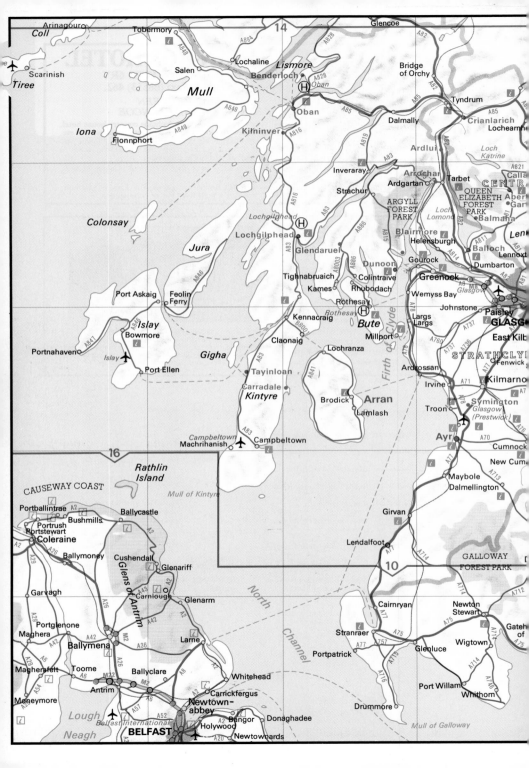

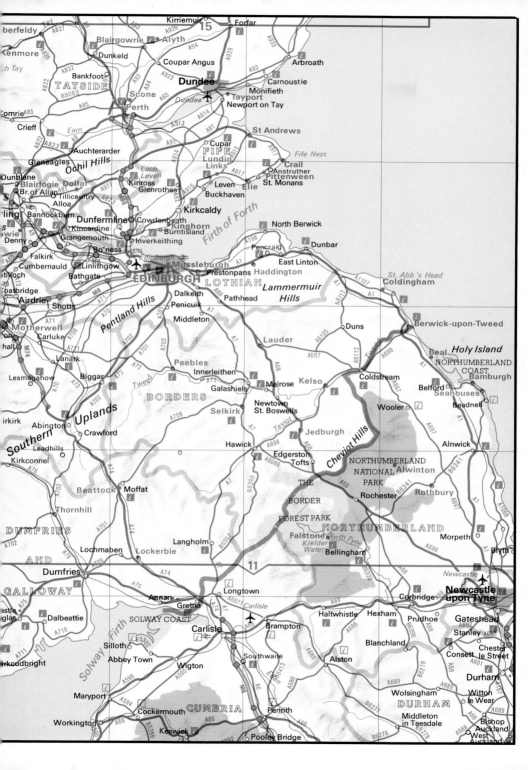

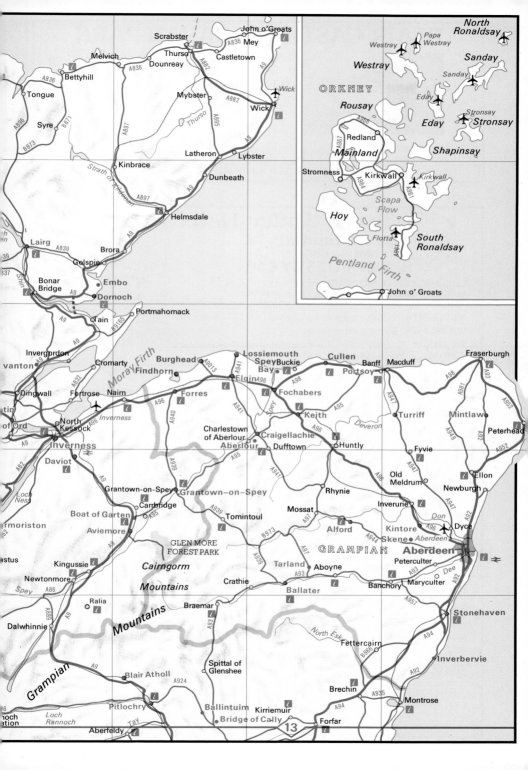

## STAY WHERE YOU SEE THE SIGN OF A REAL SCOTTISH WELCOME

**We've made sure there's a comfortable welcome waiting at hundreds of places to stay in Scotland.**

Now there's no need to puzzle over which hotel, guest house, B & B or self-catering accommodation best suits you.

We've introduced a new easy to understand classification and grading scheme so you can find at a glance *exactly* what you're looking for.

### WHAT DOES CLASSIFICATION MEAN?

The *classifications*, from 'Listed' to five crowns, are awarded according to the *range* of facilities available. In hotels, guest houses and B & Bs, a 'Listed' classification guarantees, for example, that your bed conforms to a minimum size, that hot and cold water is available at all reasonable times, that breakfast is provided and that there is adequate heating according to the season.

In self-catering accommodation, one crown means that you have a minimum size of unit, at least one twin or double bedroom, dining and cooking facilities suitable for the number of occupants, and a refridgerator.

Naturally, more crowns mean more facilities. A five crown establishment will provide many extras for your holiday comfort. To name just two, in five crown hotels *all* rooms have 'en suite' bathrooms, and five crown self-catering units provide the labour-saving fittings of home, including a dishwasher.

**All classifications have been checked by our fully-trained team of independent officers.**

# CLASSIFICATION AND GRADING OF ACCOMMODATION IN SCOTLAND

## WHAT ABOUT GRADING?

While classification is all about facilities, *grading* is solely concerned with their *quality*. The grades awarded — 'Approved', 'Commended' or 'Highly Commended' — are based upon an independent assessment of a wide variety of items, ranging from the appearance of the buildings and tidiness of the gardens, to the quality of the furnishings, fittings and floor coverings. Cleanliness is an absolute requirement — and, of course, our officers know the value of a warm and welcoming smile.

**Like classification, grading is carried out by the Scottish Tourist Board's expert team.**

You can find excellent quality in all kinds of places to stay in Scotland, irrespective of the range of facilities offered: for example, a 'Listed' B & B, with the minimum of facilities, but offering excellent quality, would be awarded a 'Highly Commended' grade while a five crown self-catering property would be graded as 'Approved' if the quality of its extensive facilities was assessed as average.

## SO HOW DOES THE NEW SCHEME HELP YOU PLAN YOUR HOLIDAY?

Quite simply, it offers a guarantee of both the range of facilities and their quality. Many of the establishments listed in this brochure have been inspected and this is highlighted in their entries. When you choose accommodation that has been classified, or classified and graded, you have the reassurance that what is being offered has been independently checked.

Equally, if you're on a touring holiday, and booking accommodation as you go, the new scheme can help you. All places to stay which have been inspected bear a distinctive blue oval sign by their entrance showing the classification and grade awarded. And if you call in at a Tourist Information Centre you can ask for a list of local establishments that have joined the scheme, which will include those which are shown in this brochure as *awaiting inspection* at time of going to press.

Whatever kind of accommodation you're looking for, you can be sure the new classification and grading scheme will help you find it.

Please note that where self-catering establishments offer a number of units of differing classifications and grades, their entry in this brochure is shown as 'Up to' the highest award held. You should ascertain the specific classification and grade of an individual unit at time of booking.

Please also note that establishments are visited annually and therefore classifications and grades may therefore change from year to year.

# CONTENTS

COLOUR MAPS ....................................................................... 2

Index to Place Names.................................................................. 10

Introduction by Jackie Stewart....................................................... 13

Touring Scotland by Elliot Mitchell................................................. 14

PLACES TO STAY etc. ............................................................... 67

Area Tourist Boards & Tourist Information Centres ............................. 99

Places of Interest...................................................................... 106

Pastime Publications Ltd gratefully acknowledge the assistance of The Scottish Tourist Board, Area Tourist Boards, Historic Buildings and Monuments, Jim Farley and others in compiling this guide.

Published by Pastime Publications Limited, 15 Dublin Street Lane South, Edinburgh EH1 3PX. Telephone: 031-556 1105/0057.

**First published by The Scottish Tourist Board 1970**

Typesetting by Newtext Composition Ltd.
Printed & Bound in the U.K.

**Worldwide distribution by
The British Tourist Authority**

# INDEX

**GENERAL** .................67

**ABERDEENSHIRE**
Aberdeen.......................67
Ballater .........................68
Balmedie ......................69
Insch ............................69

**ANGUS**
Dundee..........................70
Edzell ...........................70

**ARGYLLSHIRE**
Cairndow.......................70
Campbeltown ...............71
Glencoe ........................71
Oban.............................71
Strontian ......................72
Tarbert..........................73

**AYRSHIRE**
Kilmarnock....................73

**BERWICKSHIRE**
Duns .............................74
Lauder ..........................74

**CAITHNESS**
John o' Groats...............74
Wick..............................74

**DUMFRIESSHIRE**
Gretna...........................75

**DUNBARTONSHIRE**
Loch Lomond................75
Rhu ...............................75

**FIFE**
Kirkcaldy.......................76

**INVERNESS-SHIRE**
Aviemore.......................76
Boat of Garten .............76

Fort William .................76
Kingussie......................77
Newtonmore.................77
Onich ...........................77

**KINROSS-SHIRE**
Kinross .........................78

**KIRKCUDBRIGHTSHIRE**
Dalbeattie.....................78

**LANARKSHIRE**
Airdrie...........................79
Bothwell .......................79
Glasgow .......................79
Hamilton.......................80

**LOTHIAN**
Edinburgh ....................80
South Queensferry........81

**MORAYSHIRE**
Elgin.............................82
Fochabers.....................82
Forres ...........................83
Grantown-on-Spey........83

**PEEBLESSHIRE**
Peebles.........................83

**PERTHSHIRE**
Aberfeldy......................84
Auchterarder.................84
Blairgowrie....................84
Bruar.............................84
Callander.......................85
Crieff ............................85
Perth ............................86
Stanley .........................88

**RENFREWSHIRE**
Paisley ..........................89

**ROSS-SHIRE**
Achnasheen ........................89
Gairloch ............................89
Kyle of Lochalsh ...............90
Strathconon ......................90
Strathpeffer ......................90
Ullapool ............................90

**ROXBURGHSHIRE**
Jedburgh ...........................91
Melrose .............................91

**SELKIRKSHIRE**
Selkirk ...............................92

**STIRLINGSHIRE**
Killearn .............................92

Stirling ...............................92

**SUTHERLAND**
Kylesku ..............................93
Lairg ..................................93
Tongue ...............................93

**WIGTOWNSHIRE**
Newton Stewart ..................94

**SCOTTISH ISLANDS**
Isle of Arran ......................94
Isle of Gigha ......................95
Isle of Islay .......................95
Isle of Lewis ......................96
Isle of Mull .......................96
Isle of Skye .......................96

*ALSO SEE COLOUR ADVERTS*

# There are excellent grounds for a holiday in the Highlands and Islands.

Warmed by the gentle Gulf Stream, the Highlands and Islands of Scotland are a horticultural heaven.

At Inverewe Gardens, for example, sub-tropical plants and flowers thrive on a latitude farther north than Moscow. You'll discover equally spectacular botanical treasures throughout this beautiful area.

Of course, Highland hospitality provides even more grounds for coming here. And how do you do that? It's surprisingly easy with our excellent road network.

For holiday bookings and details on hotels, inns, guest houses and self-catering, telephone Hi-Line on 0349 63434.

*The Scottish Highlands and Islands*

# THE MARINE MOTORWAY CAR FERRY SERVICES TO THE CLYDE AND THE WESTERN ISLES

### *Year Round Services*

Gourock-Dunoon
Wemyss Bay-Rothesay (Bute)
Colintraive-Rhubodach (Bute)
Largs-Cumbrae Slip (for Millport)
Ardrossan-Brodick (Arran)
Tayinloan (Kintyre)-Gigha
Kennacraig (Kintyre)-Port Ellen/Port Askaig (Islay)
Oban-Lismore · Craignure (Mull) · Colonsay · Coll · Tiree
Castlebay (Barra) · Lochboisdale (South Uist)
Lochaline-Fishnish (Mull)
Mallaig-Armadale (Skye)*
Kyle of Lochalsh-Kyleakin (Skye)
Sconser (Skye)-Raasay
Uig (Skye)-Tarbert (Harris)-Lochmaddy (North Uist)
Kyles Scalpay (Harris)-Scalpay
Ullapool-Stornoway (Lewis)

*Passenger only service October-Easter.

### *Seasonal Services*

Claonaig (Kintyre)-Lochranza (Arran)
Kennacraig (Kintyre)-Port Askaig (Islay)-Colonsay-Oban
Mallaig-Castlebay (Barra)

### *Package Offers*

**Hebridean Driveaway** — Package Island touring holidays for motorists including ferry travel, accommodation and certain meals.

**Island Hopscotch** — A choice of attractive fares for cars and accompanying passengers on a selection (there are 23 to choose from!) of pre-planned routes on Island Hopping Holidays.

**Island Rover** — Runabout tickets, with or without car, valid for 8 to 15 days unlimited travel on most Clyde and Western Isles ferries.

Our free colour brochure gives all the details of times and fares.

**Contact:-**

# Caledonian MacBrayne
### *Hebridean and Clyde Ferries*
The Ferry Terminal, GOUROCK PA19 1QP.
Tel: (0475) 33755. Fax: (0475) 37607.
or any Tourist Information Centre

# INTRODUCTION

## By JACKIE STEWART O.B.E.

The charm of Scotland's roads, for me, has always been the variety of minor roads and byways. It seems a shame to drive from A to B by the fast route when I know there is so much to enjoy on the minor roads to either side!

On most of Scotland's roads, speed is a positive disadvantage as it distracts you from the splendour of the scenery. Even with years of experience of driving around Scotland, I always find something new and glorious about the countryside - and I don't just mean new parks and buildings.

The light and the seasons change the look of the land almost beyond belief, so that what might appear a bleak windswept moor one minute can be a magnificent swathe of muted greens and browns 10 minutes later.

Even in the central belt of Scotland, where so many people live and work, there are lots of excellent alternatives to the motorways, and often just a short distance will take you away from almost all signs of civilisation.

The real wonder of all this beauty, however, is the accessibility of remote places by roads that are kept in good repair and are often devoid of other traffic. Compared to many other countries, Scotland's roads are well cared for by the local authorities, even in the remote areas.

When I passed my driving test, at the age of 17, I drove my heart out all over Scotland. It was wonderful, a voyage of discovery that instilled in me a pride in my own country that I hold to this day.

I hope you, too, will discover the magic of Scotland by car.

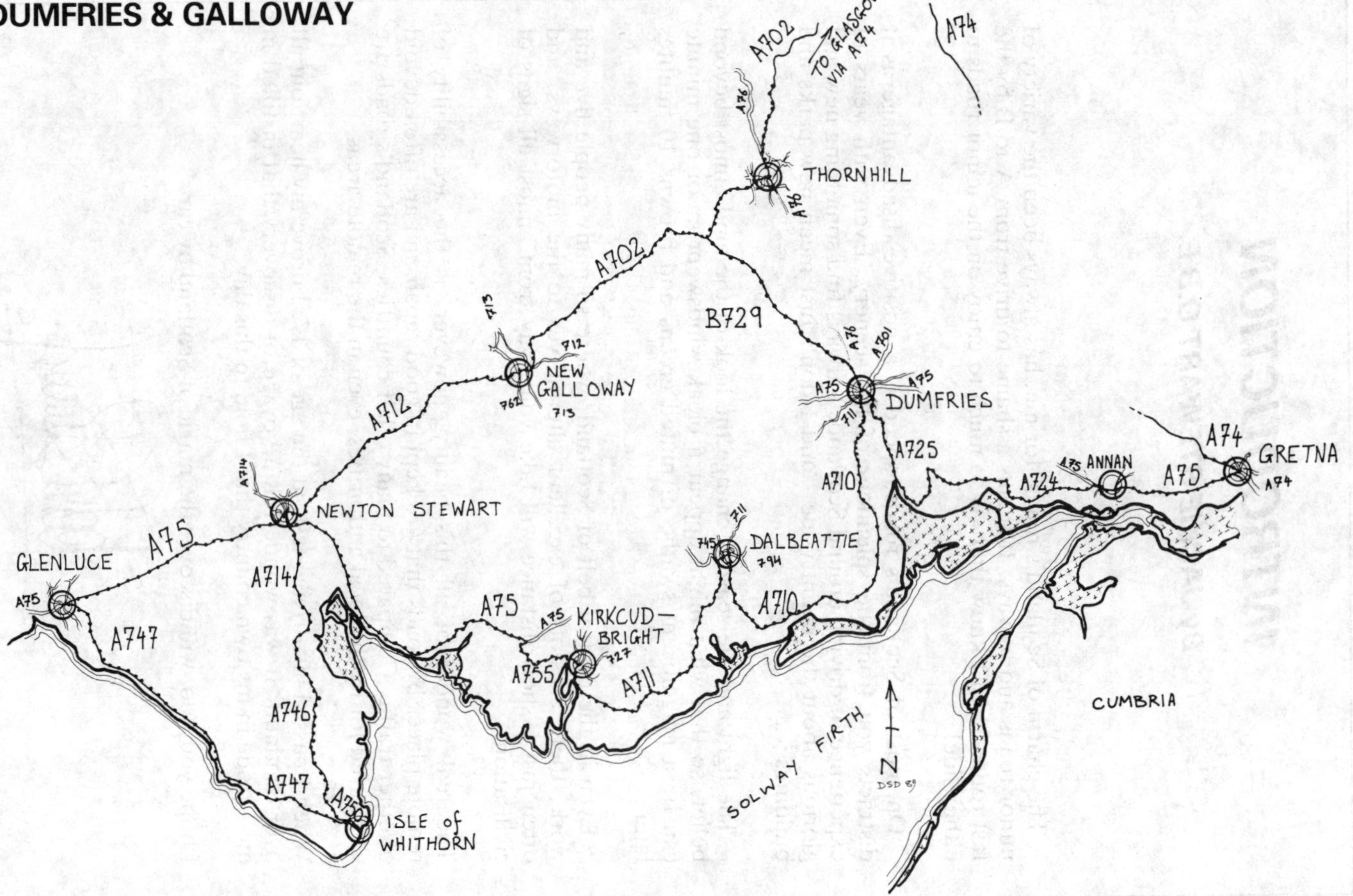

# DUMFRIES & GALLOWAY

GRETNA

A74

A74

A75

ANNAN

A75

A724

A74

CUMBRIA

A701

A75

DUMFRIES

A725

A76

A710

DALBEATTIE

A710

Solway Firth

N

TO GLASGOW VIA A74

THORNHILL

A702

A76

B729

A702

NEW GALLOWAY

KIRKCUD—BRIGHT

A711

A755

NEWTON STEWART

A75

A712

A714

A746

A747

ISLE of WHITHORN

A75

GLENLUCE

A747

# DUMFRIES AND GALLOWAY

The south west of Scotland takes a pride in being one of Scotland's most beautiful rural areas, yet all too often it is missed by tourists.

Visitors arriving in Scotland often whizz past Dumfries and Galloway on the A74 on their way to Glasgow, not realising the landscape they are missing: high hills, forests, remote moors, lochs and varied coastline.

The scenery is superb, and if you catch the area at the right season it is a riot of colour as the many gardens take advantage of the climate – that's a polite way of saying it rains a lot, but there is plenty of sunshine too.

As much as you can, keep off the main A75 Dumfries to Stranraer Euro-route with its heavy lorries, and you will often have the road to yourselves. This is old-fashioned touring country, a place to enjoy Scotland in a car.

## TOUR OF DUMFRIES AND GALLOWAY

As you enter Scotland from the south, shortly after the M6 motorway becomes the A74 dual carriageway, turn off into Gretna Green, a small village that has achieved worldwide fame for the lovers who come here to marry.

Taking advantage of Scottish law, eloping English couples could at one time marry in Scotland by a declaration before witnesses, and Gretna Green was the first place they came to across the border. Although the law changed in 1940 to end this privilege, elopers can still take advantage of Scottish law permitting marriage without parental consent from the age of 16.

The old blacksmith's shop, where couples used to marry over an anvil, is now a visitor centre, but if marriage is on your mind you can still go ahead at the Registry Office. It does a roaring trade throughout the year.

Gretna Green is the starting point of this tour, and after you leave the village you take the A75 towards Dumfries, 25 miles away.

However, rather than stay on the A75, look for the signs to the left for the start of the Solway Coast Heritage Trail just after the new Annan bypass. Much of this tour will be based on the Heritage Trail, which is signposted throughout, and you can ask for a free leaflet at any Tourist Information Centre. On occasion, however, this tour takes a different route, as the Heritage Trail sometimes tries a little bit too hard.

An early example of that is to be had by driving the extra half mile into the village of Clarencefield to see Comlongon Castle, an exceptionally well preserved 15th century castle, where, as it is attached to a hotel, you can even stay for the night!

Back on to the Heritage Trail, and a few miles further on you really should stop at Caerlaverock Castle. This unusual triangular castle comes complete with water-filled moat and drawbridge, one of the most beautiful in Scotland. Its attraction is increased by being at the entrance to Caerlaverock National Nature Reserve, over 13,000 acres of marsh and tidal areas; the birds sing from their haunts on the castle walls.

Continuing on the B725 to Dumfries, as you enter the town at the first set of traffic lights you will see on the right the Burns Mausoleum and, ahead of you, Burns House. The town centre has plenty to do and you can park in the substantial free car parks by the River Nith (although these are often full).

Dumfries is a busy town, rather too busy for motoring pleasure, so you would be better to park your car and discover it on foot. The town has a good selection of museums and historic houses, and a fine place to soak up the atmosphere with a drink and a meal is The Globe Inn, the pub where Robert Burns was a regular two hundred years ago. One unusual museum in town is at Crichton Royal Infirmary, devoted to medical history.

Leave Dumfries by the A710 to the south, still following the Heritage Trail signs, and make a first stop in New Abbey, seven miles down the road. As you enter the village, on the right is the car park for Shambellie House Museum of Costume. Then in the middle of New Abbey you should visit the beautiful ruins of Sweetheart Abbey, built in 1273 by Devorgilla Balliol (who endowed Balliol College in Oxford). It is also worth seeing New Abbey Corn Mill, a working mill.

American visitors will be sure to want to visit Arbigland, five miles further along, signposted to the left at Kirkbean. John Paul Jones' father was gardener here and Jones himself was born in a cottage nearby.

After passing through Dalbeattie, the A710 road becomes the A711, and passing attractions are Orchardton Tower (one mile down a single track road), a 15th century circular tower house whose battlements you can climb, and the North Glen Gallery at Palnackie where you can see glass blowing and sculpture in the making.

From the road you will have some excellent views to the south across the Solway Firth, with the Cumbria coast visible.

At Dundrennan there are the ruins of a 12th century abbey, then in Kirkcudbright (pronounced Kir-cood-bri) there is a wealth of historical interest, ranging from MacLellan's Castle to the Stewartry Museum with its John Paul Jones display. Park (free) in the town centre next to the Tourist Information Centre, where you may be surprised to see fishing boats moored at the quay. The sea is never far away.

Rejoin the A75 main road to the west and head for Newton Stewart, on the way perhaps stopping for the imposing Cardoness Castle on the right and Carsluith Castle to the left.

For something different visit the Creetown Gem Rock Museum, one of the world's most comprehensive gem and mineral collections.

Eventually you come to Newton Stewart and its attractive twin village of Minnigaff across the Cree River. This is the turning point of this tour.

## DETOUR

Newton Stewart is the turning point of this tour, but if you still have a thirst for more of the beautiful Galloway coastline, turn south (still on the Solway Heritage Trail) and head for Isle of Whithorn to visit sites associated with St. Ninian, who brought Christianity to Scotland in the 4th century. This peninsula is many people's favourite part of Scotland, with beautiful unspoilt scenery in a peaceful atmosphere. Further attractions include Whithorn Priory and several prehistoric sites.

From Newton Stewart, head inland to the east along the A712 to New Galloway for a complete change of scene. This is the Queen's Way, heading through Kirroughtree Forest, where it is often hard to imagine that the sea is just a short drive away.

The landscape here is constantly changing as the Forestry Commission harvest their crop of trees and plant new seedlings. They have also catered extensively for passing motorists and there is a steady succession of picnic sites and places to start walks into the hills.

The road is great fun to drive along, as you are unlikely to encounter any commercial traffic. Almost the only people using it will be tourists like yourselves.

A good place to stop and find out more on the environment is the Galloway Deer Museum, beside the main road at the wonderfully named Clatteringshaws Loch.

New Galloway is a picturesque town at the crossroads of the main routes through central Galloway.

Continue to the north east by following the signs for Crocketford, turn left off the A712 on to the A769 at Balmaclellan, then right onto the A702 for Moniaive.

Moniaive is charming, an old world town with cottages lining the main street and no pavements. Turn right two miles after Moniaive onto the B729 for the long gentle descent into Dumfries.

One prominent stopping place just after this turning is Maxwelton House, dating back to the 14th and 15th centuries, when it was a stronghold of the Earls of Glencairn. Later it was the birthplace of Annie Laurie, who was immortalised in song; you can see her boudoir in the house.

As you approach Dumfries, one final attraction is the 15th century collegiate church in Lincluden, signposted to the left shortly after the B729 joins the busy A76. Then you come into the town itself, and your tour of Galloway is at an end.

## DUMFRIES AND GALLOWAY ATTRACTIONS

Arbigland. Signposted, one mile from Kirkbean off A710, 12 miles south of Dumfries. Gardens open May-September, Tuesday, Thursday and Sunday, 1400-1800. House open occasionally in afternoons (check in advance). Admission: Adult £1.50, child 75p. Tel: Kirkbean (038788) 213.

Burns House. In Burns Street, Dumfries. Open all year, Monday to Saturday 1000-1300 and 1400-1700, Sunday 1400-1700. (Closed Sunday and Monday from October-March). Admission: Adult 50p, child 25p.

Burns Mausoleum. In St. Michael's Churchyard, Dumfries. Open all reasonable times, free admission.

Caerlaverock Castle, Signposted off B725, ten miles west of Annan. Opel April-September, Monday to Saturday 0930-1900 and Sunday 1400-1900; October-March, Monday to Saturday 0930-1600 and Sunday 1400-1600. Admission: Adult 60p, child 30p.

Caerlaverock National Nature Reserve. Entrance at Caerlaverock Castle, off B725. Open all year, free admission.

Cardoness Castle. Beside A75, one mile south west of Gatehouse-of-Fleet. Open April-September, Monday to Saturday 0930-1900 and Sunday 1400-1930; October-March, Monday to Saturday 0930-1600 and Sunday 1400-1600. Admission: Adult 60p, child 30p.

Carsluith Castle. On A75, seven miles west of Gatehouse-of-Fleet. Open April-September, Monday to Saturday 0930-1900, Sunday 1400-1900; October-March, Monday to Saturday 0930-1600, Sunday 1400-1600. No admission charge.

Comlongon Castle. In Clarencefield village, signposted at end of tree-lined drive, on B724, six miles west of Annan. Open March-November, daily 1030-1800. Admission: Adult £1.00, child 50p. Tel: Clarencefield (038787) 283.

Creetown Gem Rock Museum. In Creetown by A75, turn up street opposite clock tower and follow signs. Open daily all year, 0930-1900 (winter closing at 1700). Admission: Adult £1.00, child 50p. Tel: Creetown (067182) 357.

Crichton Royal Infirmary Museum. In Easterbrook Hall, Bankhead Road, Dumfries. Open all year, Thursday to Saturday 1330-1630. Admission free.

Dumfries Museum. In the Observatory, Dumfries. Open April-September, Monday to Saturday 1000-1300 and 1400-1700, Sunday 1400-1700; October-March, Tuesday to Saturday 1000-1300 and 1400-1700. No admission charge (Camera obscura admission: Adult 50p, child 25p).

Dundrennan Abbey. On A711, twelve miles south west of Dalbeattie. Open April-September, Monday to Saturday 0930-1900 and Sunday 1400-1900; October-March, Monday to Saturday 0930-1600 and Sunday 1400-1600. Admission: Adult 60p, child 30p.

Galloway Deer Museum. At Clatteringshaws, on A712, six miles west of New Galloway. Open Easter-mid October, daily 1000-1700. Admission free.

Globe Inn. Off High Street, Dumfries. Open all year during normal licensing hours. No admission charge. Tel: Dumfries (0387) 52335.

Gretna Green Old Blacksmith's Shop. In Gretna Green, just off A74. Open daily all year. Admission to museum: 30p.

Kirroughtree Forest. Off A712 between Newton Stewart and New Galloway. Accessible at all times, with plenty of stopping places.

Lincluden Collegiate Church. Signposted off A76, one mile north of Dumfries centre. Open April-September, Monday to Wednesday and Saturday 0930-1900, Thursday 0930-1400, Sunday 1400-1900; October-March, Monday to Wednesday and Saturday

0930-1600, Thursday 0930-1400, Sunday 1400-1600. Admission: Adult 60p, child 30p.

Maxwelton House. On B729, two miles east of Moniaive. Chapel open April-September, daily 1000-1700. Garden open April-September, Monday to Thursday 1400-1700. House and Museum open July and August, Monday to Thursday 1400-1700. Various admission charges. Tel: Moniaive (08482) 385.

MacLellan's Castle. Off High Street, Kirkcudbright. Open April-September, Monday to Saturday 0930-1900, Sunday 1400-1900; October-March, Saturday 0930-1600, Sunday 1400-1600. Admission: Adult 60p, child 30p.

New Abbey Corn Mill. In New Abbey, six miles south of Dumfries on A710. Open April-September, Monday, Tuesday, Friday, Saturday 0930-1900, Thursday 0930-1400, Sunday 1400-1900; October-March, Monday, Tuesday, Friday, Saturday 0930-1600, Thursday 0930-1400, Sunday 1400-1600. Admission: Adult 60p, child 30p.

North Glen Gallery. In Palnackie, three miles south west of Dalbeattie on A711. Open daily 1000-1800 (but best to phone first). Admission: Adult 40p, child 10p. Tel: Palnackie (055660) 200.

Old Bridge House. Old Mill Road, Dumfries (by Devorgilla's Bridge). Open April-September, Monday to Saturday 1000-1300 and 1400-1700, Sunday 1400-1700. Admission free.

Orchardton Tower. Just off A711 down narrow road, three miles south of

*Caerlaverock Castle*

Dalbeattie. Open April-September, Monday to Saturday 0930-1900, Sunday 1400-1900; October-March, Monday to Saturday 0930-1600, Sunday 1400-1600. Admission free, ask for custodian at nearby cottage if door not open.

Saint Ninian's Chapel. At Isle of Whithorn, at the end of the A750. Accessible at all times, no admission charge.

Shambellie House Museum of Costume. In New Abbey, six miles south of Dumfries on A710. Open May-September, Monday, Thursday, Friday and Saturday 1000-1730, Sunday 1200-1730. Admission free. Tel: New Abbey (038785) 375.

Stewartry Museum. In St. Mary Street, Kirkcudbright. Open Easter-October, Monday to Saturday 1100-1600 (July and August, open 1100-1700). Admission: Adult 75p, child 25p.

Sweetheart Abbey. In New Abbey, six miles south of Dumfries on A710. Open April-September, Monday to Saturday 0930-1900, Sunday 1400-1900; October-March, Monday to Saturday 0930-1600, Sunday 1400-1600. Admission: Adult 60p, child 30p.

Whithorn Priory and Museum. In Main Street, Whithorn, on A746. Open April-September, Monday to Saturday 0930-1900, Sunday 1400-1900; October-March, Saturday 0930-1600, Sunday 1400-1600. Admission: Adult 60p, child 30p.

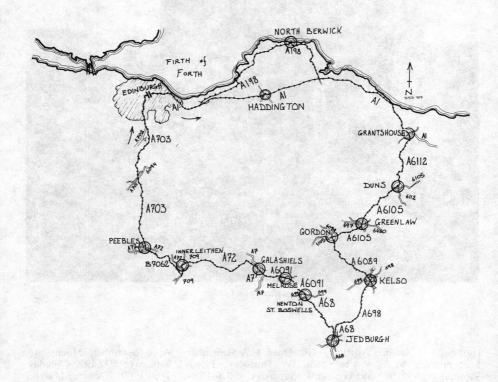

# THE SOUTH

# BORDER COUNTRY

To many people, the Borders combine all that is best of Scotland. The hills are accessible, there are busy towns and picturesque villages, the greenery is lush and mellow, there are castles and stately homes galore, and best of all the roads are excellent.

To complete this whole tour you would need to spend considerably more than one day, as there is so much variety, something to discover on and off every road. But if time is short, by following the recommended route you will at least be able to pick and choose and at any time be within an hour's drive of Edinburgh.

Accommodation is excellent and plentiful, while you will be glad to hear that Borders Regional Council have invested heavily in resurfacing many of the roads in the past few years.

For the convenience of seeing the Borders in a round tour, this route assumes you are based in Edinburgh, at least to start with. It can, of course, be picked up at any point if you are entering Scotland from the south.

If coming from the west, take the A7 from just north of Carlisle and head for Hawick and Selkirk. From the east coast, turn off the A1 at Grantshouse, 16 miles north of Berwick; and if coming from the east by the overland route, join the tour on the A68 at Jedburgh or the A697 at Greenlaw, 10 miles north of Coldstream.

The Borders have always been the buffer area between Scotland and England. Although you can drive between the two countries

today and hardly notice the change, there are plenty of ruins and relics to remind you of its turbulent past.

There are great ruined abbeys in Jedburgh, Kelso, Melrose, Dryburgh, all dating from the 12th century and built on an awesome scale for such an early age.

To guard the local people (albeit not always successfully) there are castles and fortified homes, although you will find a greater concentration of castles along the East Lothian coast in our suggested detour. And to show how far back defence was necessary, take a look at Edinshall Fort, built in the Iron Age.

The stately homes include Abbotsford, Floors Castle, Manderston, Mellerstain and Traquair, sumptuous mansions which recall days of splendour. Although still inhabited by the owners, all are open to the public and you can also tour the grounds.

There are plentiful gardens; museums in almost every town; local festivals called Common Ridings that recall the turbulent days; culinary delicacies like Selkirk bannocks that can be discovered in the many tearooms; golf; fishing and walking in abundance.

All of which are set among hills and rivers that comprise some of Scotland's finest scenery. Welcome to the Borders!

## TOUR OF THE BORDERS

Leave Edinburgh by the A1, the main road to the east. This road has been substantially upgraded in recent years and is dual carriageway for about the first ten miles out of the city. The trip to Grantshouse,

your point of entry to the Borders, is about 40 miles and should not take much more than an hour if you do not stop.

However, by not stopping you would miss out on Haddington, the East Lothian county town that has retained an old world feel by virtue of a well-preserved medieval street plan. Turn right off the A1 into the town, where you can park free in the centre.

Almost 300 of its buildings are designated as being of special architectural or historic interest, and the best way to discover them is to follow the town trail; leaflets from the Information Centre or just follow the blue signs. One mile to the south of Haddington on the B6369 is Lennoxlove, historic home of the Duke and Duchess of Hamilton.

To leave Haddington, rather than going back to the A1, continue through the town and follow the signs for Stevenson House and Hailes Castle. Stevenson House is a 16th century house with 18th century reconstruction and decoration, and an attractive garden.

Hailes Castle has a secluded site, one mile down a narrow road six miles from Haddington, with extensive ruins dating from the 13th century. Nearby you can climb Traprain Law, an Iron Age fortified site 734 feet high.

The winding minor road past Hailes Castle carries on to rejoin the A1 at East Linton. Cross straight over into the village and follow the signs to visit Preston Mill, a picturesque water mill that still works, attended by Muscovy ducks in the millpond. Then it's back on to the A1 to the east.

## DETOUR: EAST LOTHIAN

As an alternative to Haddington, you may prefer to discover the attractive coastal towns of East Lothian. Turn left at the roundabout at the end of the dual carriageway as you leave Edinburgh, and take the A198 to North Berwick.

The road passes through Aberlady, Gullane and Dirleton, fine villages where you can enjoy golf on some of Scotland's finest links courses, stroll the foreshore where generations of Edinburgh schoolchildren have gone to learn about marine life, and tuck into some of the biggest portions of fish and chips you are likely to discover anywhere. And if you are interested in cars, visit the Myreton Motor Museum, off the A198 to the right.

Just beyond North Berwick are the extensive ruins of Tantallon Castle, a spectacular clifftop stronghold dating from the 14th century. And a mile off the shore is the Bass Rock, a geological fault that sticks 350 feet out of the sea, home to thousands of birds; you can take boat trips round the rock from North Berwick.

Complete your detour through East Lothian, still on the A198, by visiting the gardens at Tyninghame House, home of the Earl of Haddington, shortly before the road rejoins the A1.

The A1 speeds past a symbol of the modern age, the huge newly-commissioned nuclear power station at Torness, just east of Dunbar, and soon you arrive in Grantshouse, a small village where you take the turning right into the Borders, signposted to Preston and Duns along the A6112.

You will instantly notice the change in scenery as you climb away from the coast into the Border foothills.

Signposted on a hill to your right after about five miles are the remains of Edinshall Fort; an Iron Age broch that continued to be occupied until Roman times; it can be reached by driving down a rough track in a picturesque valley. Just beyond it, along a minor road off the B6355, is Abbey St. Bathans, a village where you will find a Trout Farm complete with visitor centre, pottery workshop — and fresh trout for sale!

Shortly afterwards you come into the small quiet town of Duns, birthplace of two men from different eras who went on to wider fame. John Duns Scotus, a 13th century monk who became one of the greatest medieval scholars, is commemorated by a statue in the town park; while in Newton Street there is a memorial room dedicated to contemporary hero Jim Clark, twice world motor racing champion who died in 1967. There is a nature reserve at Duns Castle.

Two miles to the east on the A6105 is Manderston, one of Scotland's finest Edwardian country houses, although opening hours are rather limited.

Continuing west from Duns on the A6105, travel through Greenlaw (following signs for Earlston) to Gordon village and turn left there onto the A6089, signposted for Kelso. Before you reach Kelso, just ten miles distant, there are two magnificent properties well worth visiting.

First, Mellerstain House, signposted to the right two miles from Gordon, is one of Scotland's most attractive mansions, built between 1725 and 1778 and containing sumptuous interior decoration and plasterwork.

Then, just as you enter Kelso, is Floors Castle, another 18th century mansion which may look familiar as it was a setting in the film 'Greystoke'. Its history goes back many years, as a holly tree in the grounds marks the spot where James II of Scotland was killed in 1460 by a bursting cannon while he laid siege to Roxburgh Castle.

Kelso itself is a busy market town with a long history, and in recent times has a fine record of winning Britain in Bloom prizes. It has retained its cobbled streets and is well preserved; a good place to stop, and parking in the town centre is free. Kelso Abbey, in the town centre, is the first of the four Border abbeys you will encounter on this tour, founded in 1128.

Take the A698 south from Kelso, and when it joins the A68, turn left for the two mile journey to Jedburgh, the next stop. Here, turn right at the far end of town to see the substantial ruins of Jedburgh Abbey, still standing after almost nine centuries. And although the abbey does somewhat dominate the town, there is plenty more to discover if you walk the Jedburgh Town Trail (leaflets from the Information Centre), including the Castle Jail and Mary Queen of Scots House.

Head back to the north up the busy A68 and turn right at St. Boswells for the short trip to the tour's third (and most beautiful) abbey, Dryburgh Abbey, where Sir Walter Scott is buried. On the way you will see the signs to Scott's View, on a clear day an excellent vantage point to admire the Borders.

*Manderston*

Make your way back to the A68 by the same road and take the A6091 to the left at Newtown St. Boswells for Melrose, home of this tour's fourth abbey. It is adjacent to the National Trust for Scotland's Priorwood Garden. Also in Melrose is the Motor Museum, a short walk from the abbey, with a varied collection of cars, motorcycles, signs and memorabilia.

Continuing north west back on the A6091, just before Galashiels be sure to stop for a tour of Abbotsford House, the romantic mansion built and occupied by Sir Walter Scott, preserved very much as it was in his day.

At Galashiels, parking in the city centre is limited to just 30 minutes – how long before they install meters?

The town is famed for its textile industry, and the Scottish College of Textiles is based here. To gain a good impression of the skills involved, take a free conducted tour of the Peter Anderson Woollen Mill, signposted to the right as you come into the town, while there are plenty of mill shops in town to sell you the product; an alternative is to visit the Scottish Museum of Woollen Textiles at Walkerburn, on the A72 halfway to Peebles.

Also worth visiting in Galashiels is Old Gala House, signposted in the town centre. It dates from 1583 and has especially interesting painted ceilings and walls.

Approaching the end of your tour of the Borders, drive along the A72 to Innerleithen and Peebles, a pleasant road through delightful country, alongside the upper reaches of the River Tweed.

In Innerleithen, take the B709 to the left and visit Traquair House, thought to be the oldest continually inhabited house in Scotland. With over a thousand years of history behind it, and visits from 27 monarchs, Traquair would be the highlight of any tour. The owners work hard to provide extra attractions for visitors, and you may encounter one of their special summer events.

Leaving Traquair, you could return to Innerleithen and the A72 for the drive to Peebles; but if instead you leave Traquair and drive past the house entrance along the back road, the B7062, you will enjoy the other side of the river much more. It takes you past Kailzie Gardens, 17 acres of woodland and garden that is off the tourist track and wonderfully peaceful as a result.

There is the small Tweeddale Museum in Peebles, but far more interesting is Neidpath Castle, one mile to the west. With a dramatic setting in the Tweed valley among wooded hills, Neidpath is a well preserved medieval castle with 12 foot walls.

Peebles is the last stop on this Border tour, and here you head back to Edinburgh, 23 miles away to the north on the A703.

If you still have time, and want an upmarket souvenir of your trip, you could do worse than stop off to visit the Crystal Works in Penicuik, where Edinburgh Crystal is made.

And so it's back to Edinburgh. You won't have seen everything in the Borders on this tour – that would take a lifetime – but you will have seen the best that this fascinating area has to offer.

## BORDER ATTRACTIONS

Abbey St. Bathans Trout Farm. Five miles south of Grantshouse on the A6112, take the B6355 to the right for three miles then follow the signposted road to the right. Open all year, daily 1100-1700. Admission free (small fee for trout feeding). Tel: Abbey St. Bathans (03614) 237 or 242.

Abbotsford House. By the A7, signposted one mile east of Galashiels. Open late March-end October, Monday to Saturday, 1000-1700 and Sunday 1400-1700. Admission: Adult £1.80, child 90p. Tel: Galashiels (0896) 2043.

Bass Rock. One mile off the coast at North Berwick. Local boat trips round the rock are available from the harbour, contact the Tourist Information Centre for details. Tel: North Berwick (0690) 2197.

Castle Jail. In Castlegate, Jedburgh. Open all year, Monday to Saturday 1000-1200 and 1300-1700, and on Sunday 1300-1700. Admission: Adult 60p, child 30p.

Dirleton Castle. In Dirleton village, on southern edge. Open April-September, Monday to Saturday 0930-1900 and Sunday 1400-1900; October-March, Monday to Saturday 0930-1600 and Sunday 1400-1600. Admission: Adult £1.00, child 50p.

Dryburgh Abbey. Turn right off the A68 at St. Boswells, and follow the signs. Open April-September, Monday to Saturday 0930-1900 and Sunday 1400-1900; October-March, Monday to Saturday 0930-1600 and Sunday 1400-1600. Admission: Adult £1.00, child 50p.

Edinshall Fort. On a hilltop, signposted from A6112, five miles south of Grantshouse. Park at end of rough track by bridge. Accessible at all times, no admission charge.

Floors Castle. On B6089, well signposted on northern edge of Kelso. Open end April-end September, daily except Friday and Saturday (also open on Fridays in July and August), 1130-1730. Admission: Adult £2.50, child £1.50.

Haddington. Town 17 miles east of Edinburgh, just off the A1. To discover the town, buy the 'Walk Around Haddington' booklet available locally. Free parking in the main street.

Hailes Castle. Off A1 on minor road to the right at East Linton; or by following signs on minor road, five miles east of Haddington. Open April-September, Monday to Saturday 0930-1900 and Sunday 1400-1900; October-March, Monday to Saturday 0900-1600 and Sunday 1400-1600. Admission: Adult 60p, child 30p.

Jedburgh Abbey. In Jedburgh High Street. Open April-September, Monday to Saturday 0930-1900 and Sunday 1400-1900; October-March, Monday to Wednesday and Saturday 0900-1600, Thursday 0930-1300, Sunday 1400-1600. Admission: Adult £1.00, child 50p.

Jim Clark Memorial Room. At 44 Newtown Street, Duns. Open Easter to end September, Monday to Saturday 1000-1300 and 1400-1700, Sunday 1400-1700. Admission: Adult 50p, child 25p.

Kailzie Gardens. On B7062, two miles east of Peebles and five miles west of Traquair House. Open daily all year, 1100-1730. Admission: Adult £1.00, child 50p. Tel: Peebles (0721) 20007.

Kelso Abbey. In Bridge Street, central Kelso. Open April-September, Monday to Saturday 0930-1900 and Sunday 1400-1900; October-March, Monday to Saturday 0930-1600 and Sunday 1400-1600. Admission free.

Lennoxlove House. On B6369, one mile south of Haddington. Open May-September, Wednesday, Saturday and Sunday 1400-1700. Admission: Adult £2.00, child £1.00. Tel: Haddington (062082) 3720.

Manderston. Off A6105, two miles east of Duns. Open mid May-September, Thursday and Sunday 1400-1730. Admission: House and grounds £3.50, grounds only £1.50. Tel: Duns (0361) 88450.

Mary, Queen of Scots House. In Queen Street, Jedburgh. Open Easter-October, daily 1000-1700. Admission: Adult £1.00, child 50p.

Mellerstain House. Off A6089 signposted to the right, two miles south of Gordon (eight miles north of Kelso). Open at Easter and May-September, daily except Saturday 1230-1630. Admission charged.

Melrose Abbey. In Main Square, Melrose. Open April-September, Monday to Saturday 0930-1900 and Sunday 1400-1900; October-March, Monday to Saturday 0930-1600 and Sunday 1400-1600. Admission: Adult £1.00, child 50p.

Melrose Motor Museum. 200 yards from Melrose Abbey towards Newstead. Open mid May-mid October, daily 1030-1730. Admission: Adult £1.00, child 40p. Tel: Melrose (089682) 2624.

Myreton Motor Museum. Signposted off A198, six miles south west of North Berwick. Open May-October, daily 1000-1800; November-April, daily 1000-1700. Admission: Adult £1.50, child 50p.

Neidpath Castle. Off A72, one mile west of Peebles. Open Easter-September, Monday to Saturday 1100-1700, Sunday 1300-1700. Admission: Adult £1.00, child 50p.

Old Gala House. Signposted in Galashiels. Open April-October, Monday to Saturday 1000-1600 (opens 1200 in October), Sunday 1400-1600. Admission by donation.

Peter Anderson Woollen Mill. At Nether Mill in Galashiels. Open all year, Monday to Saturday 0900-1700, also July-September on Sunday 1200-1700. Free conducted tours April-September, Monday to Friday, begin at 1030, 1130, 1330 and 1430. Admission: Adult £1.00, child free. Tel: Galashiels (0896) 2091.

Preston Mill. Off A1 at East Linton, five miles east of Haddington, follow signposts in town. Open April-October, Monday to Saturday 1000-1300 and 1400-1700, Sunday 1400-1700 (October closes at 1630); November, Saturday 1000-1230 and 1400-1630, Sunday 1400-1630. Admission: Adult £1.20, child 60p.

Priorwood Gardens. By Melrose Abbey. Open July-October, Monday to Saturday 1000-1730, Sunday 1330-1730; April, May, November and December, Monday to Saturday 1000-1300 and 1400-1730. Admission by donation.

Scottish Museum of Woollen Textiles. On A72 at Walkerburn, two miles east of Innerleithen. Open all year, Monday to Friday 1000-1700;

also April-September, Saturday 1100-1600, Sunday 1200-1600. Admission: Adult 50p, child 25p.

Stevenson House. Four miles east of Haddington on minor road (signposted). Open July-mid August, Thursday, Saturday and Sunday 1400-1700. Admission: Adult £1.50, child 75p. Tel: Haddington (062082) 3376.

Tantallon Castle. By A198, three miles east of North Berwick. Open April-September, Monday to Saturday 0930-1900, Sunday 1400-19.00; October-March, Monday, Wednesday to Saturday 0930-1600, Sunday 1400-1600. Admission: Adult £1.00, child 50p.

Traprain Law. Hill just south of the A1, five miles east of Haddington. Accessible at all times, no admission charge.

Traquair House. On B709, half mile off A72, take Traquair Road in Innerleithen. Open Easter and late May-September, daily 1330-1730; earlier opening at 1030 in July and August. Admission: Adult £2.50, child £1.50. Tel: Innerleithen (0896) 830323.

Tweeddale Museum. High Street, Peebles. Open all year, Monday to Friday 0900-1700. Also April-October, Saturday and Sunday 1400-1700. Admission free.

Tyninghame House Gardens. One mile north of A1, six miles east of Haddington. Open June-September, Monday to Friday 1030-1630. Admission: Adult £1.00, child 50p. Tel: East Linton (0620) 860330.

*Scott's View, Borders*

# CENTRAL SCOTLAND

Edinburgh to Glasgow. Scotland's two great cities, just 45 miles apart. You could, of course, drive there in an hour, foot down, on the M8 motorway. But it wouldn't be much fun, would it?

You are a tourist, after all, and there is so much to discover between Scotland's two greatest cities that you will find it highly rewarding to travel the slow way.

Visit the nation's historic capital, Stirling, and the site of Scotland's greatest battlefield victory at Bannockburn. Enjoy the Trossach hills, a sample of the Highlands just a few miles from Glasgow. And see the lake that's really a loch.

Central Scotland for many years controlled the nation. While Edinburgh came to prominence thanks to its castle and palace, and Glasgow for its industrial power, the centre of the country held sway throughout medieval times.

Stirling dominated the land, its castle high above the city, with easy access to the River Forth and to the sea. The sea to the east was Scotland's link with the outside world in times of hostility with England, and ships from Scotland's allies like France and Norway could often be seen in the Forth.

Trade, therefore, grew on both sides of the Forth, giving prominence to Fife towns like Dunfermline and Culross. Parts of the latter have hardly changed in hundreds of years.

To the west of Stirling, it was a different story altogether. This was a comparative wilderness before roads were built, and you can still admire the unspoilt countryside and a network of lochs that includes one of the world's most famous stretches of water, Loch Lomond.

You will never be far from Edinburgh or Glasgow on this tour, so it can be accomplished easily enough in a day, or however much time you have.

Obviously you could drive the tour from either end, but for the purposes of this guide we shall start in Edinburgh. Enjoy the variety of Scotland's heart.

## TOUR OF CENTRAL SCOTLAND

Leave Edinburgh on the A90 Queensferry Road from the city centre, signposted to the Forth Road Bridge. This is a good fast route out of the city, but as it is also a main commuting route it does get rather clogged up during the rush hour, about 4pm to 6pm each day.

Right at the edge of the city, at Barnton, there is a confusing double roundabout that has been mystifying the locals for the past ten years. Don't worry too much about it, however daunting it looks: take one of the two middle lanes and head straight across both mini roundabouts for the A90 exit.

The road becomes a dual carriageway that stops only for the toll booths for the Forth Road Bridge. This mile-long suspension bridge was opened in 1964, at the time the biggest bridge in Britain, a companion for the original railway bridge built in 1890.

As you cannot stop or turn on the bridge itself, turn off to the services signposted just before you reach it, where there is a viewpoint (albeit with a 20p parking charge).

Alternatively, you could head down to the commuter town of South Queensferry which lives under the shadow of the bridges; as you will gather from the name, it used to be the southern terminal of the main ferry across the Forth.

Two miles to the west of South Queensferry, well signposted, is Hopetoun House, one of Scotland's finest stately homes, built in the early 18th century on a grand scale. As well as the sumptuous interior there are extensive grounds.

Back on the A90, pay your 40p toll to cross the bridge, and try to admire the view as you drive over, with the Rail Bridge to your right and Rosyth Royal Dockyard on the Fife coast to your left.

Immediately across the bridge there is a Tourist Information caravan off the first turning, a good place to stop and brief yourself before touring Fife.

For this tour, keep on the A90 over the first rise until it becomes the motorway M90, then take the next turning off (junction 2) towards Dunfermline, and follow the signs into the town centre, two miles away, on the A823.

As you come towards the town, you will see Dunfermline Abbey on the hill in front of you. Where the road goes under a railway bridge, turn left (following signs for the abbey), then right at the first set of lights. Follow this road up the hill and it will take you right past the abbey entrance; there is a small pay and display car park there, 10p for an hour.

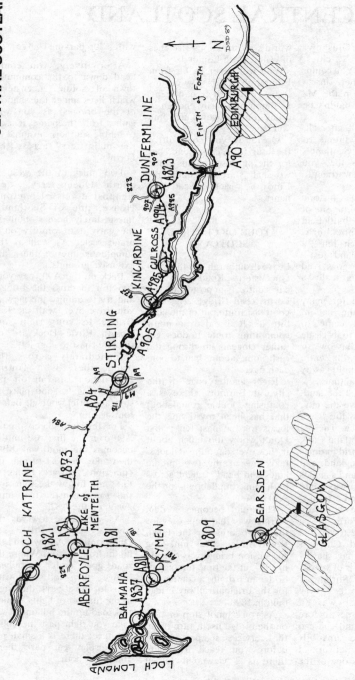

The abbey is certainly the main attraction in Dunfermline, with a history going back 900 years. From an origin as a modest church it grew to a great size, and its influence may be judged by the fact that here Robert the Bruce is buried and Charles I was born.

Also in Dunfermline there are four museums: one devoted to Robert Burns in the central library, one to Andrew Carnegie, and two others on local history at Pittencrieff House and Dunfermline District Museum.

All these are close together, so it would be best to leave the car and walk around. There is plentiful parking in the town centre, although you will probably have to pay for it. However, it is currently cheap at only 10p for one hour and 20p for three hours, long enough to see most things.

When it comes to leaving Dunfermline, the signposting out of the town centre is virtually non-existent, so you may be unsure where you are going.

From the abbey, follow the road into the city centre, go past the entrance to Pittencrieff Park, and turn left at the lights at the top of the hill. This is the A994, your road out of town; in fact, there is a sudden end to Dunfermline and you are soon in the country again.

Drive through Crossford and Cairneyhill to a large roundabout. Drive right over towards the coast onto the B9037, signposted for Torreyburn and Culross.

Three miles down this road you come to the village of Culross, which will be something of a revelation. Culross (pronounced Kew-ross)

is a remarkable example of a 16th and 17th century small town, which has changed little in 300 years. It is now a conservation area, and you may have trouble stopping your car in the town centre: better to park at the free car park at the far end of town than take your chances in the narrow cobbled streets.

In Culross there are several buildings worth visiting, of which the most impressive is the palace, finished in 1611 by Sir George Bruce, who developed the sea-going trade in salt and coal from the town. Also visit The Study, a 17th century tower house, and the 16th century Town House, former meeting place of the town council.

On leaving Culross, continue along the B9037 to Kincardine. Across the water you will see the huge petrochemical complex at Grangemouth, while closer at hand you pass by the huge Longannet Power Station on your left. Kincardine is rather dominated by its power stations, and although it has a long history there is little to recommend it today.

Turn left onto the A876 for the Kincardine Bridge, which before the Forth Road Bridge opened in 1964 was the only way for heavy vehicles to travel between Edinburgh and Fife. Kincardine Bridge is a fairly simple structure dating from 1936.

Over the bridge, head straight on to the first roundabout and turn right along the A905 towards Airth. On the left you will see Airth Castle among the trees on the hill; this is now a hotel.

A couple of miles further, follow the sign to the left for the B9124 to Cowie, and up

the lane to the right to the Pineapple, one of Scotland's strangest buildings. This curious structure was built by the Earl of Dunmore in 1761 as a garden retreat for his wife. It is now leased as a holiday home through the Landmark Trust, so you can only see it from the outside, but is still well worth a look, with an attractive modern orchard next to it.

Continuing along the A905, keep straight on and drive into Stirling, which even today has an impressive skyline, little changed in hundreds of years. There is parking in the city centre but you will have to pay for it, whereas if you head up to the top of the castle hill (signposted as you enter the city) you will have free parking on the esplanade or surrounding streets, and be much closer to all the visitor attractions.

Stirling Castle dominates the city and the surrounding area with its 250-foot great rock and you can see why the castle was for many years the key to Scotland. It changed hands several times before taking on a more settled role as a royal palace in later medieval times.

On the approaches to the castle there is a great deal to see. Even the youth hostel is a 17th century town house! Of particular note is the Church of the Holy Rude, built in 1414, which witnessed a coronation in 1567 and is still in use for worship (although currently undergoing substantial restoration). The graveyard contains some rather bizarre memorials.

From the castle you will be able to see the Wallace Monument across the valley on the next hill, and once you have had your fill of old Stirling this is another essential place to visit. This tower was completed in 1869 to commemorate William Wallace's victory over the English at the Battle of Stirling Bridge in 1297.

To go there from the castle, take the road through the city and follow the signs to the North, across the river; keep on this road and head straight over the roundabout at the end. The car park for the Wallace Monument is up a short hill, on your right, with the monument itself still a considerable climb above you.

For a further view of Scotland's turbulent birth, you can visit the site of Bannockburn, well signposted two miles south of Stirling, where Robert the Bruce defeated the English army in 1314. As well as an imposing mounted statue of Bruce, there is a Heritage Centre.

Leave Stirling to the north west by the A84, signposted for Crianlarich and Doune. Almost immediately on leaving town you will notice a marked change in scenery, as you are surrounded by farmland and there is no sign of the industry of the east.

Three miles along you may be surprised to find signs for a Safari Park to your right, but this is no joke. Scotland's Safari Park, as it is now called, is at Blair Drummond, and you can drive round it in your car. Animals range from lions and tigers to monkeys and elephants, and there are plenty of other amusements on offer.

Just beyond the Safari Park, turn left onto the A873, signposted for Thornhill and Aberfoyle. Continue to Port of Menteith on the Lake of Menteith. These names are a little confusing as the Port (a church, a hotel and not much

else) takes its name from the Gaelic poirt, or ferry, while the Lake (Scotland's only loch that takes the English name) comes from laicht, or low-lying land – so don't expect to find an English colony!

At Port of Menteith you can take a boat across to the island of Inchmahome, where there is a ruined Augustinian priory dating from 1238.

Continue west along the A81 to Aberfoyle, then turn right for a little trip to Loch Katrine and the Trossachs, one of Scotland's most scenic spots. It does get rather busy in summer, being a short trip from Glasgow, so you may find yourself stuck behind a coach on a particularly twisting road, but even so it is well worth it. There is even a special drive through the forest with excellent views, operated by the Forestry Commission.

At the end of the road, drive to the car park at Trossachs Pier on Loch Katrine. There are regular sailings along the loch on the SS Sir Walter Scott, a fine old steamer.

Drive back to Aberfoyle and continue south on the A81, through the excellent scenery of the Queen Elizabeth National Forest Park, 45,000 acres of forest, moor and mountain with many walks. Stop at the David Marshall Lodge just north of Aberfoyle for full information.

Turn to the right along the A811 to Drymen, and right again up the B837 to Balmaha for a superb view of Loch Lomond. There is a car park here, and this is probably a good spot to turn round, although the road does wind its way another few miles up the lochside to Rowardennan.

Another attraction, just after Drymen, is Buchanan

Smithy, where you can watch a traditional blacksmith and swordsmith working at his forge.

From Drymen, head south along the A809 towards Glasgow, the final leg of this tour, with a worthwhile stopping place at the Queen's View on the right for a last look back to Loch Lomond.

Then you enter the affluent north west of the city, with the suburbs of Milngavie (pronounced Mul-guy) and Bearsden, and their attendant golf courses. Bearsden has been a good place to be for a long time, as you will discover at the Roman Bath House there, one of Scotland's best surviving Roman buildings.

Then it is in to Glasgow and all that fine city has to offer. Signposting as you come into the city centre is pretty poor, so it is worth having a street map handy before you get caught up in the maze of fly-overs and one way streets.

Glasgow is rather a shock after the open roads of the country. Aren't you glad you didn't take the motorway?

## CENTRAL SCOTLAND ATTRACTIONS

Bannockburn Heritage Centre. Two miles south of Stirling, well signposted, at junction of A9 and A872. Open April-October, daily 1000-1800. Admission: Adult £1.10, child 55p.

Buchanan Smithy. One mile west of Drymen on B837. Open all year, daily 1000-1700.

Carnegie Birthplace Museum. In Moodie Street, Dunfermline. Open April-October, Monday to Saturday 1100-1700, Sunday 1400-1700; November-March, daily 1400-1600. Admission free.

*Culross*

Church of the Holy Rude. Near castle, St. John Street, Stirling. Open May-September, Monday to Friday 1000-1700, Sundays for worship at 1100. Admission free.

Culross Palace. In Culross, on B9037, six miles west of Dunfermline. Open April-September, Monday to Saturday 0930-1900, Sunday 1400-1900; October-March, Monday to Saturday 0930-1600, Sunday 1400-1600. Admission: Adult £1.00, child 50p.

Culross Town House. In Culross, on B9037. Open May-September, Monday to Friday 1100-1300 and 1400-1700, Saturday and Sunday 1400-1700. Admission: Adult 70p, child 35p.

David Marshall Lodge. Off A821, one mile north of Aberfoyle. Open mid March-mid October, daily 1000-1800. Admission 10p per car.

Dunfermline Abbey and Palace. Monastery Street, Dunfermline. Open April-September, Monday to Saturday 0930-1900, Sunday 1400-1900; October-March, Monday to Saturday 0930-1600, Sunday 1400-1600. (Closed on Thursday afternoons and Fridays) Admission: Adult 60p, child 30p.

Dunfermline District Museum. Viewfield Terrace, Dunfermline. Open all year, Monday to Saturday 1100-1700. Admission free.

Dunmore Pineapple. Signposted left one mile west of Airth on A905, take B9124 then track to car park. Can be viewed from outside only, but available for holiday lets through Landmark Trust. Tel: Stirling (0738) 31296.

Forth Road Bridge. Can be seen from viewpoint at south end of bridge at Services.

Hopetoun House. Signposted one mile west of South Queensferry along minor road. Open May-September, daily 1100-1700. Admission: Adult £2.80, child £1.40.

Inchmahome Priory. On an island in the Lake of Menteith, reached by boat from Port of Menteith, on A81. Open April-September, Monday to Saturday 0930-1900, Sunday 1400-1900. Admission free, but ferry charge is Adult £1.00, child 50p.

Murison Burns Collection. In Dunfermline Central Library, Abbot Street. Open all year, Monday to Saturday 1000-1300 and 1400-1900 (except closed on Wednesday afternoon and from 1700 on Saturday). Admission free.

Pittencrieff House Museum. In Pittencrieff Park, Dunfermline. Open May-August, daily (except Tuesday) 1100-1700. Admission free.

Queen Elizabeth Forest Park. In the countryside around Aberfoyle, on the A81 and A821, with numerous stopping places for walks into the hills. Accessible at all times, no admission charge.

Queen's View. Park on A809 six miles south of Drymen, and walk down short path to viewpoint. Open all times. Admission free.

Roman Bath House. Roman Road, Bearsden, off A809. Open at all times, admission free.

Scotland's Safari Park. At Blair Drummond on A84, five miles west of Stirling. Open April-September, daily 1000-1700. Admission charge per car or per head.

SS Sir Walter Scott. Steamer based at Trossachs Pier, off A821 eight miles north of Aberfoyle. Leaves May-September, Monday to Saturday at 1100, 1345 and 1515; Sunday at 1400 and 1530. Charge: Adult £2.00 (morning) or £1.75 (afternoon), child £1.20 or £1.00.

Stirling Castle. Open all year, Monday to Saturday 0930-1715, Sunday 1030-1645 (closes one hour earlier October-March). Admission: Adult £1.50, child 75p.

The Study. In Culross, on B9037. Open April, June-August and October, Saturday and Sunday 1400-1600. Admission: Adult 50p, child 25p.

Wallace Monument. Off A997, two miles north east of Stirling. Open April-September, daily 1000-1730 (1830 May-August); February, March and October, open daily except Wednesday and Thursday, 1000-1630. Admission: Adult £1.00, child 50p.

**PAGES 2-5 FOR COLOUR MAPS**

# THE KINGDOM OF FIFE

Fife has always been proud of its identity as an ancient Scottish kingdom, and the area has several other distinct claims to fame.

It was home to kings of Scotland for hundreds of years, a heritage reflected today in the grandeur of some of the remaining monuments: in particular the highly impressive Falkland Palace, while you can experience the romance and tragedy of Loch Leven Castle.

St. Andrews University was founded in 1411 and now has a worldwide reputation as a seat of learning, a remarkable achievement for a university in such a small town.

And that same small town is the home of the Royal and Ancient Golf Club, the world ruling body of the game. The links at St. Andrews, a Mecca for golfers, are still owned by the local authority so anyone can play there.

Around the coast, the small fishing ports have avoided the excesses of modernisation and you can wander down their narrow streets, following your nose to the harbour and the sea.

Inland, the prime agricultural land of Fife gives a constantly changing view as you drive along the country roads, and it is often worth turning off the beaten track to explore the rural back streets.

### TOUR OF FIFE

Leave Edinburgh along the A90 Queensferry Road from the city centre, signposted to the Forth Road Bridge. It is a good fast road all the way to the bridge, where you pay your 40p toll to cross to Fife.

(See the Tour of Central Scotland for full details of this part of the trip.)

Across the bridge, keep on the A90 until it becomes the motorway, just over the first rise. Turn off here, at junction 1 signposted to Kirkcaldy, and turn right at the roundabout at the bottom of the slip road. There are also signs for the Fife Tourist Route.

Keep going along this road, the A921, until you come to a roundabout signposted straight on for Aberdour, but left for Kirkcaldy. Head into Aberdour, an attractive little town with a fine medieval castle, mostly still complete. The entrance is to the right of the station by the clocktower.

Continuing along the coast, as the road climbs up the hillside you have excellent views across the Forth to Edinburgh.

## KINGDOM OF FIFE

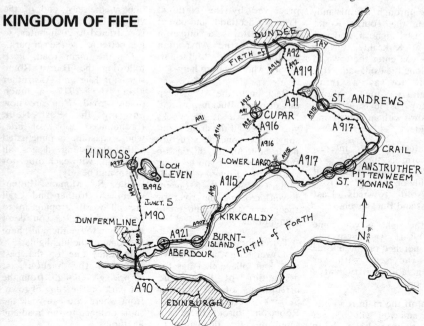

*Pittenweem, Fife*

Drive through Burntisland, following the Tourist Route signs, past Kinghorn, and you arrive at Kirkcaldy, turning right as you enter the town to drive along the esplanade. It is difficult to say anything particularly nice about Kirkcaldy, as it is a rather bleak town with an uninspiring esplanade.

Of much greater interest and charm is the village of Dysart, at the far end of Kirkcaldy on the A955, a road signposted towards East Wemyss and Buckhaven.

On the right as you come into Dysart is Ravenscraig Castle, perched on the hillside above the sea, with car parking about fifty yards further on.

Turn off the main road into Dysart and you will discover many houses have been preserved by the National Trust for Scotland, and one of them contains a museum relating to the Australian explorer John McDouall Stuart, who was born here.

Back on to the A955, keep on through Buckhaven and Methil. Down at the docks you will see all the cranes, and sometimes a massive structure being built for the oil rigs on the North Sea, if you take the road to Lower Methil. Otherwise, just keep on for Leven, crossing the river by the power station, and on to Lundin Links.

Turn right at the hotel down to Lower Largo, an attractive close-knit village that has the distinction of being the birthplace of Alexander Selkirk, better known as Robinson Crusoe. There is a small museum dedicated to

him at the east end of the village. Parking in the village is restricted to 20 minutes, so it is better to use the car park.

On the main road, keep following the Tourist Route signs for Elie and Anstruther along the A917, a much quieter road. You are now entering the East Neuk (pronounced nook) of Fife, whose coastline is punctuated with little fishing villages, all competing with each other for charm and beauty.

Elie, St. Monans, Pittenweem, Anstruther and Crail are all worth stoping in to visit, but in case you don't have time to see them all, here are some of the highlights.

In Elie, one of the best views of the harbour is, surprisingly enough, from the car park on the edge of town, from where you can walk the short distance to the headland lighthouse.

St. Monans has a superb ancient church at the east end of town, by a little stream outlet to the beach, and this is a good place to start a walk along the shore. By the harbour, you can park in the street to enjoy the view.

At Pittenweem, have a look at St. Fillan's Cave, down a path beside the church. This was created in the 12th century by Augustinian monks as a shrine to St. Fillan. Just outside the town you will see signs to Kellie Castle, three miles north, a fine restored medieval fortified house.

Anstruther is the biggest and busiest of the fishing villages, with ample parking along the harbour front at a cost of 25p. To discover more about the local fishing industry, visit the Scottish Fisheries Museum at the east end of the esplanade, and also the North Carr Lightship in the harbour. If you are feeling adventurous, you can take a boat trip out to the Isle of May.

Finally, Crail has the most charming harbour, surrounded by little fishermen's cottages and their neat gardens. Although you can drive right down to the harbour you cannot park there, so leave your car in the town centre and walk the last hundred yards.

This is the eastermost point of this tour, and you can now hit the road again to St. Andrews, ten miles away along the A917.

St. Andrews has enough to keep you busy for a whole holiday, let alone a brief motoring tour. As you enter the town, with the old city wall on your right, turn right at the T junction, follow the road round past the cathedral entrance and park in North Street. Parking is free but can be busy.

Walking around St. Andrews is great fun as there is so much to see and do in a small area. With an ancient university, castle and cathedral, the town reeks of history, and your best plan if you intend to explore properly is to take advice from the Tourist Information Centre.

When the time comes to leave St. Andrews, take the A91 to Cupar, driving past the famous golf courses on your right.

In Cupar, turn left onto the A92 signposted to Kirkcaldy, then on the edge of town take the A916 up the hill to Hill of Tarvit, an Edwardian country house with a notable art collection and lovely gardens. The entrance to Hill of Tarvit is two miles along this road on your left, with Scotstarvit Tower directly opposite.

Now it is time for a bit of exploring, off the beaten track. Just after the entrance to Hill of Tarvit on the A916, drive through the village of Craigrothie and take the next right, signposted to Chance Inn. The next few miles will be on narrow minor roads, giving fascinating views of the Fife countryside as you wind and climb through the fields and forest.

At the first T junction bear right, then at the crossroads head straight on (signposted Kettle and Burnturk). Keep on this road, high above the fields, until you come to another T junction, where you take the road to the right, signposted to Freuchie.

You must cross over two main roads (the A92 then the A914) just before you enter Freuchie (pronounced Frookie), a small village that is proud home of one of Scotland's top cricket clubs. Drive straight through Freuchie and you come to Falkland, where there is a magnificent palace.

Falkland Palace is a superb structure, one of the historical highlights of this tour. Built in the early 16th century, it was a favourite residence for several Scottish monarchs, and most of the Renaissance buildings are still kept in good order, while there are charming gardens outside.

Turn left out of Falkland towards Strathmiglo on the A912, and rejoin the A91 to the west. Just before it joins the motorway, take the left fork on the B996 into Milnathort, where you can turn off left to see Burleigh Castle, a medieval tower house.

Unfortunately there is no parking here, but you should be able to stop at the farm opposite.

After Milnathort you come to Kinross, a sizeable county town, from where you can take a boat across Loch Leven to the island castle where Mary, Queen of Scots imprisoned in 1567. Her escape one year later, when Willy Douglas locked everyone into the great hall, is one of Scottish history's great romantic episodes.

The track to the pier for the castle ferry is signposted to the left in the middle of Kinross, opposite the market cross. Drive right down the track to its end by the loch. You can wander round the ancient cemetery there while you wait for a boat.

Loch Leven is now renowned as a nature reserve, which can be entered at Vane Farm, on the south side of the loch,

*Alexander Selkirk, Lower Largo*

signposted along the B9097, left from the B996 south of Kinross. After visiting the nature centre, you can watch the vast numbers of wild geese and duck.

This is an attractive and relaxing spot to end this tour. Back on the B996 you can drive onto the M90 motorway at junction 5, south to Edinburgh, a quick 20 miles away.

## FIFE ATTRACTIONS

Aberdour Castle. In Aberdour, signposted entrance by station. Open April-September, Monday to Saturday 0930-1900, Sunday 1400-1600; October-March, Monday to Wednesday and Saturday 0930-1600, Thursday 0930-1230, Sunday 1400-1600. Admission: Adult 60p, child 30p.

Burleigh Castle. Off A911 half mile east of Milnathort, signposted. Open April-September, Monday to Saturday 0930-1900, Sunday 1400-1900; October-March, Monday to Saturday 0930-1600, Sunday 1400-1600. Admission free (ask for key at farm opposite).

Crail Heritage Centre. Beside Tolbooth in Crail town centre. Open June-September, daily 1000-1700. Admission: Adult 50p, child 25p.

Falkland Palace. In centre of Falkland, just off A912. Open April-September, Monday to Saturday 1000-1800, Sunday 1400-1800; October, Saturday 1000-1800, Sunday 1400-1800. Admission: Adult £2.40, child £1.20p.

Hill of Tarvit. To left of A916, two miles south of Cupar. Grounds open all year, 1000 to sunset. House open May-September, daily 1400-1800; April and October, Saturday and Sunday 1400-1800. Admission: Adult £2.20, child £1.10.

John McDouall Stuart Museum. In Rectory Lane, Dysart, just off A955 two miles east of Kirkcaldy. Open June-August, daily 1400-1700. Admission free.

Kellie Castle. On B9171, three miles north of Pittenweem. Gardens open all year, 1000 to sunset. Castle open May-October, daily 1400-1800; April and October, Saturday and Sunday 1400-1800. Admission: Adult £2.20, child £1.10.

Kinross House Gardens. In Kinross, just off town centre towards loch. Open May-September, daily 1000-1900. Admission: Adult £1.00, child 50p.

Loch Leven Castle. On an island on Loch Leven; access by boat from Kinross. Open April-September, Monday to Saturday 0930-1900, Sunday 1400-1900. Admission: Adult £1.00, child 50p.

Ravenscraig Castle. Beside A955 between Kirkcaldy and Dysart, car park just beyond castle. Open all year, Monday, Tuesday, Friday and Saturday 0930-1230 and 1330-1900, Wednesday 0930-1230, Sunday 1400-1900 (October-March, closes at 1600).

St. Andrews Castle. North side of St. Andrews beside road. Open April-September, Monday to Saturday 0930-1900, Sunday 1400-1900; October-March, Monday to Saturday 0930-1600, Sunday 1400-1600. Admission: Adult 60p, child 30p.

St. Andrews Cathedral. East end of St. Andrews. Cathedral ruins open at all times. Museum and St. Rule's Tower open April-September, Monday to Saturday 0930-1900, Sunday 1400-1900; October-March, Monday to Saturday 0930-1600, Sunday 1400-1600. Admission to museum and tower: Adult 60p, child 30p.

St. Andrews University. Most college courtyards are open at all reasonable times. Guided tours operate in July and August, twice daily; ask at Tourist Information Centre.

St. Fillan's Cave. Down lane by church in Pittenweem, off A917. Open all year, 1000-1300 and 1430-1730. (Ask for key at shop opposite). Admission: Adult 25p.

St. Monans Church. West end of St. Monans; follow narrow road from harbour. Open at all reasonable times. Admission free.

Scotstarvit Tower. Off A916, two miles south of Cupar, down track opposite entrance to Hill of Tarvit. Open April-September, Monday to Saturday 0930-1900, Sunday 1400-1900; October-March, Monday to Saturday 0930-1600, Sunday 1400-1600. Admission free.

Scottish Fisheries Museum. In Anstruther, overlooking harbour. Open all year, daily 1000-1730 (1700 in winter and on Sundays). Admission: Adult £1.50, child 60p.

Vane Farm Nature Reserve. On south shore of Loch Leven, signposted on B9097 from B996, five miles south of Kinross. Open all year, daily 1000-1700 (1600 in winter). Admission: Adult £1.00, child 50p.

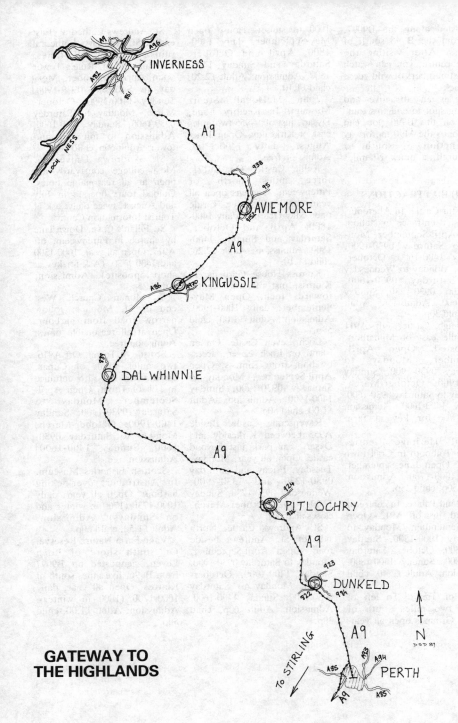

INVERNESS

LOCH NESS

A9

AVIEMORE

A9

KINGUSSIE

DALWHINNIE

A9

PITLOCHRY

A9

DUNKELD

A9

N

DSD 81

To STIRLING

PERTH

**GATEWAY TO
THE HIGHLANDS**

# THE GATEWAY TO THE HIGHLANDS

If you want to drive north to Inverness, there is really only one way to go, on the A9. This road has been substantially upgraded in the past 15 years, with numerous sections of dual carriageway, while all the towns have now been bypassed.

The result is a fast road to the north, so that on a good day the journey between Edinburgh or Glasgow and Inverness can be done in three hours for a distance of 160 miles.

The drawback is that the road has lost none of its old reputation for being dangerous, and accidents are still all too common. So watch out for cars overtaking at speed in risky conditions.

Between Stirling and Inverness, two large towns that have long and distinguished histories, you will be passing through some of Britain's most inhospitable landscapes.

The A9 follows a route along valleys through the Grampian Mountains, with the Cairngorms to the east and the Monadhliath Mountains to the west.

It can seem bleak indeed. But there are numerous communities just off the road, the largest being Perth while others of particular note are Pitlochry, Kingussie and Aviemore. You will probably have to pull off the main road at some time, as there are no petrol stations on it – a deliberate policy to pull people into the towns.

The small towns have their charms and rely heavily on the tourist trade for their survival. So you can generally be sure of a welcome whether you are stopping for petrol or looking for a bed for the night.

If you are planning on driving direct to Inverness, you won't really need to follow this tour. But should you feel the desire to pull off and explore, there is always plenty to see within a few minutes drive and you will quickly forget the thundering traffic of the main road.

## THE ROUTE

If you have come from the south, you will drive past Stirling on the M9 motorway; from Stirling itself, leave the town on the A9 to the north.

These two roads merge a couple of miles north of Stirling at a roundabout where the motorway ends, and this is where this tour begins.

From here to Perth, the first 33 miles, the only town of note is Dunblane, three miles up the road, with its fine restored cathedral and the neighbouring Dean's House with a museum.

Meanwhile, if you want to take a look at how the other half lives, stop off for a look at The Gleneagles Hotel on the A823 after 17 miles. This is Scotland's finest – and most expensive.

The A9 bypasses Perth to the west of the city, but there is plenty to see there if you venture in. Perth has a particularly attractive setting, with the city centre bordered by the River Tay to the east and a huge park called the South Inch to the south.

Attractions in the town include the Branklyn Garden, generally considered Scotland's finest small garden; factories where you can see glass-making and whisky production; a horse centre

where Clydesdales work and breed; and several historical buildings of interest.

Two miles north east of Perth, requiring a detour from the A9 along the A93, is Scone Palace, a place of great historical importance for Scotland. Although the present palace was finished in 1803 it incorporates earlier palaces. The Moot Hill at Scone was the site of the coronation Stone of Scone, brought there in the 9th century; it was stolen by the English in 1296 and now resides in Westminster Abbey, although many people would like to see it back in Scotland.

Continuing north from Perth on the A9, the next stop could be at Dunkeld, 15 miles further. Dunkeld Cathedral, founded in the 12th century, has a beautiful setting by the River Tay, while next to it in the town centre are the Little Houses, charmingly restored by the National Trust for Scotland to give a flavour of 17th century life.

If you want to stretch your legs a little, follow the riverside path down river from the superb Dunkeld Bridge to Birnam Oak, last relic of Macbeth's Birnam Wood.

A further 18 miles north takes you to Pitlochry, a town which has had to shed its title of Gateway to the Highlands since it was bypassed by the new road. The turning to Pitlochry is three miles before the town to the right, along the A924.

Much of the charm of Pitlochry comes from its excellent location as a centre for walking and touring holidays: the scenery is superb hereabouts. But while you are in town, stop for a look at the salmon leaping (in season) up the fish ladder in the hydro-electric power station; and perhaps go on a tour of Blair Atholl Distillery. Parking is not easy in town.

At the north end of Pitlochry, the road soon rejoins the A9 and almost immediately you come to the Pass of Killiecrankie, a famous wooded gorge where in 1689 government troops were routed by Jacobites under 'Bonnie Dundee'. The pass is on a network of walks which extend 20 miles in the area.

Next stop is Blair Atholl, six miles further on to the right. Just outside the town is the white turreted, baronial Blair Castle, seat of the Duke of Atholl. Parts date back to 1269, and this was the last castle in Britain to be besieged. The Duke is the only British subject allowed to maintain a private army, the Atholl Highlanders, who can be seen on special occasions.

One place perhaps worth mentioning if you want to find out about your family history is the Clan Donnachaidh Museum in Calvine, four miles north of Blair Atholl. The clan includes the surnames Reid, Robertson, MacConnachie, Duncan and others.

The next forty or so miles see the road climb through the beginnings of the Grampian Mountains, which rise steeply on both sides of the road. They may look tall and threatening, but the grandest are still a long way off. The summit of the road comes at last at Drumochter Pass, 1516 feet above sea level.

The A889 forks off to the left and Dalwhinnie, joining up with an alternative route to Fort William and the west along the winding A86.

Keeping on the A9, turn off to Newtonmore and Kingussie. These two attractive towns suffered from the new road as they no longer benefit from passing trade. Yet they are good places to stop, if only to mark the half way point in your journey to Inverness.

Newtonmore is the smaller of the two, a good base for hill walking expeditions and also home of the Clan Macpherson Museum. As you come into the town, on the left is the shinty pitch, home of one of Scotland's top clubs and a source of much pride in the village.

At Kingussie you can discover what life was really like in the area before modern times at the Highland Folk Museum. It covers all sides of life, from farming to travelling salesmen, and has a look at the landed gentry as well. Turn right in the main street at the railway station, along the B970, for Ruthven Barracks, the considerable ruins of an 18th century barracks built to keep the rebellious Highlanders in check.

Three miles north of Kingussie on the left is the Highland Wildlife Park, where you can see breeding groups of Highland animals and birds in a beautiful natural setting. The drive-through section includes red deer, bison and other species.

Aviemore, ten miles on to the right, has achieved fame as an all year holiday resort, offering skiing in winter and excellent leisure facilities all the time. If you fancy a change of transport, take the Strathspey Railway steam service to Boat of Garten and back, while in the town you won't be short of things to do.

There is a highly profess-ional Landmark Visitor Centre at Carrbridge, ten miles beyond Aviemore. This was the first of its kind in Europe and has built on its attractions over the years, with a superb three screen audio visual show and a dramatic permanent exhibition. It is also home of the Scottish Forestry Heritage Centre.

From here it is a straight-forward drive the last 25 miles to Inverness. However, to complete your education of Scottish life in this part of the world, turn off onto the B851 some five miles before Inverness and have a look at Culloden Moor.

Culloden was the place where Prince Charles Edward's (Bonnie Prince Charlie) cause was crushed in 1746 by the Duke of Cumberland's army. The battlefield looks much as it was 250 years ago, a haunting place where it is easy to imagine the two sides in battle. The visitor centre there tells the full story.

As you drive down the final descent towards Inverness you will see the new Kessock Bridge, opened in 1984, spanning the Beauly Firth to the north. That is the starting point of the next tour, The Far North; but for now you should turn into Inverness, the Highland capital, and relax a little.

### GATEWAY TO THE HIGHLANDS ATTRACTIONS

Aviemore Centre. In Aviemore. Open all year, daily, from 1000 to late. Admission free, but charges for use of facilities.

Blair Atholl Distillery. Just south of Pitlochry centre. Open all year, daily 0930-1700

(November-February, closed Sunday). Admission free.

Blair Castle. Just north of Blair Atholl. Open April-late October, daily 1000-1700 (April, May and October, Sunday opening at 1400). Admission: Adult £3.00, child £2.00.

Branklyn Garden. In Perth on the A85 Dundee Road. Open March-October, daily, 0930-sunset. Admission: Adult £1.20, child 60p.

Caithness Glass, Perth. On A9 north of Perth, at Inveralmond. Open July and August, daily 0900-1800; rest of year, Monday to Friday 0900-1630. Admission free.

Clan Donnachaidh Museum. In Calvine, four miles north of Blair Atholl. Open mid April-mid October, Monday and Wednesday to Saturday 1000-1300 and 1400-1700, Sunday 1400-1700. Admission free.

Clan Macpherson Museum. In Newtonmore. Open May-September, Monday to Saturday 1000-1730, Sunday 1430-1730. Admission free.

Culloden Moor. Beside B9006, five miles east of Inverness. Site open all year. Visitor centre open April-October, 0930-1930 (closes 1730 in April, May and from mid September). Admission: Adult £1.20, child 60p.

Dean's House. Cathedral Square, Dunblane. Open June-September, Monday to Saturday 1030-1230 and 1430-1630. Admission free.

Dunkeld Cathedral. In High Street, Dunkeld. Open April-September, Monday to Saturday 0930-1900, Sunday 1400-1900; October-March, Monday to Saturday 0930-1600, Sunday 1400-1600. Admission free.

Fairways Heavy Horse Centre. Two miles east of Perth, by A85. Open April-September, daily 1000-1800. Admission free.

Highland Folk Museum. In Kingussie. Open April-October, Monday to Saturday 1000-1800, Sunday 1400-1800; November-March, Monday to Friday 1000-1500. Admission: Adult £1.50, child 75p.

Highland Wildlife Park. Three miles north off Kingussie on B9152. Open April-October, daily 1000-1700 (1800 in July and August). Admission: car and passengers £6.50.

Landmark Visitor Centre. In Carrbridge. Open all year, daily, 0930-2130 in summer, 0930-1730 in winter. Admission: Adult £2.95, child £1.75.

Lower City Mills. Signposted as 'working water mill' from Perth inner ring road. Admission: Adult £1.00, child 70p.

Pass of Killiecrankie. Site open all day, admission free. Visitor centre open April-October, daily 1000-1700 (June-August 0930-1800). Admission: Adult 30p, child free.

Pitlochry Power Station and Dam. In Pitlochry. Open April-October, daily 0940-1730. Admission free.

Ruthven Barracks. On B970, half mile from Kingussie main street. Open all reasonable times. Admission free.

Scone Palace. Off A93 Braemar Road, two miles north of Perth. Open April-October, Monday to Saturday 0930-1700, Sunday 1330-1700 (from 1000 in July and August). Admission: Adult £3.00, child £2.00.

Strathspey Steam Railway. Park car in Dalfaber Road, Aviemore. Train services run June-August, daily; April-October on Sundays; May-October on Saturdays; April and May on Wednesdays; but ask for timetables locally. Various fares.

*Dunkeld Bridge*

# GLASGOW TO OBAN

# THE WEST: GLASGOW TO OBAN

From Glasgow, the magnificence of Scotland's west coast scenery is not far away, and on the drive to Oban you will never cease to be amazed at the variety and beauty.

This tour includes a lengthy drive along the banks of Loch Lomond, one of the world's most famous stretches of water and rightly so.

The road then winds its way past Inveraray and along Loch Fyne, an arm of the sea that penetrates many miles inland, while the mountains and forest rise high above.

The final leg of the journey gives you glimpses of secret islands and beyond them the Atlantic Ocean. On a sunny day, the view can hardly be bettered.

Oban itself is a holiday resort par excellence. There are car ferries to the islands, and in the town you will be well catered for and entertained, with a huge selection of accommodation.

This is a part of Scotland that dreams are made of.

## THE ROUTE

Your road from Glasgow is the A82, the Great Western Road out of the city. It is a reasonably fast road, a tree-lined dual carriageway through some of the city's more attractive suburbs.

It does not take long to feel out of town and in the country, and you will soon see the gracious sweep of the Erskine Bridge across the Clyde to your left.

The road bypasses Dumbarton but if you turn to your left you could visit the castle there, perched on the massive rock that dominates the town to such an extent

that the locals are called 'Sons of the Rock'. The castle is mainly a modern barracks, but older parts dating back to the 12th century have been preserved.

Keep following the signs to Loch Lomond, which beckons on your right. If you turn right along the A811 at Balloch you can catch the traditional cruise ship 'Countess Fiona' for a leisurely five hour journey, or one of many other smaller cruisers. This is one of Scotland's most popular excursions; it would probably be better to go on it by a day trip from Glasgow rather than stop on the way to Oban.

While the 'Countess Fiona' cruises on the water, you can still enjoy the beauty of the loch from the road, which hugs the loch for much of the next 20 miles. Although the dual carriageway stops at Balloch, the road north has been substantially upgraded in the past couple of years and there are frequent stopping places if you don't want to divert your attention from the road.

You spend 17 miles on the lochside before coming to Tarbet, where the loch has become much narrower, turn left onto the A83 to the west, signposted for Crianlarich. Tarbet means a narrow isthmus, and sure enough just two miles down the road at Arrochar you see the next stretch of water, Loch Long, which is connected to the sea.

Quickly the road climbs from the water to the aptly named Rest and Be Thankful, where there is a viewpoint. Then you have the long descent to Cairndow, where you can visit Strone Gardens, with the tallest tree in Britain.

The road stays at sea level for many miles now, following the contours of Loch Fyne, whose produce can be sampled at a roadside oyster bar.

An early opportunity to stop comes at Inveraray, visible across the water before you arrive, where the main attraction is the fine 18th century castle, home of the Duke of Argyll. It has superb interiors and historic portraits, and is set in notable grounds. You get your first view of the castle as you come into town over the little humpbacked bridge.

Worth seeing in Inveraray is the Combined Operations Museum, near the castle, which shows the work of the Training Centre there during World War II. You may also like to climb the 126-feet bell tower which dominates the town.

For a look at the local wildlife, try the Argyll Wildlife Park, just two miles from Inveraray. It contains not only Scottish but also some foreign species.

Continuing along Loch Fyne, five miles to the south west there is a fascinating museum of a small Highland township at Auchindrain, on the left of the road, where the buildings have been preserved and furnished.

Then at Crarae Lodge, another five miles on as you enter the village of Minard, is a garden among the loveliest open to the public in Scotland. It is set in a Highland glen with rhododendrons, azaleas conifers and ornamental shrubs.

The road reaches the headland and turns north

again just before it comes into Lochgilphead, a small town that boasts a helicopter pad for those in a hurry to reach Glasgow. Here the A86 turns south to Kintyre, and you should join the A816 to Oban, either by driving right along the seafront or through the main street. Parking is difficult in this busy town, so use one of the car parks if you are stopping.

On a hill to the left of the road you will see the signs to Dunadd Fort, one of the ancient capitals of prehistoric Scotland. This is probably where the early kings were invested. There are a number of other prehistoric remains in the area, including the sculptured stones in Kilmartin Church, on the left of the road.

A fortification of slightly more modern times is Carnasserie Castle, dating back at least to the 16th century. Its present ruinous state is the fault of the rebellion of 1685, when it was captured and blown up, but for all that it is well preserved. Park by the main road and walk up the hill to the castle, and you will be rewarded by fine views from the top of the battlements.

To your left you will see the B8002 to Ardfern, which is a popular and sheltered place to stay, not only for motorists but also for sailors. At last from the main road you have a clear view of the sea to the west, and there is a particularly fine viewpoint at Arduaine. The islands immediately in front of you are Shuna and Luing, while you should have a first sight of Mull in the distance.

The road then leaves the coast for a few miles, and here it could be a frustrating place to be stuck behind a slow

vehicle. The road has been substantially resurfaced in recent years but there is no real room to widen it.

You should consider taking a detour to the left along the B844, signposted for Easdale. It leads to Seil, which is an island but only just, and is reached by the single arch bridge at Clachan, famous as the 'Bridge over the Atlantic', which is bending the truth a little! It was built as long ago as 1791.

Continuing to the other side of Seil, on little Easdale Island there is a folk museum with a pictorial history of life in the days when this was an important slate quarrying area.

Back on to the A816, you are just a short distance from Oban, which will reveal itself as you drive down into town. The harbour will probably have one of the Caledonian MacBrayne ferries by the quay, the town centre will be bustling, and overlooking it all is McCaig's Tower, a bizzare hilltop folly on a grand scale.

You will enjoy Oban, stay there a while. A word of warning about parking, however: The town is always busy so you may have trouble finding anywhere central other than the dreaded pay and displays.

## GLASGOW TO OBAN ATTRACTIONS

Arduaine Gardens. At Arduaine, joint entrance with Loch Melfort Hotel, on A816, 20 miles north of Lochgilphead. Open April-September, Saturday to Wednesday 1000-1800. Admission: Adult £1.00, child free.

Argyll Wildlife Park. Two miles from Inveraray, on A83. Open Easter-September, daily 0930-1800.

Auchindrain Township. On A83, five miles south west of Inveraray. Open June-August, daily 1000-1700; April, May and September, daily except Saturday, 1000-1600. Admission: Adult £2.00, child £1.20.

Carnasserie Castle. Car park to left of A816, nine miles north of Lochgilphead, and walk up hill. Open at all reasonable times. Admission free.

Clachan Bridge. On B844, three miles off A816 at Kilninver. Open all times. No admission charge.

Combined Operations Museum. In Cherry Park, near Inveraray Castle. Open July-August, Monday to Saturday 1000-1800, Sunday 1300-1800; mid May-June and September, Monday to Thursday and Saturday 1000-1300 and 1400-1800, Sunday 1300-1800. Admission: Adult 80p, child 50p.

Crarae Garden. By A83 in Minard, ten miles south west of Inveraray. Open all year, daily 0900-1800. Admission: Adult £1.70, child 70p.

Dumbarton Castle. Signposted off A814, on Dumbarton Rock. Open April-September, Monday to Saturday 0930-1900, Sunday 1400-1900; October-March, Monday to Saturday 0930-1600, Sunday 1400-1600. Admission: Adult 60p, child 30p.

Dunadd Fort. On hill west of A816, four miles north of Lochgilphead. Open all reasonable times. Admission free.

Easdale Folk Museum. Easdale Island, at end of B844, five miles from A816 at

*Carnasserie Castle*

Kilninver. Open April-October, Monday to Saturday 1030-1730, Sunday 1030-1630. Admission: Adult 70p, child 20p.

Inveraray Bell Tower. Central Inveraray. Open May-September, Monday to Saturday 1000-1300 and 1400-1700; Sunday 1400-1800. Admission: Adult 60p, child 30p (exhibition free).

Inveraray Castle. Half mile north of Inveraray. Open July-August, Monday to Saturday 1000-1730, Sunday 1300-1730; April-June and September-mid October, Monday to Thursday and Saturday 1000-1230 and 1400-1730, Sunday 1300-1730. Admission: Adult £2.20, child £1.10.

Inveraray. Jail. Central Inveraray. Open all year, daily 0930-1800. Admission: Adult £2.20, child £1.00.

Loch Lomond Cruises. Include 'Countess Fiona' from Balloch Pier, in town just off A82. Cruises depart daily, April, May and September at 1015, June, July and August at 0930 and 1410. Tickets: Adult £10.00 and £8.50, child half fare.

McCaig's Tower. On a hill overlooking Oban. Open at all times. Admission free.

Oban Distillery. Oban town centre. Open all year, Monday to Friday 0900-1630, and Easter-October, Saturday 0930-1630. Admission free.

Oban Glass. On Lochavullin Estate, Oban. Factory open all year, Monday to Friday 0900-1700. Admission free.

Strone Gardens. By A83 at Cairndow. Open April-October, daily 0900-2100. Admission: Adult £1.00, child free.

World in Miniature. In Kilninver, seven miles south of Oban on A816. Open April-mid October, Monday to Saturday 1000-1800, Sunday 1200-1800. Admission: Adult 80p, child 50p.

# GLENCOE

The name of Glencoe is one of the most evocative of Scottish history, along with the likes of Bannockburn and Culloden.

In the early hours of February 13, 1692, the order was given for soldiers under Campbell of Glen Lyon to massacre the inhabitants of the village; of 200 occupants at least 40 were killed straight away, while others who fled to the hills died from exposure and starvation.

The massacre was carried out on the orders of King William III, to punish the lateness of the Macdonalds of Glencoe in swearing allegiance to him. The dreadful deed caused outrage all over Scotland and is still remembered.

Today there is a visitor centre in Glencoe and the glen is visited as much for its outstanding natural beauty as in remembrance of the massacre. It is also excellent hillwalking and skiing country.

This tour from Oban to Fort William drives in a circle through some of Scotland's finest hills and glens, and can easily be finished within a day. You could use it as a stepping stone to a drive further north, or return to Oban.

## THE TOUR

Leave Oban to the north on the A85 for Connel, which used to be a bottleneck when it had a joint railway and road bridge across the narrow neck of Loch Etive. Now, however, the whole of the bridge is used for motor traffic and looks like a giant Meccano kit. Leave it for the moment and continue on the open road to the east on the south side of the loch, still along the A85, signposted for Crianlarich.

The sheltered south bank of Loch Etive makes it an excellent place for gardens, and you will see signs to some of them to your left. The more impressive ones include Achnacloich and Barguillean.

At Taynuilt, seven miles east of Connel, signposted to the left there is a restored iron furnace for smelting, built in the 18th century; then at Inverawe, a few miles further, you can see a fire of a more delicate hue, in the shape of a fish curing and smoking business that is in daily operation.

Loch Awe appears to your right, hiding behind a dam, as you drive through the narrow Pass of Brander, a short but impressive road with bare hills rising steeply above you on both sides.

You can take a cruise on Loch Awe, lasting about an hour, at Lochawe Village, on

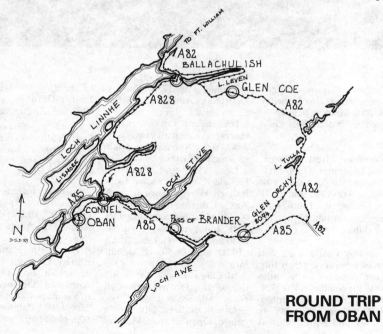

**ROUND TRIP FROM OBAN**

*Oban*

the Lady Rowena steam launch. Overlooking the northern point of Loch Awe is Kilchurn Castle, not signposted but reached along a track on the right just after the road crosses the river. It was built in 1440 and 1693, but as it is in a ruinous state there is little of the inside to see.

At Inverlochy, rather than continue on the A85 to the east, turn left onto the B8074, a scenic alternative through Glen Orchy. This is a delightful gem of a road, running alongside the fast flowing River Orchy for about ten miles before it joins the A82 to the north, just before Bridge of Orchy.

As the road climbs into the mountains, it gradually levels off and the road touches the west edge of Rannoch Moor. This bleak and inhospitable moor is virtually unspoilt and

has a beauty all of its own.

The road stays in the hills, and on your left you could take a trip up the Glencoe Chairlift at White Corries, about a mile away. Although intended mainly for the winter skiing season, there is an access chairlift in summer which you can ascend to over 2,000 feet for the superb views.

Then as you come over the rise, you begin the descent into the majesty of Glencoe, confirmed by the sign on the left. You can stop at the laybys to the side of the road, or at the National Trust for Scotland visitor centre, which is on the main road just after the turning right to Glencoe village. The visitor centre will give you the complete story, not just of the massacre but

also of the wildlife in the area.

In Glencoe village, at the foot of the glen, there is a folk museum in a number of thatched cottages, with Jacobite relics and a history of domestic life in later days.

At Glencoe, instead of continuing along the A82, take instead the B863 round Loch Leven. This little used road gives you excellent views from high above the loch on the way to Kinlochleven at the head of the loch. This is a surprisingly busy town, largely thanks to the hydro electric scheme there. Return to the main road along the north side of the loch, rejoining at North Ballachulish.

Here you must decide whether to continue north to Fort William, or drive south and return to Oban.

If you are going south, cross the bridge at Ballachulish, which although essential for crossing the water, rather spoils the beauty of the area. But cross it you must if you wish to return to the A828 south. Beyond here, the drive for the last 35 miles to Oban on the A828 is excellent, with fine views across Loch Linnhe and the smaller Loch Creran.

There is still plenty of opportunity to enjoy the local flora and fauna. At Dalnashean there is a three acre 'field of fairies', an attractive beach and spruce lined garden. Then at Appin, the retired ranger has collected many specimens of local wildlife to let visitors know what to look for in the area. And nearby, at Kinlochlaich House Gardens, you can visit the West Highland's largest nursery garden.

Then in Barcaldine itself, just north of Connel Bridge, there is the impressive Sea Life Centre. This is Britain's largest display of native marine life, with over 100 species in a beautiful lochside setting. And then it is back to Oban.

If you are going north to Fort William, it is a 12 mile drive along the east bank of Loch Linnhe. There is little really to see other than the view across the loch, although if the scenery on the other side takes your fancy, you could take the short car ferry at Corran.

Fort William is not now the most attractive of towns, and seems to cater primarily for coach parties. However, it is a good centre for touring and here you can decide where to go next.

## GLENCOE TOUR ATTRACTIONS

**Achnacloich Woodland Garden.** Three miles east of Connel on A85. Open April-mid June during daylight hours. Admission: Adult £2.00, child £1.00.

**Appin Wildlife Museum.** At Appin Home Farm, ten miles south of Ballachulish on A828. Open all year, daily 1000-1800. Admission by donation.

**Barguillean Garden.** Three miles south of Taynuilt on minor road through Glen Lonan. Open April-October, daily during daylight hours. Admission: Adult 50p, child free.

**Bonawe Ironworks.** At Bonawe, eight miles east of Connel, off A85 at Taynuilt. Open April-September, Monday to Saturday 0930-1900, Sunday 1400-1900. Admission: Adult 60p, child 30p.

**Castle Stalker.** Off A828, 12 miles south of Ballachulish. Open March-September by appointment. Admission: Adult £4.00, child £2.00 (including boat trip). Tel: Upper Warlingham (08832) 2768.

**Cruachan Power Station.** Off A85, 18 miles east of Oban. Open April-October, daily 0900-1630. Admission: Adult £1.25, child 50p.

**Dalnashean.** By Port Appin, on minor road off A828. Open mid April-mid September, Sunday and Monday 1000-dusk. Admission: Adult 50p, child free. free.

**Glencoe Folk Museum.** In Glencoe village, off A82. Open May-September, Monday to Saturday 1000-1700. Admission: Adult 50p, child 25p.

**Glencoe Visitor Centre.** In Glencoe, to right of A82. Open June-August, daily 0930-1830; April, May, September, October, daily 1000-1730. Admission: Adult 30p, child 15p.

**Inverawe Smokery and Fisheries.** On A85 at Lochawe. Smokehouses open all year, daily 0900-1700. Fisheries open April-October, daily 0900-1800. Admission free.

**Kilchurn Castle.** At northern tip of Loch Awe, by A85. Open April-September, daily 0930-1900; October-March, daily 0930-1600. Admission free.

**Kinlochlaich House Gardens.** At Appin on A828, entry by police station. Open April-October, Monday-Saturday 0930-1800, Sunday 1030-1800; November-March, Monday-Friday 1000-1700. Admission: Adult 50p, child free.

**Lady Rowena.** Sails from pier at Lochawe, by A85. Sails June-September, daily 1030-1600. Fare: Adult £2.75, child £1.50.

**Sea Life Centre.** At Barcaldine, on A828 just north of Connel. Open March-November, daily 0900-1700. Admission charge.

**White Corries Chairlift.** Off A82 by Kingshouse. Open January-April, Thursday to Monday 1000-1700; June-September, daily 1000-1730. Admission: Adult £1.90, child £1.50.

# ROYAL DEESIDE

If the Royal Family go there for their holidays, there can't be much wrong with it! Royal Deeside, the long and beautiful valley stretching inland from Aberdeen, has long been a favourite haunt of royalty and there is nothing to stop you enjoying it, too.

This part of the country has a great deal of variety, and your tour from Dundee to Aberdeen will take you through farmland, mountains and forest in a fairly short distance, including the highest main road in Britain.

The farmland north of Dundee is among Scotland's most fertile, a gentle undulating plain with small hills and a traditional way of life.

In the distance, however, the Grampian Mountains are always present, and this tour takes you high up through the pass of Glenshee, famous now for its skiing.

You emerge at the far side in upper Deeside, and the long gentle 60 miles descent through superb wooded countryside to Aberdeen.

## THE ROUTE

Drive north from the Dundee ring road on the A929, the main road to Aberdeen which is a dual carriageway. Stay on it for only six miles before turning off left on the A928, signposted to Kirriemuir and Glamis.

Almost instantly you find yourself away from the main road and in a country setting. This area is called the Mearns, and is renowned for its agricultural excellence.

Cross over the A94 just as you come into the village of Glamis, which has been famous since Shakespeare wrote 'Macbeth', and there is evidence of a long royal connection. Glamis Castle is just north of the village as you head for Kirriemuir, and parts of the existing castle may indeed be contemporary. Most of it, however, owes its present appearance to the late 17th century, and it is a fascinating building to tour.

In Glamis itself, if you turn right into the village and go to the far end of the main street, is the Angus Folk Museum, a row of 19th century cottages containing many relics of domestic and agricultural life in the olden days.

Leave Glamis still on the A928 for Kirriemuir, a few miles north. In Kirriemuir is the birthplace of J.M.Barrie, the author of 'Peter Pan', and there is a small museum there to commemorate his life. It can be reached by following the one-way system to the other side of the town, and it is on the right of the road.

Retrace your steps through Kirriemuir and head towards the hills on the B951, signposted to the right to Glenisla. After one mile you pass Loch of Kinnordy Nature Reserve, which contains large numbers of nesting birds. There is a small car park and observation hides.

This small road carries on, meandering pleasantly for several miles through the foothills to the west, through the little village of Kirkton of Glenisla and following the Isla river until it eventually joins up with the A93, where you turn right to the north.

The road climbs and climbs into Glenshee, which has built an excellent reputation in recent years as a ski resort, and there are several chairlifts on the surrounding hills. Snow is generally good enough for skiing between December and April, although the season varies considerably with the weather.

The chairlift at Glenshee, just by the main road at the summit, is open all year round, as are the huge car parks and cafe, so it is a good opportunity to climb Cairnwell mountain, which seems high at 3,059 feet, but the road itself is the highest main road pass in Britain at 2,199 feet.

From here there is a long descent until you come to Braemar, the highest town on Deeside, and this is the first stop of your royal tour.

Each summer, the Royal family can be found at the Braemar Gathering, one of the most sumptuous and prestigious highland games meetings. It will be held in 1990 on Saturday, September 1st.

Braemar is an archetypal highland town, with elegant hotels, shops and a fast-flowing river to complement the attractive houses. One mile to the north, just off the A93 to the left, is Braemar Castle, a fine turreted residence that dates from 1748, although there was a castle on the site for many years before then. Another castle in the town is the ancient Kindrochit, not much more than a scant ruin today.

Six miles along the road from Braemar is Balmoral Castle, the royal residence, which has been their holiday home for over a century since Queen Victoria rebuilt it.

# ROYAL DEESIDE
# & THE MEARNS

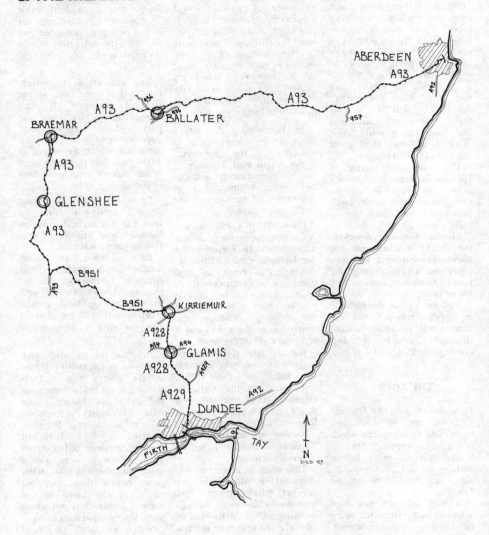

Most of the castle is closed to the public but you can tour the gardens, although they will be closed when the Royal family are in residence. You will catch a glimpse of the castle through the trees as you approach, and this is the only time it is visible from a distance.

Continuing the royal theme, across the road from the Balmoral car parks you can also visit the little church in Crathie where they attend services. Drive through the car parks and across the river and follow the signs for Royal Lochnagar Distillery, a couple of miles away, where you can go on a free tour.

Back on the main road, the next town is Ballater. As you come into the town, you will see the signs to the left to the McEwan Gallery, an interesting art collection, and then the Craigendarroch Country Club, one of Scotland's poshest. The town itself has an attractive church and shops, and you turn left at the end of the main street to continue down through Dee Valley with the forests covering the hills to both sides.

A couple of miles after Aboyne it is worth making the detour to the north to Craigievar Castle, one of Scotland's most enchanting fortified houses. From the A93, take the turning on to a minor road to the left (signposted) and when it joins with the A980 head towards Alford. The castle is on a hill to your left.

On the way, to the right, you pass the Peel Ring at Lumphanan, a hugh medieval earthwork where legend has it that Macbeth was killed.

Back on the A93, continue down the Dee Valley, and three miles after Banchory

you will come to Crathes Castle on the left, another outstanding tower house which was completed in 1660 although the tower dates from 1533. The gardens are also magnificent, with many miles of wayfaring walks.

Five miles later is another fine castle, at Drum, signposted one mile off to the left, up a minor road. A massive granite tower built towards the end of the 13th century joins onto a mansion of 1619, and again there are pleasant grounds.

It is fairly obvious you are approaching Aberdeen at this point, as the amount of housing grows along with the traffic. Just after you come into Peterculter you also cross the Aberdeen city boundary. The final stretch of road into the city is usually pretty busy, but at least it goes right into the centre and the traffic is bearable until you reach Union Street in the centre.

This is Aberdeen, the end of the tour, a fine old city with a great deal to see and do.

## ROYAL DEESIDE TOUR ATTRACTIONS

Angus Folk Museum. Off A94 in Glamis main street. Open mid April-September, daily 1100-1700. Admission: Adult £1.30, child 60p.

Balmoral Castle. On A93, nine miles east of Braemar. Grounds and castle ballroom open May-July, Monday to Saturday 1000-1700 (except when Royal family in residence). Admission: Adult £1.50, child free.

Barrie's Birthplace. In Brechin Road, north side of Kirriemuir. Open May-September, Monday to Saturday 1100-1730, Sunday 1400-1730. Admission: Adult £1.00, child 50p.

Braeloine Interpretive Centre. Signposted, two miles from Aboyne. Open April-September, daily 1000-1700. Admission by donation.

Braemar Castle. At Braemar on A93. Open May-early October, daily 1000-1800. Admission: Adult £1.30, child 65p.

Craigievar Castle. On A980, seven miles north of A93 east of Aboyne. Grounds open all year, daily 0930-sunset. Castle open May-September, daily 1400-1800 (opens 1100 in July and August). Admission: Adult £2.40, child £1.20.

Crathes Castle. Off A93, three miles east of Banchory. Grounds open all year, daily 0930-sunset. Castle open May-September, daily 1100-1800; April and October, Saturday and Sunday 1100-1800. Admission: Adult £3.00, child £1.50.

Crathie Church. To left of A93 at Crathie, seven miles east of Braemar. Open April-October, Monday to Saturday 0930-1730, Sunday 1400-1800 (services at 1100). Admission free.

Drum Castle. Beside A93, one mile down track. Castle open mid April-September, daily 1400-1800; October, Saturday and Sunday 1400-1800. Grounds open all year, daily 0930-sunset. Admission: Adult £2.40, child £1.20.

Glamis Castle. Just north of Glamis, on A928. Open mid April-mid October, daily 1200-1730. Admission: Adult £3.00, child £1.50

Glenshee Chairlift. Beside A93, with car park. Open all year, daily 0900-1700. Admission charge.

Kindrochit Castle. In Balnellan Road, Braemar. Open all reasonable times. Admission free.

*Craigievar Castle*

Loch of Kinnordy Nature Reserve. On B951, one mile west of Kirriemuir. Open all year, daily 0900-sunset (except closed Saturdays in September and October). Admission free.

Lumphanan Peel Ring. Signposted off minor road, two miles north of A93 east of Aboyne. Open all reasonable times. Admission free.

Royal Lachnagar Distillery Centre. Off A93 at Crathie. Open March-October, Monday to Saturday 1000-1700, Sunday 1100-1600; November-March, Monday to Friday 1000-1700. Admission free.

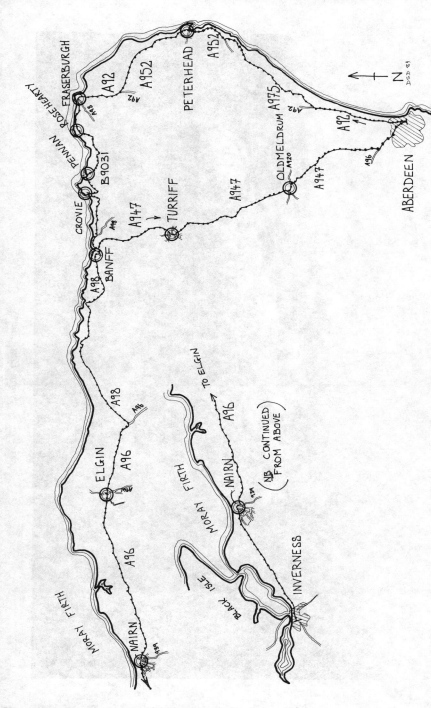

**NORTH EAST COAST**

*North-East Coast*

# NORTH EAST COAST

The cold east wind bites fiercely across the land nowhere more than the north east coast of Scotland, where for centuries the inhabitants have made their living from the sea.

There are many charming little fishing villages strung along the coast, some of them in seemingly impossible positions, but while many of them still have boats, most of the industry is now centred on the larger ports of Fraserburgh and Peterhead.

This tour from Aberdeen to Inverness takes you past or through a great number of tight-knit communities that have a great deal of charm.

There are other attractions, too, such as the massive ruins of Slains Castle, where Dracula was inspired, and the mighty cathedral of Elgin, not to mention the haunting battlefield of Culloden near Inverness.

On its lighter side, if you have ever seen the film 'Local Hero' be sure to stop at the village of Pennan, where much of it was filmed.

This is a part of Scotland with a character all of its own, where determination to win through against ht elements has shaped the communities to the way they are today.

## NORTH EAST COAST TOUR

Leave Aberdeen by the road to the north, signposted for Ellon and Peterhead, the A92 dual carriageway. After ten miles, turn right onto the quieter and more picturesque A975, which will take you the scenic route to Peterhead.

This small road takes you through Forvie Nature Reserve, bridging the estuary of the River Ythan, and a couple of miles beyond the village of Cruden Bay to the glorious and extensive ruins of Slains Castle, overlooking the sea. So dramatic is the setting that it inspired Bram Stoker for the creaton of Dracula. There is a small carpark on the right of the road, then a walk down a bumpy track.

Half a mile further on is another dramatic sight, this time entirely natural. The Bullers of Buchan is an extraordinary 200 feet deep chasm in the cliffs, carved out by the sea. There are no guard rails by the sheer drop – not recommended for sufferers of vertigo!

Rejoin the main road, by now the A952, and drive the last few miles to Peterhead. This is one of the world's busiest fishing ports, built round a huge natural bay, and a visit to the docks is almost always worthwhile as it will be a hive of activity, especially when the catches are being landed.

To introduce you to the fishing industry of the north east, visit the Peterhead Arbuthnot Museum, with fascinating displays on the development of this local trade. Peterhead is also home to Scotland's maximum security prison, and the high walls are much in evidence as you come into the town.

Leave the town to the north, following the signs for North Traffic, and rejoin the A952 for Fraserburgh. On the way you pass the huge complex at St. Fergus, where most of Britain's natural gas comes on shore from the North Sea.

Fraserburgh is another busy fishing port, pivoted around the old castle on the headland which is now a lighthouse. The oldest building in the town goes back to the 16th century, and there are a number of other old buildings including a fine market cross.

West of Fraserburgh, follow the B9031 to Rosehearty, which takes the coastal route past a succession of fascinating little villages.

Sandhaven and Rosehearty are the first two, with the latter having the further attraction of the ruins of Pitsligo Castle, an impressive ruin of 1424. In the middle of Rosehearty turn left for New Aberdour.

The road leaves the coast for a few miles, going through New Aberdour, one of many planned villages for agricultural workers in the 18th century.

Then it's back to the coast and Pennan. It is entirely hidden from the main road, and can be reached only by a steep descent down a single track road. At the sea front, turn left for the car park.

This village achieved fame through its starring role in the film 'Loca Hero', but be warned that some artistic licence was used when making the film. Those glorious sandy beaches were actually over on the west coast near Oban! For all that, it is still a charming little village.

Two miles to the west round the headland, and even more dramatic, is Crovie, perched on a narrow strip of land between the cliffs and the sea. Although it can be reached by road, there really is no room for visiting cars, so park instead at the viewpoint overlooking the village.

Gardenstown, the next village across the bay, seems ridiculously large for its precarious situation on the hillside. It has an attractive walled harbour and steep winding roads.

The B9031 a few miles later rejoins the A98 main road in time to enter the twins towns of Macduff and Banff, split by the River Deveron. Macduff has an attractive harbour but far more interesting, across the river, is Banff. This old town contains Duff House, one of the finest mansions in Britain with its rich details, on your left as you enter town. There is also a museum in the town.

If you are returning to Aberdeen, this is a good place to turn south. Take the A947 to Turriff and on to Aberdeen itself, 45 miles away. There are some excellent castles on the way, including Delgatie, Fyvie and Tolquhon.

However, to carry on towards Inverness and the west, stay on the A98, with charming towns to look out for including Portsoy, with its 17th century harbour, Sandend and Cullen.

Just after Portsoy, signposted to the left is Fordyce, and it is well worth making the detour here for a look at this tiny village built round a 16th century castle and church.

Cullen has some interesting features, but it is rather dominated by the old railway viaduct above the town.

The A98 joins the A96 at Fochabers and this is now the main road from Aberdeen to Inverness. Consequently, traffic will be heavier from here onwards. Fochabers has a number of interesting little antique shops scattered along its main street.

Fochabers is also famed for its food, as the traditional Scottish firm of Baxters is based here. They have a visitor centre on the right as you leave the town, with a restaurant where you can sample their produce.

Drive on to Elgin, where you will hardly fail to be impressed by the magnificent cathedral; turn right at the roundabout as you enter town. Much of the original 13th century architecture remains, although it is a ruin. Elgin also has an award-winning museum in the centre that specialises in fossils alongside the more modern exhibits.

At the west end of Elgin, to the right off the main road are the Old Mills, which used to grind meal using the waters of the River Lossie. It now has a visitor centre and you can tour the mills.

At Forres, which has a new bypass, you can see Sueno's Stone as you come into the town, down a road on the right. This is a remarkable sculptured 9th or 10th century monument standing 20 feet high. Forres itself is a small market town that has become much more pleasant since the bypass opened.

Four miles west of Forres, just off the A96 down a tree-lined drive, is Brodie Castle, a 17th century structure noted for its fine collections of paintings and furniture. The woodland grounds are attractive, too, with a substantial pond and an adventure playground.

Nairn, your next sizeable town, is a popular resort, although its nickname of 'the Brighton of the north' is perhaps pushing its luck a little. However, there are splendid beaches and a fine harbour.

Inverness is now just 16 miles away, but there are important sights worth seeing off the main road.

Five miles south west of Nairn, on the B9090, is Cawdor Castle and its gardens. This has been a family home for over 600 years, although it probably goes back further; this was traditionally the setting for Macbeth's murder of Duncan.

Up the A9006 to the right is Fort George, a huge defensive fortification built in 1748 to guard the entrance to the Beauly Firth against a Jacobite invasion; it was never needed. It also contains a museum for the Queen's Own Highlanders Regiment.

Finally, a few miles before Inverness, turn left off the A96 and follow the signs to visit the site of the Battle of Culloden. The moor here has been restored to look as it might have done on 16th April, 1746, when Bonnie Prince Charlie's army was crushed. It is a haunting place, with headstones for the clans that fell and a great memorial cairn. There is also a visitor centre that explains what happened at the battle.

And so you come into Inverness, capital of the Highlands, and a great place to stay awhile. Then you can choose whether to go further north, to the west, or return to the south.

## NORTH EAST COAST ATTRACTIONS

Banff Museum. In Banff, on A947. Open June-September, daily except Thursday, 1400-1715. Admission free.

Baxters Visitor Centre. Half mile west of Fochabers on A96. Open Easter-October, Monday to Friday 1000-1200 and 1300-1600 (Friday 1400). Also Saturday and Sunday,

*Crovie*

mid May-mid September. Admission free.

Brodie Castle. Off A96, four miles west of Forres. Open April-September, Monday to Saturday 1100-1800, Sunday 1400-1800; October, Saturday 1100-1800 and Sunday 1400-1800. Grounds open all year, daily 0930-sunset. Admission: Adult £2.40, child £1.20.

Bullers of Buchan. On right of A975, two miles north of Cruden Bay. Accessible at all times. Admission free.

Cawdor Castle. At Cawdor on B9090, five miles south of Nairn. Open May-September, daily 1000-1700. Admission: Adult £2.90, child £1.50.

Culloden Moor. Beside B9006, five miles east of Inverness. Site open all year. Visitor centre open April-October, 0930-1930 (closes 1730 in April, May and from mid September). Admission: Adult £1.20, child 60p.

Duff House. In Banff, to left of bridge. Open April-September, Monday to Saturday 0930-1900, Sunday 1400-1900. Admission: Adult 60p, child 30p.

Elgin Cathedral. In central Elgin. Open April-September, Monday to Saturday 0930-1230 and 1330-1900, Sunday 1400-1900; October-March, Monday to Saturday 0930-1230 and 1330-1600, Sunday 1400-1600. Admission: Adult 60p, child 30p.

Fort George. At end of B9039, off A96 to west of Nairn. Open April-September, Monday to Saturday 0930-1900, Sunday 1400-1900; October-March, Monday to Saturday 0930-1600, Sunday 1400-1600. Admission: Adult £1.50, child 75p.

Forvie Nature Reserve. Off A975, 15 miles north of Aberdeen. Accessible at all times. Admission free.

Old Mills. In Elgin, at west end of town, half mile off A96 (signposted). Open all year,

Tuesday to Sunday 0900-1700. Admission: Adult 30p, child 15p.

Peterhead Arbuthnot Museum. St. Peter Street, Peterhead. Open all year, Monday to Saturday 1000-1200 and 1300-1700. Admission free.

Pitsligo Castle. By Rosehearty, on B9031, three miles west of Fraserburgh. Open all reasonable times. Admission free.

Queen's Own Highlanders Museum. At Fort George. Open April-September Monday to Saturday 1000-1800, Sunday 1400-1800; October-March, Monday to Friday 1000-1600. Admission free.

Slains Castle. Off A975, one mile north of Cruden Bay, car park on right of road. Open all reasonable times. Admission free.

Sueno's Stone. At east end of Forres. Accessible at all times. Admission free.

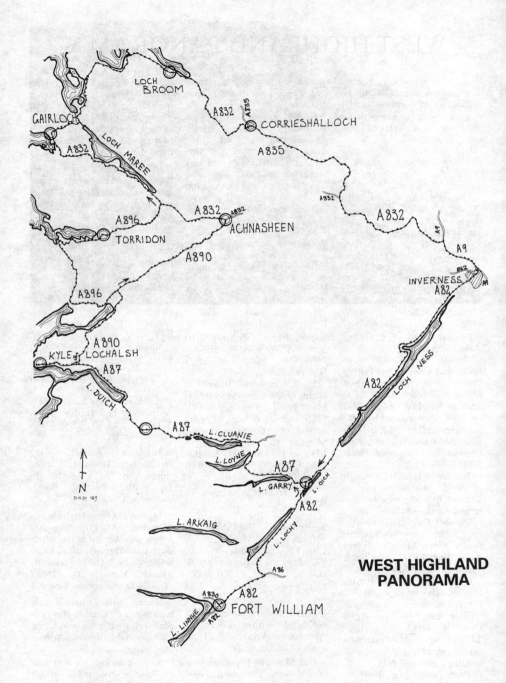

LOCH BROOM

GAIRLOCH

A832

A835

CORRIESHALLOCH

A835

LOCH MAREE

A832

A832

A832

A832

A9

A9

INVERNESS

A896

TORRIDON

A832

A832

ACHNASHEEN

A82

A890

A896

A82

LOCH NESS

A890

KYLE of LOCHALSH

A87

L. DUICH

A82

A87

L. CLUANIE

L. LOYNE

A87

L. GARRY

L. OICH

A82

L. ARKAIG

L. LOCHY

N

DSD 89

A86

**WEST HIGHLAND PANORAMA**

A830

A82

FORT WILLIAM

L. LINNHE

A82

58

# WEST HIGHLAND PANORAMA

This is a lengthy tour, if only because the attraction of the north west of Scotland is that you can drive for long distances with little to stop for.

Visitor attractions are few and far between, although those that are there are certainly impressive.

The enchanting Eilean Donan Castle, for instance, ppears on more tourist literature than any other Scottish building. Its setting really is magical, on an island in a loch with wonderful mountain backdrop.

The gardens at Inverewe are awesome: Palm trees in northern Scotland! You won't believe it till you have been there.

But the real attraction of this part of Scotland is all around you. The scenery really is second to none, from sweeping golden beaches through dramatic glens to the tall mountains.

Enjoy the quality of the light, so clean and pure. Make the most of the quiet roads, with a different view round every corner. Watch the Wildlife, undisturbed by modern civilisation.

This will be a drive to remember the rest of your life, so take your time and savour it.

## THE TOUR

Start at Fort William, which is just 14 miles north of Ballachulish (see the Glencoe tour). This town, as you would guess from the name, began its life as a fort, although there is no sign of it today. Although there is plenty to do here, it seems to be a town dominated by coach parties and the tourist industry has taken over.

Rising steeply above Fort William, its top usually shrouded in mist, but visible from time to time, is Ben Nevis, Britain's tallest mountain at 4,406 feet. You don't need to climb to the top to find out more, as there is an exhibition all about it in the town.

Head north from Fort William on the A82, and after only two miles there is the turning left towards Mallaig, an alternative road to Skye by the A830. However, stay on the A82 towards Spean Bridge, signposted for Kyle of Lochalsh and Inverness.

Just after Spean Bridge, as you approach Loch Lochy, there is an impressive monument to the Commandos of World War II who trained in this area. Stop there for fine views of Ben Nevis and Lochaber, if the weather is clear.

Continue alongside Loch Lochy to Invergarry, passing over the Caledonian Canal at the foot of Loch Oich. This canal joins Inverness with the west coast, using the networks of lochs that lie in the natural geological fault called the Great Glen, joining each of them with a short stretch of canal.

On the right of the road you will see the curious little monument called the Well of the Seven Heads, which recalls the grisly story of the execution of four brothers in the 17th century.

Turn left at Invergarry onto the A87, signposted for Kyle of Lochalsh. For the next 30 or 40 miles the road makes its way past Lochs Garry, Loyne and Cluanie amidst magnificent mountain and glen scenery. Civilisation (apart from the road) seems almost to have been left behind.

Not until you arrive at Loch Duich is there another visitor attraction, the National Trust for Scotland visitor centre at Morvich, a mile off the road to the right. It explains and introduces you to the Kintail area, through which you have just driven.

As you drive along Loch Duich, the fairytale castle of Eilean Donan comes into view, just off the shore but connected by a causeway. Now completely restored, it perhaps isn't as enchanting inside as it is from the outside, but that is a small complaint. Have your camera ready.

If you are considering visiting the Isle of Skye, continue on the A87 all the way to Kyle of Lochalsh, where you can catch the short but pricey ferry trip across the water.

This tour heads north, turning right onto the A890, signposted simply to 'The North'. As the road climbs steeply from the valley, you will immediately notice the change in tempo from busy main road to winding country lane, even though it is still classified as an A road.

In fact, soon it becomes so narrow that there is no room for two vehicles to pass. This may be your first encounter with single track roads, so you should know there is a simple code of conduct for all vehicles.

Always give way to oncoming traffic by pulling in at the marked passing places to let them pass, unless they have already done so for you. And always pull in to let the traffic behind you pass, if they are travelling faster than you. It may take a little getting used to, especially as you have to watch out for oncoming traffic, but it shouldn't prove too difficult.

Another point to remember is that petrol stations are much further apart and probably won't stay open in the evenings, so always try to make sure you have plenty of petrol in reserve.

Follow the A890 for 16 miles alongside Loch Carron to Strathcarron junction, where you turn right along the A890 signposted to Achnasheen. You may be surprised to find a road alongside a railway, but this is the famous West Highland line from Inverness to Kyle.

There is an 18 mile drive through Glen Carron, with hills and mountains to either side, and some attractive gardens at Achnashellach Lodge. At Achnasheen turn left onto the A832 for Kinlochewe and Gairloch.

Just after Kinlochewe, ten miles away, the road follows the shore of Loch Maree, a long and particularly beautiful loch. The road has been rebuilt here, but ends rather abruptly with another stretch of single track. There is an award-winning heritage museum in Gairloch with displays of all aspects of Highland life, and you may decide to stay in the town to explore the surrounding area.

However, if you drive on, still with the A832, five miles north at Poolewe are the great Inverewe Gardens, started 120 years ago. Plants from all

around the world thrive here, giving an almost continuous display of colour all year, making the most of the comparatively warm waters brought by the Gulf Stream.

The road continues its way along the coastline, with views of Loch Ewe, Gruinard Bay and Little Loch Broom in turn. The scenery never fails to impress.

After Little Loch Broom the road heads inland and joins up with the larger A835 route at Corrieshalloch. If you want to carry on exploring the north west coast, turn left here for Ullapool, but we are going to take the right turn and head towards Inverness.

Before you go, however, stop for a look at Corrieshalloch Gorge, a spectacular mile long crevasse, with a waterfall, that plunges 200 feet below the suspension bridge and precarious viewpoint. Park half a mile down the Ullapool road.

You are now driving south east on the A835, which after 20 miles becomes the A832, with a transformation in the scenery from mountain to farmland. Follow the signs to Strathpeffer and Dingwall by turning right onto the A834.

Strathpeffer, two miles up the road, has retained the atmosphere of the Victorian spa town that it once was, and you can see the original sulphur wells at the Pump Room. The railway station is particularly well preserved and contains a visitor centre.

Next stop is Dingwall, your first point of contact with the east coast. Drive up the hill in the town to the Sir Hector MacDonald monument, which gives a superb view down the Cromarty Firth. Dingwall is the county town of Ross-shire and has an air of aloof superiority.

Turn right at Dingwall to rejoin the A835 then the A9 for the few miles drive to Inverness. This is largely a new road, built to take the extra traffic created by the superb bridge at Kessock which you are about to cross, over the Beauly Firth into Inverness.

The capital of the Highlands dominates the north of Scotland, both administratively and culturally. Inverness, with a population of about 40,000, is the only place north of Perth or west of Aberdeen that has any pretentions to calling itself a city, and a very attractive city it is, too.

The River Ness cuts a swathe through the city centre, and that's not a new railway bridge you see being built across it: the old one was swept away in a flood a couple of years ago and this is the reconstruction work.

For all Inverness's history, little remains from before Victorian days; even the castle and cathedral are both 19th century creations. But as a centre for touring the surrounding area it has all the facilities a visitor could wish for.

The River Ness is, of course, a link with famous Loch Ness to the south, where thousands of visitors – no matter how sceptical – will keep an eye open for an appearance by Nessie the Monster. You can start your monster-spotting activities by going to the Loch Ness Monster Video Show in Inverness; and if you prefer to get closer to the loch than the road, you could take a cruise on the Scot II which leaves from the town.

The lochside road, however, provides plenty of good vantage points as it follows

*Loch Shiel – Above to West: Below to East*

Loch Ness for the full extent of its 24 miles. Take the A82 out of Inverness, the road you will stay on for the rest of this tour, back to Fort William.

At Drumnadrochit there is the official Loch Ness Monster Exhibition Centre, a comprehensive and fascinating place that will tell you anything and everything there is to know about Nessie.

Close by are the extensive medieval ruins of Urquhart Castle on a headland overlooking the loch. This is an atmospheric place that gives Loch Ness a touch of drama, so perhaps it is not surprising that more monster sightings are made here than anywhere else.

Loch Ness comes to an end at Fort Augustus, formerly a garrison town but now famous for its Benedictine abbey and school. In the town you can visit the Great Glen Highland Heritage Museum.

Invergarry is where you complete this circular tour of the north west of Scotland. Continue south to Fort William, retracing your route at the start, or cut across on the A86 from Spean Bridge to Newtonmore to reach the central Highlands.

You have seen some of the best and most unspoilt scenery that Scotland has to offer, and if the weather was good it will have been a memorable experience.

## WEST HIGHLAND ATTRACTIONS

Ben Nevis Exhibition, In Fort William. Open July and August, daily 0900-2200; Easter-June and September-November, daily 0900-1730. Admission: Adult 10p, child free.

Commando Memorial. Beside A82, 11 miles north east of Fort William. Accessible at all times, admission free.

Corrieshalloch Gorge. Beside A835 at Braemore, by junction with A832. Accessible at all times, admission free.

Eilean Donan Castle. Beside A87, overlooking Loch Duich. Open Easter-September, daily 1000-1230 and 1400-1800. Admission: £1.00.

Gairloch Heritage Museum. In Gairloch. Open Easter-end September, Monday to Saturday 1000-1700. Admission: Adult 50p, child 10p.

Great Glen Highland Heritage Museum. In Fort Augustus beside the canal. Open April-October, daily 0930-1700. Admission free (or by donation).

Inverewe Gardens. On A832, six miles north of Gairloch. Gardens open all year, daily 0930-sunset. Visitor Centre open May-early September, Monday to Saturday 0930-1800, Sunday 1200-1800; April and early September-October, Monday-Saturday 1000-1700, Sunday 1200-1700. Admission: Adult £2.20, child £1.10.

Inverness Museum and Art Gallery. In Castle Wynd, central Inverness. Open all year, Monday-Friday 0900-1700. Admission free.

Kintail Visitor Centre. At Morvich, one mile from A87. Open June-September, Monday to Saturday 1000-1800, Sunday 1400-1800. Admission by donation.

Loch Ness Monster Exhibition Centre. At Drumnadrochit on A82, 14 miles south of Inverness. Open June-September, daily 0900-2130; October-May, Monday to Saturday 0900-1700. Admission: Adult £1.65, child £1.00.

Loch Ness Monster Video Show. In Huntly Street, Inverness. Open June-September, daily 0930-2130; October-May, Monday to Saturday 0900-1700.

Pump Room. The Square, Strathpeffer. Open May-October, Monday to Saturday 1000-1200 and 1430-1630. Admission: Adult 50p, child free.

Saint Andrew's Cathedral. Inverness. Open in daylight hours, in summer 0800-2100; daily services at 1230 and 1730. Admission free or by donation.

Scot II Cruises. Depart from Muirton Locks in Inverness. Cruises depart April-September, Monday to Friday 1015; May-September, Monday to Friday 1415. Fare: Adult £6.00 and £3.50; child £3.00 and £1.75.

Sir Hector MacDonald Monument. On Mitchell Hill above Dingwall, signposted from town centre. Open all times. Admission free. For keys to tower, tel: Dingwall (0349) 62391.

Strathpeffer Visitor Centre. In renovated railway station in Strathpeffer. Audio/visual programme runs May-September in evenings. Admission free.

Urquhart Castle. Two miles south east of Drumnadrochit, by A82. Open April-September, Monday to Saturday 0930-1900, Sunday 1400-1900; October-March, Monday to Saturday 0930-1600, Sunday 1400-1600. Admission: Adult £1.00, child 50p.

Well of the Seven Heads. By A82 on west shore of Loch Oich. Accessible at all times, no admission charge.

West Highland Museum. In Cameron Square, Fort William. Open all year, Monday to Saturday 1000-1300 and 1400-1700 (July and August 0930-2100, June and September 0930-1730). Admission: Adult 50p, child 20p.

# THE FAR NORTH

North of Inverness is an area rarely visited by tourists, where the scenery is radically different from the Highlands.

The mountains give way to the wind-swept hills and lochs of Sutherland and Caithness, where there are few roads and fewer villages away from the main coastal routes.

It is scenery that has a splendour all of its own, a rugged wilderness where you can feel truly alone, then suddenly come across a hamlet or a remote roadside inn.

In recent years the hills have to some extent been tamed by the Forestry Commission, who have planted millions of trees that are bred for their hardiness. Little else could grow here apart from grass and heather.

As you drive, be prepared for a windy ride, especially on the A9 main east coast route.

It is what might once have been called 'frontier country'. But the welcome is much too friendly for that.

## THE ROUTE

From Inverness to the northern tip of the Scottish mainland is just over 140 miles, all of it on the A9 and most of it clinging tenaciously to the eastern coast.

Almost surprisingly, it is actually quite a good road for most of the way, with a considerable amount having been spent in recent years of resurfacing and widening.

The most tangible benefits to drivers, however, are the two bridges across the Beauly and Cromarty Firths, which save driving the meandering roads inland.

The first of these bridges, the Kessock Bridge from Inverness, is a fine sweeping structure that takes you north into the Black Isle, a name which is a little bit misleading as it is neither black nor an isle. This is a fertile peninsula with many farms, which you can admire from the new fast road over the hill and down to the Cromarty Firth.

The Cromarty Bridge is rather disappointing, in contrast, being merely a causeway, but it gets you there all the same.

The A9 sweeps along past Invergordon and Nigg Bay, which witnessed a boom period during the heady days of North Sea oil exploration due to the happy coincidence of deep water, shelter and proximity to the oilfields. You can still often see rigs just offshore for construction or repair.

The road has to make a substantial loop inland via Bonar Bridge to cross the Dornoch Firth, but there are plans to build a bridge across the mouth of the firth to cut out a good ten miles journey. Whether or when it is ever built is another story.

Driving back along the north side of the Dornoch Firth, it is worth making the short detour to the town of Dornoch itself, a couple of miles down the A949.

Dornoch is renowned for the quality of its golf course, which is of championship quality, and has allowed the town to develop as a fully-equipped holiday resort. It is also a place with a history, the most prominent building being the cathedral, which although founded in 1224 was beautifully restored in the 1920s. Across the road, in the unlikely setting of the old town jail, there is a craft centre.

Go back to the A9 from Dornoch by the B9168, turning right at the war memorial as you come out of town. Continuing north, just after Golspie is the superb Dunrobin Castle, home of the Earls of Sutherland since the 13th century, although most of the current building is 19th century. It is set in a great park overlooking the sea.

The main attraction of this road is the view out to sea, although you do drive through a succession of small towns like Brora, Helmsdale and Berriedale.

At Dunbeath, efforts have been made to preserve the character of the town, and there is a heritage exhibition in the town. The bridge and bypass may have opened by the time you read this, but make the trip down the steep hill into the village. One mile north on the A9 is the Laidhay Croft Museum, an 18th century croft complex furnished entirely in the style of the time.

The Clan Gunn has its heritage centre in the old parish church at Latheron, dating from 1735.

Next stop is Wick, a sizeable town after all the little villages along the coast. This is a busy place with a long history and no fewer than three castles to protect it, although all are now ruins.

Old Wick Castle, a mile to the south, dates from the 14th century, but more spectacular are the twin medieval castles

Wick itself used to base its prosperity on the harbour, which although still active is a shadow of its former self. The industry of today is the Caithness Glass factory, which you can tour.

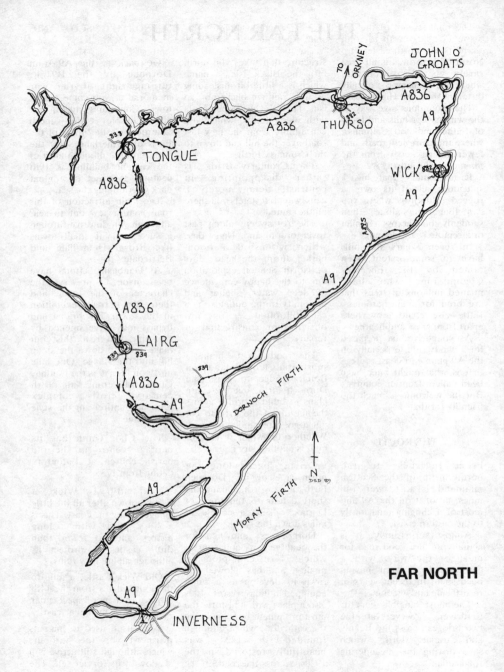

JOHN O'
GROATS

TO ORKNEY

A836

THURSO

A9

A836

WICK

A9

TONGUE

A836

A836

A835

A9

A836

LAIRG

A836

A9

DORNOCH FIRTH

N
DSD 89

A9

MORAY FIRTH

A9

INVERNESS

**FAR NORTH**

The final stretch of the A9 is the 17 miles north to John o'Groats, the north eastern tip of the British mainland and scene of a thousand charity marathons departing for Land's End, 873 miles away. The name derives from a Dutchman, John de Groot, who came to run the Orkney ferry in the 15th century.

The actual end of land is Duncansby Head, two miles further, where there is a lighthouse overlooking the dramatic cliffs, as well as the inevitable souvenir stalls. The views of the Orkney islands are excellent on a clear day.

Turn west from here along the A836 to Thurso, passing on the way the turning to Dunnet Head, the true northernmost point in Britain. The promontary here rises to over 400 feet, again giving terrific views over to Orkney.

Thurso keeps busy, as the neighbouring village of Scrabster is the ferry terminal for Orkney. If you want, you could take your car across the water to Stromness; the trip takes two hours.

The road to the west of Thurso, still the A836, becomes progressively more remote, winding its way along the north coast through a succession of little windswept villages. From Thurso to Tongue, your next turning point, is 43 miles, much of it on narrow single track road.

At Crosskirk, six miles west, there is an interesting ruined chapel, probably of the 12th century. In complete contrast nearby is Dounreay Nuclear Power Station, which has an exhibition area and tours of the prototype fast reactor.

Another small attraction, at the village of Bettyhill, is Strathnaver Museum, housed in the 18th century church. Just as you enter Bettyhill, you could make a short detour

to Farr, signposted to the right, where there is a viewing area at the end of the road.

Tongue is really just a village but has a fair degree of importance by being the largest place for miles. It overlooks a sheltered bay, and you can see the causeway bridge that continues to the west.

Driving south from Tongue you leave the coast behind you for a complete change of scenery on the 37 miles to Lairg. There are few buildings apart from the hotels at Altnaharra and Crask, which keep going largely due to the popularity of the area for anglers.

Lairg, at the head of Loch Shin, marks the end of the vast expanses of moorland you have just driven through, and also the end of the single track roads.

At Invershin, a few miles further, the huge building across the river is Carbisdale Castle, one of Scotland's more exotic youth hostels.

You leave the A836 at last when you rejoin the A9 at Bonar Bridge. The main road comes as quite a shock after all those miles of open country, so if you relish another cross-country stretch you could get back onto the A836 four miles later, signposted as the direct route to Dingwall, and head over the hills instead. This will actually save you 12 miles.

And so you return to Inverness, having seen a part of the country that is largely unknown to many people, including a large proportion of Scots.

The far north of Scotland is not picturesque in the traditional tourist fashion, but its remote ruggedness gives it a quality all of its own.

## FAR NORTH OF SCOTLAND ATTRACTIONS

Caithness Glass. Harrowhill, Wick. Open all year, Monday to Friday 0900-1630. Admission and tour free.

Clan Gunn Heritage Centre. On A9 at Latheron. Open June-September, Monday to Saturday 1100-1800. Admission: Adult 60p, child 40p.

Dornoch Cathedral. In Dornoch, just off A9. Open all year, daily. Admission free.

Dornoch Craft Centre. In old town jail, Dornoch. Open April-September, Monday to Saturday 0930-1700, Sunday 1200-1700; October-March, Monday to Friday 0930-1700. Admission free.

Dounreay Nuclear Power Station. At Dounreay, ten miles west of Thurso on A836. Open Easter-September, daily 0900-1630. Admission and tour free.

Dunrobin Castle and Gardens. Off A9, 12 miles north of Dornoch. Open June-September, Monday to Saturday 1030-1730, Sunday 1300-1730. Admission: Adult £2.40, child £1.20.

Girnigoe and Sinclair Castles. Three miles north of Wick, take the airport road towards Noss Head. Park near lighthouse and walk across fields. Open at all times. Admission free.

Laidhay Croft Museum. On A9, one mile north of Dunbeath. Open Easter-September, daily 0900-1700. Admission: Adult 50p, child 15p.

Old Wick Castle. One mile south of Wick by minor road, signposted. Open at all times. Admission free.

Strathnaver Museum. Beside A836 at Bettyhill, in village church. Open June-September, Monday to Saturday 1400-1700. Admission by donation.

*View from Tongue*

*Tweed Bridge near St. Boswells*

 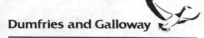

**ABERDEENSHIRE**

## KINCARDINE & DEESIDE DISTRICT COUNCIL
## ANDERSON ROAD CARAVAN PARK, BALLATER

Set in an area of oustanding natural beauty, the site is 300 metres from the town square, on the banks of the River Dee. Touring pitches, caravans to let, camping site available.

Open April-October

Adjacent to Ballater Golf Course, close to Balmoral Castle and woodland walks.

## QUEEN ELIZABETH CARAVAN PARK, STONEHAVEN

Set at the north of the town, half mile from the town centre, this site is easily reached from the A92 Aberdeen — Dundee road. Adjacent to Stonehaven Leisure Centre and the outdoor swimming pool. Near to the golf course and harbour. Touring pitches and caravans to let.

Open April-October

*Enquiries to* **Leisure & Recreation Section,**
**Kincardine & Deeside District Council, Viewmount, Stonehaven   Tel: (0569) 62001**

---

 *White Horse* **INN**

# BALMEDIE, ABERDEEN AB4 0XR
**Tel: Balmedie 42404 (STD Code 0358)**
ON A92 ABERDEEN-ELLON ROAD

Modern motel 5 miles (8 km) north of Aberdeen, situated adjacent to Balmedie Beach and Grampian Castle Trail with local golf courses nearby. All bedrooms have:

★ Private bathroom, shower
★ Colour TV, radio
★ Tea/coffee making facilities
★ Full central heating

A la carte & table d'hote meals served daily in the Whitehorse Grill. Children welcome. All major credit cards acceptable.

---

Westhall, with views of Benachie and its 11th Century Keep, combines the history and character of a Medieval Castle.

Bedrooms: 7 Double, 1 Twin, 4 Family. All with private facilities.

Prices: B & B £20-£30, double, twin and family. Open all year.

We have indoor tennis court, sauna & solarium. We are set in a secluded 500 acres with nice country walks, whisky trails and within easy reach of pony-trekking.

**Oyne, Insch, Aberdeenshire AB5 6RW.**
**Tel: (04645) 225.**

---

# TRADES DESCRIPTION ACT

*The accommodation mentioned in this holiday guide has not been inspected, and the publishers rely on information provided. The publishers have every confidence in their advertisers but cannot be held responsible for the accuracy of the descriptions published.*

---

---

74

**DUMFRIESSHIRE**

**DUNBARTONSHIRE**

# The Scot House Hotel

Newtonmore Road
**KINGUSSIE**
Inverness-shire PH21 1HE

*Telephone 0540 661351*

Resident Proprietors
Alasdair and Kathleen
Buchanan

The Buchanan family welcome you to our 19th Century country house style hotel which is the perfect base for the many attractions of the Spey Valley.

Each of our large well furnished bedrooms is en-suite with colour TV, tea making facilities and central heating. Our dining room offers a wide selection of carefully prepared dishes using the finest of local produce and our welcoming bar boasts an extensive range of fine wines and malt whiskies. Open all year with a range of off season packages from £27.50 per person half board. Children welcome. Advance booking recommended.

---

AA★★
RAC★★
## *Glen Hotel*

*Newtonmore (05403) 203 Reservations*

*Newtonmore Inverness-shire PH20 1DD*

Ideally situated for touring - near where the A9 meets the A86, opposite the Clan MacPherson Museum in the pretty village of Newtonmore. 9 comfortable bedrooms - most with private bathrooms. An enviable reputation for good food and good value. Lots to do all the year round. Please send for our fully descriptive brochure now, or call in and see for yourself.

---

Marine Guest House

# MARINE GUEST HOUSE
## Onich (08553) 251

Personally run by the MacKinnon family, the Marine Guest House offers a warm and friendly atmosphere. You can have a bedroom with or without private facilities, also a good Scottish breakfast or evening meal. We are situated in the picturesque village of Onich overlooking Loch Linnhe. We also have ample car parking and pets are very welcome. An ideal stopping area for the motorist.

**For brochure contact: Mrs. MacKinnon or telephone.**

---

## TO ASSIST WITH YOUR BOOKINGS OR ENQUIRIES YOU WILL FIND IT HELPFUL TO MENTION THIS

# Pastime Publications Guide

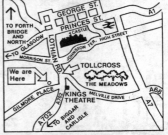

**Please mention this Pastime Publications Guide**

LOTHIAN

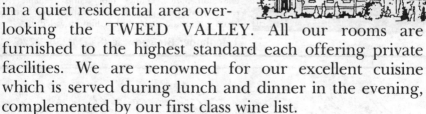

# TO ASSIST WITH YOUR BOOKINGS OR ENQUIRIES YOU WILL FIND IT HELPFUL TO MENTION THIS

# Pastime Publications Guide

TO ASSIST WITH YOUR BOOKINGS
OR ENQUIRIES YOU WILL FIND IT HELPFUL
TO MENTION THIS

# Pastime Publications Guide

# THE ISLE OF GIGHA

*Only the view will take your breath away.*

Relax and unwind in the tranquil atmosphere of Gigha - the fairest Isle in the Hebrides.

Stroll along the magnificent sandy beaches, visit the legendary gardens of Achamore and observe the brilliant array of wild flowers and birds.

For more active pursuits, sample our nine hole Golf Course, Clay Pigeon Shoot and Trout fishing. Stay at the Gigha Hotel and sample some real Island hospitality.

*We look forward to welcoming you.*

**For reservations please call: (05835) 254**

Gigha is only 20 minutes away from the mainland by car ferry from Tayinloan.

# PORT ASKAIG HOTEL

Port Askaig Hotel is a picturesque Island Inn situated on the shore of the Sound of Islay.

All bedrooms have colour TV, radio, tea/coffee making facilities, some have private bathrooms.

Menus feature the best of Scottish fare, local pheasant, venison, lobster and home garden produce.

An ideal base for exploring this magical island on miles of good roads. Easily accessible by car ferry from Kennacraig (5 miles south of Tarbert on the A83) 2½ hours drive from Glasgow.

Inclusive holiday package with car ferry tickets.

**Details from Mavis Spears, Port Askaig Hotel, Isle of Islay PA46 7RD.**
**Tel: 049 684 245/295.**

**L E W I S**

# Tower Guest House

### 32 James Street, Stornoway
### Tel: Stornoway (0851) 3150.

This comfortable and friendly guest house is an ideal base for a motoring holiday. Situated on direct route to Airport. It is within easy reach of every part of the island. Peaceful surroundings with beautifully clean white beaches. Fine golf course only 10 mins walk away situated in the Castle grounds, once the home of Sir James Matheson. Complex sports centre nearby.

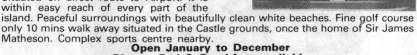

**Open January to December**
**Dinner, Bed & Breakfast available**
**For further details write to Mrs D. Hill**

---

**M U L L**

# THE WESTERN ISLES HOTEL

Under the personal direction of the resident proprietor the Western Isles Hotel offers true Highland hospitality, a warm friendly atmosphere, comfort and good food. Superbly situated overlooking Tobermory Bay, the hotel can be a haven of relaxation or a centre for outdoor activities. Many of our 24 rooms have private bathrooms. There is an elegant lounge and a terrace lounge embracing a breathtaking view of the Bay. The Cocktail Bar boasts many of Scotland's finest malt whiskies. The hotel has free use of golf courses, and guests enjoy free trout fishing. Cruises go to the Isles of Staffa, Iona, Tiree and Coll.

**For full colour brochure contact:**
**Reception, Western Isles Hotel, Tobermory, Isle of Mull PA75 6PR. Tel: 0688 2012.**

---

**S K Y E**

# Clan Donald Centre
## ARMADALE · ISLE OF SKYE

*Visitor Services Manager, Clan Donald Centre*
*Armadale, Sleat, Isle of Skye Tel: 04714 305*
**SKYE'S AWARD-WINNING VISITOR CENTRE**

### THE GARDEN OF SKYE
Over 40 acres of beautifully restored and sheltered woodland gardens.

### MUSEUM OF THE ISLES
The Story of 'The Lordship of the Isles'

STABLES RESTAURANT AND SHOP
COUNTRYSIDE RANGER SERVICE

Guided walks and Children's Events

*Suitable for the disabled.*

*LUXURY SELF-CATERING*
*ACCOMMODATION*

---

# Misty Isle Hotel
### Dunvegan, Isle of Skye. IV55 8WA.

The Misty Isle Hotel, situated at the edge of Loch Dunvegan, is an ideal touring centre.

Dunvegan Castle is near and on the other side of the Loch are craft centres, the Black House Museum, piping centre and imposing scenery.

**Telephone: 047 022 208.**

## TRADES DESCRIPTION ACT

*The accommodation mentioned in this holiday guide has not been inspected, and the publishers rely on information provided. The publishers have every confidence in their advertisers but cannot be held responsible for the accuracy of the descriptions published.*

*Passing place near Achnasheen*

*Glen Maree*

# TOURIST INFORMATION CENTRES

E: = Written enquiries to

## 1

### Angus

**ARBROATH**
Angus Tourist Board
Information Centre
Market Place
Tel: Arbroath (0241) 72609/76680
Jan-Dec

**BRECHIN**
Angus Tourist Board
Information Centre
St Ninian's Place
Tel: Brechin (03562) 3050
Jun-Sep
E: Arbroath

**CARNOUSTIE**
Angus Tourist Board
Information Centre
24 High Street
Tel: Carnoustie (0241) 52258
Jan-Dec
E: Arbroath

**FORFAR**
Angus Tourist Board
Information Centre
The Myre
Tel: Forfar (0307) 67876
Jun-Sep
E: Arbroath

**KIRRIEMUIR**
Angus Tourist Board
Information Centre
Bank Street
Tel: Kirriemuir (0575) 74097
Jun-Sep
E: Arbroath

**MONTROSE**
Angus Tourist Board
Information Centre
212 High Street
Tel: Montrose (0674) 72000
Jan-Dec
E: Arbroath

## 2

### Aviemore and Spey Valley

**AVIEMORE**
Aviemore and Spey Valley
Tourist Board
Main Road
Tel: Aviemore (0479) 810363
Jan-Dec

**BOAT OF GARTEN**
Boat Hotel Car Park
Tel: Boat of Garten (047 983) 307
May-Sep
E: Aviemore

**CARRBRIDGE**
Information Centre
Village Car Park
Tel: Carrbridge (047 984) 630
May-Sep
E: Aviemore

**GRANTOWN-ON-SPEY**
Information Centre
54 High Street
Tel: Grantown-on-Spey (0479) 2773
Jan-Dec
E: Aviemore

**KINGUSSIE**
Information Centre
King Street
Tel: Kingussie (054 02) 297
May-Sep
E: Aviemore

**NEWTONMORE**
Information Centre
Main Street
Tel: Newtonmore (054 03) 274
May-Sep
E: Aviemore

**RALIA PICNIC SITE**
Nr Newtonmore
Tel: Newtonmore (054 03) 253
Apr-Oct
E: Aviemore

## 3

### Ayrshire and Burns Country

**AYR**
Information Centre
39 Sandgate
Tel: Ayr (0292) 284196 (24-hr answering service)
Jan-Dec

**CULZEAN CASTLE**
Tel: Kirkoswald (0656) 293
Apr-Oct
E: Ayr

**GIRVAN**
Information Centre
Bridge Street
Tel: Girvan (0465) 4950
Apr-Oct
E: Ayr

**PRESTWICK**
Information Centre
Boydfield Gardens
Tel: Prestwick (0292) 79946
Jun-Sep
E: Ayr

**PRESTWICK AIRPORT**
British Airports Authority
Information Desk
Tel: Prestwick (0292) 79822
Jan-Dec
E: Ayr

**TROON**
Information Centre
Municipal Buildings
South Beach
Tel: Troon (0292) 317696
Apr-Oct
E: Ayr

## 4

### Ayrshire Valleys

**CUMNOCK**
Tourist Information Centre
Glaisnock Street
Tel: Cumnock (0290) 23058
Jan-Dec
E: Kilmarnock

**NEW CUMNOCK**
Tourist Information Centre
Town Hall
Tel: New Cumnock (0290) 38581
Apr-Sep
E: Kilmarnock

**DALMELLINGTON**
Tourist Information Centre
Tel: Dalmellington (0292) 550145
Apr-Sep
E: Kilmarnock

**DARVEL**
Tourist Information Centre
Tel: Darvel (0560) 22780
Apr-Sep
E: Kilmarnock

**KILMARNOCK**
Ayrshire Valley Tourist Board
Tourist Information Centre
62 Bank Street
Tel: Kilmarnock (0563) 39090
Jan-Dec

## 5

### Banff and Buchan

**BANFF**
Information Centre
Collie Lodge
Tel: Banff (026 12) 2419
Mid Apr-Mid Oct

**FRASERBURGH**
Information Centre
Saltoun Square
Tel: Fraserburgh (0346) 28315
Mid May-Sep
E: Banff

**FYVIE**
Information Centre
Fordoun
Tel: Fyvie (065 16) 597
End Apr-Sep
E: Banff

**PETERHEAD**
Information Centre
71 Broad Street
Tel: Peterhead (0779) 71904
Jul-Aug incl
E: Banff

## 6

### Caithness

**JOHN O'GROATS**
Information Centre
Tel: John o'Groats (095 581) 373
May-Sep

**THURSO**
Information Centre
Car Park
Riverside
Tel: Thurso (0847) 62571
May-Sep

**WICK**
Caithness Tourist Board
Whitechapel Road
off High Street
Tel: Wick (0955) 2596
Jan-Dec

## 7

### City of Aberdeen

**ABERDEEN**
City of Aberdeen Tourist Board
St Nicholas House
Broad Street
Tel: Aberdeen (0224) 632727/637353
Telex: 73366
Jan-Dec

Tourist Information Kiosk
(local bed-booking only)
Concourse
Railway Station
Guild Street
Jan-Dec

## 8

### City of Dundee

**DUNDEE**
Information Centre
4 City Square
Tel: Dundee (0382) 27723
Jan-Dec

## 9

### City of Edinburgh

**EDINBURGH**
City of Edinburgh Tourist Information
and Accommodation Service
Waverley Market
Princes Street
Tel: 031-557 1700
Telex: 727143 (Mon-Fri only)
Jan-Dec

**EDINBURGH AIRPORT**
City of Edinburgh Tourist Information
and Accommodation Service
Tel: 031-333 2167
Jan-Dec

## 10

### Clyde Valley

**ABINGTON**
'Little Chef'
(A7 Northbound)
Tel: Crawford (086 42) 436
May-Sep

**BIGGAR**
Information Centre
Main Street
Tel: Biggar (0899) 21066
May-Sep

**Nr HAMILTON**
(M74 Northbound)
Roadchef Service Area
Tel: Hamilton (0698) 285590
May-Sep

**LANARK**
Clyde Valley Tourist Board
Horsemarket
Ladyacre Road
Tel: Lanark (0555) 61661
Jan-Dec

**LESMAHAGOW**
The Resource Centre
New Trows Road
Tel: Lesmahagow (0555) 894449
May-Sep

**MOTHERWELL**
The Library
Hamilton Road
Tel: Motherwell (0698) 51311
May-Sep

## 11

### Cunninghame

**LARGS**
Information Centre
Promenade KA30 8BQ
Tel: Largs (0475) 673765
Jan-Dec

**MILLPORT**
Information Centre
Guildford Street
Tel: Millport (0475) 530753
Apr-Oct
E: Largs

## 12

### Dumfries and Galloway

**CASTLE DOUGLAS**
Information Centre
Markethill
Tel: Castle Douglas (0556) 2611
Easter-Oct

**DALBEATTIE**
Information Centre
Car Park
Tel: Dalbeattie (0556) 610117
Easter-Oct

**DUMFRIES**
Information Centre
Whitesands
Tel: Dumfries (0387) 53862
Easter-Oct

**GATEHOUSE OF FLEET**
Information Centre
Car Park
Tel: Gatehouse of Fleet (05574) 212
Easter-Oct

**GRETNA**
Information Centre
Annan Road
Tel: Gretna (0461) 37834
Easter-Oct

**KIRKCUDBRIGHT**
Information Centre
Harbour Square
Tel: Kirkcudbright (0557) 30494
May-Sep

**LANGHOLM**
Town Hall
Tel: Langholm (0541) 80976
Easter-Oct

**MOFFAT**
Information Centre
Church Gate
Tel: Moffat (0683) 20620
Easter-Oct

**NEWTON STEWART**
Information Centre
Dashwood Square
Tel: Newton Stewart (0671) 2431
Easter-Oct

**STRANRAER**
Information Bureau
Port Rodie
Tel: Stranraer (0776) 2595

## 13

### Dunoon and
### The Cowal Peninsula

**DUNOON**
Dunoon & Cowal Tourist Board
7 Alexandra Parade
Tel: Dunoon (0369) 3785
Jan-Dec

## 14

### East Lothian

**DUNBAR**
Information Centre
Town House
High Street
Tel: Dunbar (0368) 63353
Jan-Dec

**MUSSELBURGH**
Brunton Hall
East Lothian
Tel: 031-665 6597
Jun-Mid Sep

**NORTH BERWICK**
Information Centre
Quality Street
Tel: North Berwick (0620) 2197
Jan-Dec

**PENCRAIG**
A1
East Linton
Tel: East Linton (0620) 860063
Mid May-Mid Sep
E: Dunbar

# 15

## Forth Valley

DUNFERMLINE
Information Centre
Glen Bridge Car Park
Tel: Dunfermline (0383) 720999
May-Sep
E: Linlithgow

FORTH ROAD BRIDGE
Information Centre
Tel: Inverkeithing (0383) 417759
Easter-Sep
E: Linlithgow

KINCARDINE BRIDGE
Tourist Information Centre
Pine 'n' Oak
Kincardine Bridge Road
Airth
Falkirk
Tel: Airth (032 483) 422
May-Sep
E: Linlithgow

LINLITHGOW
Burgh Halls
The Cross
Tel: Linlithgow (0506) 844600
Jan-Dec

# 16

## Forth William and Lochaber

BALLACHULISH
Tourist Office
Tel: Ballachulish (08552) 296
Apr-Sep
E: Fort William

FORT WILLIAM
Fort William and Lochaber Tourist
Board
Tel: Fort William (0397) 3781
Jan-Dec

MALLAIG
Information Centre
Tel: Mallaig (0687) 2170
Apr-Sep
E: Fort William

SALEN
Tourist Office
Tel: Salen (096 785) 622
Mid Jun-Mid Sep
E: Fort William

# 17

## Gordon

ALFORD
Information Centre
Railway Museum
Station Yard
Tel: Alford (0336) 2052
Apr-Sep
E: Aberdeen

ELLON
Information Caravan
Market Street Car Park
Tel: Ellon (0358) 20730
Mid May-Sep
E: Aberdeen

HUNTLY
Information Centre
The Square
Tel: Huntly (0466) 2255
Mid May-Sep
E: Aberdeen

INVERURIE
Information Centre
Town Hall,
Market Place
Tel: Inverurie (0467) 20600
Mid May-Sep
E: Aberdeen

# 18

## Greater Glasgow

GLASGOW
Tourist Information Centre
35-39 St Vincent Place
Tel: 041-227 4880
Telex: 779504
Jan-Dec

PAISLEY
Town Hall
Abbey Close
Tel: 041-889 0711
Jan-Dec
E: Glasgow

GOUROCK
Information Centre
Municipal Buildings
Shore Street
Tel: Gourock (0475) 39404
Jan-Dec

GREENOCK
Information Centre
Municipal Buildings
23 Clyde Street
Tel: Greenock (0475) 24400

# 19

## Inverness, Loch Ness and Nairn

DAVIOT
By Inverness
Daviot Wood Information Centre
Tel: Daviot (0463 85) 203
Apr-Sep
E: Inverness

FORT AUGUSTUS
Information Centre
Car Park
Tel: Fort Augustus (0320) 6367
May-Sep
E: Inverness

INVERNESS
Inverness, Loch Ness and Nairn Tourist
Board
23 Church Street
Tel: Inverness (0463) 234353
Telex: 75114
Jan-Dec

NAIRN
Information Centre
62 King Street
Tel: Nairn (0667) 52753
May-Sep
E: Inverness

# 20

## Isle of Arran

BRODICK, Isle of Arran
Tourist Information Centre
The Pier
Tel: Brodick (0770) 2140/2401
Jan-Dec

# 21

## The Isle of Skye and
## South West Ross

BROADFORD, Isle of Skye
The Isle of Skye and South West Ross
Tourist Board
Tel: Broadford (047 12) 361/463
Easter-Sep
E: Portree

KYLE OF LOCHALSH
The Isle of Skye and South West Ross
Tourist Board
Tel: Kyle (0599) 4276
Easter-Sep
E: Portree

PORTREE, Isle of Skye
The Isle of Skye and South West Ross
Tourist Board
Tourist Information Centre
Tel: Portree (0478) 2137
Jan-Dec

SHIEL BRIDGE
Information Caravan
Tel: Glenshiel (0599) 81264
Easter-Sep
E: Portree

# 22

## Kincardine and Deeside

ABOYNE
Information Caravan
Ballater Road Car Park
Tel: Aboyne (0339) 2060
Easter-Sep

BALLATER
Information Centre
Station Square
Tel: Ballater (0338) 55306
Easter-Mid Oct

BANCHORY
Information Centre
Dee Street Car Park
Tel: Banchory (033 02) 2000
Easter-Sep

BRAEMAR
Information Centre
Balnellan Road
Tel: Braemar (033 83) 600
Easter-Oct

STONEHAVEN
Information Centre
The Square
Tel: Stonehaven (0569) 62806
Easter-Sep

# 23

## Kirkcaldy

**BURNTISLAND**
4 Kirkgate
Tel: Burntisland (0592) 872667
Jan-Dec

**KIRKCALDY**
Information Centre
Esplanade
Tel: Kirkcaldy (0592) 267775
Jan-Dec

**LEVEN**
Information Centre
South Street
Tel: Leven (0333) 29464
Jan-Dec

# 24

## Loch Lomond, Stirling and The Trossachs

**ABERFOYLE**
Information Centre
Main Street
Tel: Aberfoyle (087 72) 352
Apr-Sep

**BALLOCH**
Information Centre
Balloch Road
Tel: Alexandra (0389) 53533
Apr-Sep

**BANNOCKBURN**
Motorway Services Area
By Stirling
Tel: Bannockburn (0786) 814111
Mar-Oct

**CALLANDER**
Tourist Information Centre
Leny Road
Tel: Callander (0877) 30342
Apr-Sep

**DUNBLANE**
Tourist Information Centre
Stirling Road
Tel: Dunblane (0786) 824428
Apr-Sep

**HELENSBURGH**
Tourist Information Centre
The Clock Tower
Tel: Helensburgh (0436) 2642
Apr-Sep

**KILLIN**
Tourist Information Centre
Main Street
Tel: Killin (056 72) 254
Apr-Sep

**STIRLING**
Tourist Information Centre
Dumbarton Road
Tel: Stirling (0786) 75019
Jan-Dec

**TARBET**, Loch Lomond
Information Caravan
Pier Road
Tarbet
Loch Lomond
Tel: Arrochar (03012) 260
Apr-Sep
E: Stirling

**TILLICOULTRY**
Information Centre
Clock Mill
Upper Mill Street
Tel: Tillicoultry (0259) 52176
Apr- Sep

**TYNDRUM**
Information Centre Car Park
Tel: Tyndrum (083 84) 246
Apr-Sep

# 25

## Mid Argyll, Kintyre and Islay

**BOWMORE**, Isle of Islay
Information Centre
Tel: (049 681) 254
Apr-Mid Oct
E: Campbeltown

**CAMPBELTOWN**
Mid Argyll, Kintyre and Islay Tourist
Board
Tel: Campbeltown (0586) 52056
Jan-Dec

**INVERARAY**
Information Centre
Tel: Inveraray (0499) 2063
Apr-Mid Oct
E: Campbeltown

**LOCHGILPHEAD**
Information Centre
Tel: Lochgilphead (0546) 2344
Apr-Mid Oct
E: Campbeltown

**TARBERT**, Loch Fyne
Information Centre
Tel: Tarbert (088 02) 429
Apr-Mid Oct
E: Campbeltown

# 26

## Moray

**CULLEN**
Information Centre
20 Seafield Street
Tel: Cullen (0542) 40757
Jun-Sep
E: Elgin

**DUFFTOWN**
Information Centre
The Clock Tower
The Square
Tel: Dufftown (0340) 20501
May-Sep
E: Elgin

**ELGIN**
Information Centre
17 High Street IV30 1EG
Tel: Elgin (0343) 3388/2666
Jan-Dec

**FORRES**
Information Centre
Falconer Museum
Tolbooth Street
Tel: Forres (0309) 72938
May-Sep
E: Elgin

**KEITH**
Information Centre
Church Road
Tel: (054 22) 2634
Jun-Sep
E: Elgin

**TOMINTOUL**
Information Centre
The Square
Tel: Tomintoul (080 74) 285
Apr-Oct
E: Elgin

# 27

## Oban, Mull and District

**OBAN**
Oban. Mull and District Tourist Board
Argyll Square
Tel: Oban (0631) 63122
Jan-Dec

**TOBERMORY**. Isle of Mull
Information Centre
48 Main Street
Tel: Tobermory (0688) 2182
Jan-Dec (9-11 in winter months)

# 28

## Orkney

**KIRKWALL**, Orkney
Orkney Tourist Board
Information Centre
Broad Street KW15 1DH
Tel: Kirkwall (0856) 2856
Jan-Dec

**STROMNESS**. Orkney
Information Centre
Ferry Terminal Building
Pierhead
Tel: Stromness (0856) 850716
May-Sep
(also 2 hours per day Oct-Apr)
E: Kirkwall

# 29

## Outer Hebrides

**CASTLEBAY**. Isle of Barra
Information Centre
Tel: Castlebay (087 14) 336
May-Sep
E: Stornoway

**LOCHBOISDALE**, Isle of South Uist
Information Centre
Tel: Lochboisdale (087 84) 286
May-Sep
E: Stornoway

**LOCHMADDY**. Isle of North Uist
Information Centre
Tel: Lochmaddy (087 63) 321
May-Sep
E: Stornoway

**STORNOWAY**. Isle of Lewis
Outer Hebrides Tourist Board
Administration and Information Centre
4 South Beach Street
Tel: Stornoway (0851) 3088
Jan-Dec

**TARBERT**. Isle of Harris
Information Centre
Tel: Harris (0859) 2011
May-Sep
E: Stornoway

# 30

## Perthshire

**ABERFELDY**
Aberfeldy and District Tourist
Association
8 Dunkeld Street
Tel: Aberfeldy (0887) 20276
Easter-Mid Sep

**AUCHTERARDER**
Auchterarder and District Tourist
Association
High Street
Tel: Auchterarder (076 46) 3450
Apr-Oct
(Oct-Apr open 1000-1400 daily)

**BLAIRGOWRIE**
Blairgowrie and District Tourist
Association
Wellmeadow
Tel: Blairgowrie (0250) 2960
Jan-Dec

**CRIEFF**
Crieff and District Tourist Association
James Square
Tel: Crieff (0764) 2578
Apr-Oct
(Nov-Mar open 4 hrs per day)

**DUNKELD**
Dunkeld and Birnam Tourist
Association
The Cross
Tel: Dunkeld (035 02) 688
Easter-Oct

**GLENSHEE**
Information Officer
Glenshee Tourist Association
Corsehill
Upper Allan Street
Blairgowrie
Tel: Blairgowrie (0250) 5509

**KINROSS**
Kinross-shire Tourist Association
Information Centre
Kinross Service Area
Off Junction 6, M90
Tel: Kinross (0577) 63680 (62585 when
closed)
Apr-Oct

**PERTH**
Perth Tourist Association
The Round House
Marshall Place
Tel: Perth (0738) 38353
Jan-Dec

**PITLOCHRY**
Pitlochry and District Tourist
Association
22 Atholl Road
Tel: Pitlochry (0796) 2215/2751
Jan-Dec

# 31

## Ross and Cromarty

**GAIRLOCH**
Ross & Cromarty Tourist Board
Information Office
Achtercairn
Gairloch IV21 2DN
Tel: Gairloch (0445) 2130
Jan-Dec

**NORTH KESSOCK**
Ross & Cromarty Tourist Board
Tourist Office
North Kessock IV1 1XB
Tel: Kessock (0463 73) 505
Jan-Dec

**STRATHPEFFER**
Ross & Cromarty Tourist Board
Information Centre
The Square
Tel: Strathpeffer (0997) 21415
Easter, May-Sep
E: North Kessock

**ULLAPOOL**
Ross & Cromarty Tourist Board
Information Centre
Tel: Ullapool (0854) 2135
Easter-Sep
E: Gairloch

# 32

## Rothesay and Isle of Bute

ROTHESAY, Isle of Bute
Rothesay & Isle of Bute Tourist Board
The Pier
Tel: Rothesay (0700) 2151
Jan-Dec

# 33

## St Andrews and North East Fife

**ANSTRUTHER**
East Neuk Information Centre
Scottish Fisheries Museum
Tel: Anstruther (0333) 310628
May-Sep
E: St Andrews

**CUPAR**
Information Centre
Fluthers Car Park
Tel: Cupar (0334) 55555
Mid Jun-Sep
E: St Andrews

**ST ANDREWS**
Information Centre
South Street
Tel: St Andrews (0334) 72021
Jan-Dec

# 34

## Scottish Borders

COLDSTREAM
Henderson Park
Tel: Coldstream (0890) 2607
Apr-Oct

**EYEMOUTH**
Auld Kirk
Tel: Eyemouth (08907) 50678
Apr-Oct

**GALASHIELS**
Bank Street
Tel: Galashiels (0896) 55551
Apr-Oct

**HAWICK**
Common Haugh
Tel: Hawick (0450) 72547
Apr-Oct

**JEDBURGH**
Information Centre
Murray's Green
Tel: Jedburgh (0835) 63435/63688
Feb-Nov

**KELSO**
Turret House
Tel: Kelso (0573) 23464
Apr-Oct

**MELROSE**
Priorwood Gardens
Nr Abbey
Tel: Melrose (089 682) 2555
Apr-Oct

**PEEBLES**
Chambers Institute
High Street
Tel: Peebles (0721) 20138
Apr-Oct

**SELKIRK**
Halliwell's House
Tel: Selkirk (0750) 20054
Apr-Oct

# 35

## Shetland

LERWICK, Shetland
Shetland Tourist Organisation
Information Centre
Tel: Lerwick (0595) 3434
Telex: 75119
Jan-Dec

# 36

## Sutherland

**BETTYHILL**
Information Centre
Tel: Bettyhill (064 12) 342
May-Sep
E: Dornoch

**BONAR BRIDGE**
Information Centre
Tel: Ardgay (08632) 333
May-Sep
E: Dornoch

**DORNOCH**
Sutherland Tourist Board
The Square
Tel: Dornoch (0862) 810400
Jan-Dec

**DURNESS**
Information Centre
Tel: Durness (097 181) 259
Apr-Oct
E: Dornoch

**HELMSDALE**
Information Centre
Tel: Helmsdale (043 12) 640
May-Sep
E: Dornoch

**LAIRG**
Information Centre
Tel: Lairg (0549) 2160
May-Sep
E: Dornoch

**LOCHINVER**
Information Centre
Tel: Lochinver (057 14) 330
Apr-Oct
E: Dornoch

# FOR FURTHER INFORMATION

The offices on this page will be pleased to send you further information at any time of year.
Details are correct at time of going to press. Pastime Publications cannot accept responsibility for subsequent omissions or alterations.

1 Angus Tourist Board
Tourist Information Centre
Market Place
Arbroath DD11 1HR
Tel: Arbroath (0241) 72609/76680

2 Aviemore & Spey Valley Tourist
Board
Main Road
Aviemore PH22 1PP
Tel: Aviemore (0479) 810363 (24 hours)

3 Ayrshire & Burns Country Tourist
Board
Tourist Information Centre
39 Sandgate
Ayr KA7 1BG
Tel: Ayr (0292) 284196 (24 hours)

4 Ayrshire Valleys Tourist Board
62 Bank Street
Kilmarnock
Ayrshire KA1 1ER
Tel: Kilmarnock (0563) 39090

5 Banff & Buchan Tourist Board
Collie Lodge
Banff AB4 1AU
Tel: Banff (026 12) 2789

6 Caithness Tourist Board
Tourist Office
Whitechapel Road
Wick, Caithness
Tel: Wick (0955) 2596

7 Grampian Highlands & Aberdeen
Freepost
Aberdeen AB9 7AR
Tel: Aberdeen (0224) 632727

8 City of Dundee Tourist Board
The Tourist Information Centre
Nethergate Centre
Dundee DD1 4ER
Tel: Dundee (0382) 27723

9 City of Edinburgh District Council
Department of Public Relations and
Tourism
Waverley Market
Princes Street
Edinburgh
Tel: Edinburgh (031) 557 2727

10 Clyde Valley Tourist Board
Horsemarket
Ladyacre Road
Lanark ML11 7LQ
Tel: Lanark (0555) 2544

11 Cunninghame District Council
Tourist Information Centre
The Promenade
Largs KA30 8BG
Tel: Largs (0475) 673765 (24 hours)

12 Dumfries & Galloway Tourist
Board
Douglas House
Newton Stewart DG8 6DQ
Tel: Newton Stewart (0671) 2549/
3401

13 Dunoon & Cowal Tourist Board
Tourist Information Centre
Dunoon
Argyll PA23 7HL
Tel: Dunoon (0369) 3785 (24 hours)

14 East Lothian Tourist Board
Tourist Information Centre
Town House
Dunbar
Tel: Dunbar (0368) 63353

15 Forth Valley Tourist Board
Burgh Halls
The Cross
Linlithgow
West Lothian EH49 7AH
Tel: Linlithgow (0506) 844600

16 Fort William & Lochaber Tourist
Board
Cameron Centre
Cameron Square
Fort William PH33 6AJ
Tel: Fort William (0397) 3781 (24 hours)

17 Aberdeen & Gordon Tourist
Boards
St Nicholas House
Broad Street
Aberdeen AB9 1DE
Tel: Aberdeen (0224) 632727

18 Greater Glasgow Tourist Board
35-39 St Vincent Place
Glasgow G1
Tel: Glasgow (041) 227 4880

19 Inverness, Loch Ness & Nairn
Tourist Board
23 Church Street
Inverness IV1 1EZ
Tel: Inverness (0463) 234353 (24 hours)

20 Isle of Arran Tourist Board
Tourist Information Centre
Brodick Pier
Brodick
Isle of Arran
Tel: Brodick (0770) 2140/2401

21 The Isle of Skye & South West Ross
Tourist Board
Tourist Information Centre
Portree
Isle of Skye IV51 9BZ
Tel: Portree (0478) 2137

22 Kincardine & Deeside Tourist
Board
45 Station Road
Banchory AB3 3XX
Tel: Banchory (033 02) 2066

23 Kirkcaldy District Council
Tourist Information Centre
South Street
Leven KY8 4PF
Tel: Leven (0333) 29464

24 Loch Lomond, Stirling & Trossachs
Tourist Board
PO Box 30
Stirling
Tel: Stirling (0786) 75019 (24 hours)

25 Mid Argyll, Kintyre & Islay Tourist
Board
Area Tourist Office
The Pier
Campbeltown
Argyll PA28 6EF
Tel: Campbeltown (0586) 52056

26 Moray District Tourist Board
17A High Street
Elgin
Morayshire IV30 1EG
Tel: Elgin (0343) 2666 or 3388

27 Oban, Mull & District Tourist
Board
Boswell House
Argyll Square
Oban
Argyll
Tel: Oban (0631) 63122

28 Orkney Tourist Board
Freepost
Kirkwall
Orkney KW15 1BR
Tel: Kirkwall (0856) 2278

29 Outer Hebrides Tourist Board
4 South Beach Street
Stornoway
Isle of Lewis PA87 2XY
Tel: Stornoway (0851) 3088

30 Perthshire Tourist Board
PO Box 33
Perth PH1 5LH
Tel: Perth (0738) 27958

31 Ross & Cromarty Tourist Board
Tourist Information Centre
Gairloch
Ross-shire IV21 2DN
Tel: Gairloch (0445) 2130 (24 hours)

32 Rothesay & Isle of Bute Tourist
Board
The Pier
Rothesay
Isle of Bute PA20 9AQ
Tel: Rothesay (0700) 2151 (24 hours)

33 St Andrews & N E Fife Tourist
Board
Information Centre
South Street
St Andrews
Fife KY16 9JX
Tel: St Andrews (0334) 72021

34 Scottish Borders Tourist Board
Municipal Buildings
High Street
Selkirk TD7 4JX
Tel: Selkirk (0750) 20555

35 Shetland Tourist Organisation
Market Cross
Lerwick
Shetland
Tel: Lerwick (0595) 3434

36 Sutherland Tourist Board
Area Tourist Office
The Square
Dornoch IV25 3SD
Tel: Dornoch (0862) 810400

# EDITORIAL CONTENT

This information is divided into the following geographical sections:-

Borders
Edinburgh
Lothian
Fife
Perth
Angus
Aberdeen
North East
The Northern Highlands
Western & Central Highlands
Scotland's Islands
Central & South West Scotland
Glasgow

Within these sections the places of interest are listed alphabetically.

**READERS ARE ADVISED TO CHECK ADMISSION TIMES AND OTHER DATA.**

## ABBREVIATIONS
The abbreviations used in the entries are listed below, together with the head offices of the organisations concerned.

**AM**
Ancient Monuments in the care of the Secretary of State for Scotland and maintained on his behalf by the Scottish Development Department, Ancient Monuments Division, 3-11 Melville Street, Edinburgh EH3 7PE. Tel: 031-244 3101

**FC**
Forestry Commission (Scotland), 231 Corstorphine Road, Edinburgh EH12 7AT. Tel: 031-334 0303.

**NCC**
The Nature Conservancy Council, 12 Hope Terrace, Edinburgh EH9 2AS. Tel: 031-447 4784.

**NTS**
The National Trust for Scotland, 5 Charlotte Square, Edinburgh EH2 4DU. Tel: 031-226 5922.

**RSPB**
The Royal Society for the Protection of Birds, 17 Regent Terrace, Edinburgh EH7 5BN. Tel: 031-556 5624.

**SWT**
The Scottish Wildlife Trust, 25 Johnston Terrace, Edinburgh EH1 2NH. Tel: 031-226 4602.

**OPENING STANDARD**
This refers to the hours during which Ancient Monuments are open to the public: April to September: Mon-Sat 0930-1900, Sun 1400-1900. October to March: Mon-Sat 0930-1600, Sun 1400-1600.

**DISTANCES**

The distances indicated in the location of entries are approximate and are normally the shortest by road, except in a few remote places where they are "as the crow flies".

TO ASSIST WITH YOUR BOOKINGS
OR ENQUIRIES
YOU WILL FIND IT HELPFUL TO MENTION THIS
## Pastime Publications Guide

# PLACES OF INTEREST

## BORDERS

**Abbotsford House:** *A7, 2½m SSE of Galashiels. Late Mar-end Oct. Mon-Sat 1000-1700, Sun 1400-1700. (Mrs. P Maxwell-Scott, OBE). Tel: Galashiels (0896) 2043.* Sir Walter Scott's romantic mansion built 1817-1822. Much as in his day, it contains the many remarkable historical relics he collected, armouries, the library with some 9,000 volumes and his study. He died here in 1832. Free car park, with private entrance for disabled drivers. Teashop and gift shop.

**Bowhill:** *Off A708, 3m W of Selkirk. Grounds and playground open 30 Apr-29 Aug (not Fri). House open 9 Jul-21 Aug. Daily (incl Fri) 1200-1700, Sun 1400-1800. (House 1300-1630). Dates subject to slight alteration each year. Please telephone for precise information. Tel: Selkirk (0750) 20732.* For many generations Bowhill has been the Border home of the Scotts of Buccleuch. Inside the house, begun in 1812, there is an outstanding collection of pictures, including works of Van Dyck, Reynolds, Gainsborough, Canaletto, Guardi, Claude Lorraine, Raeburn, etc. Also porcelain and furniture, much of which was made in the famous workshop of Andre Boulle in Paris. In the grounds are an adventure woodland play area, a riding centre, garden, nature trails, tearoom and gift shop.

**Dawyck Botanic Gardens:** *B712, 8m SW of Peebles. Apr-Sep inclusive, daily 1000-1700. No animals (except guide dogs). (Royal Botanic Garden, Edinburgh). Tel: Peebles (0721) 6254.* All year round colour from spring bulbs to autumn tints. Rare trees, including many very fine conifers, shrubs, rhododendrons and narcissi, among woodland walks. In the woods is Dawyck Chapel, designed by William Burn.

**Dryburgh Abbey:** *Off A68, 6m SE of Melrose. Opening standard. (AM). Tel: 031-244 3101.* Peacefully situated on the banks of the Tweed, Dryburgh Abbey is one of the four famous Border abbeys founded in the reign of David I by Hugh de Morville, Constable of Scotland. Though little save the transepts has been spared of the church itself, the cloister buildings have survived in a more complete state than in any other Scottish monastery, except Iona and Inchcolm. Much of the existing remains are 12/13th century. Sir Walter Scott is buried in the church.

**Estate Exhibition Centre:** *The Hirsel, Coldstream.* Interesting exhibition of life and work of a large Borders estate. Extensive walks in grounds (and Dundock Wood) particularly noted for ornithological interest.

**Floors Castle:** *B6089, 2m NW of Kelso. (Castle and grounds) Open Easter Sun and Mon, from early May-late Sep, 1030-1750. (Garden centre) all year, daily 0930-1700. (Duke and Duchess of Roxburghe). Tel: Kelso (0573) 23333.* A large and impressive mansion, built by William Adam in 1721, with additions in the 1840s by William Playfair. A holly tree in the grounds is said to mark the spot where James II was killed by the bursting of a cannon in 1460. Location of the film 'Greystoke'.

**Greenhill Covenanters' House:** *In Biggar on A702 26m from Edinburgh, A74 (South) 12m. Easter, then mid May-mid Oct, daily 1400-1700. (Biggar Museum Trust). Tel: Biggar (0899) 21050.* Burns Braes Farmhouse, rescued in ruinous condition and rebuilt at Biggar, ten miles from the original site. Exhibits include relics of local Covenanters, Donald Cargill's bed (1681), 17th century furnishings, costume dolls, rare breeds of animals and poultry. Reduced price for joint admission to Gladstone Court Street Museum. Audio-visual programme.

**Grey Mare's Tail:** *Off A708, 10m NE of Moffat. (NTS). Tel: 031-226 5922.* A spectacular 200-feet waterfall formed by the Tail Burn dropping from Loch Skene. The area is rich in wild flowers and there is a herd of wild goats.
NB. Visitors should keep to the path to the foot of the falls: there have been serious accidents to people scrambling up and care should be exercised.

**Halliwell's House Museum and Gallery:** *Off main square, town centre, Selkirk. Apr-Oct, Mon-Sat 1000-1700, Sun 1400-1600. Jul & Aug open daily until 1800. Nov-Dec, Mon-Fri 1400-1630. (Ettrick and Lauderdale District Council). Tel: Selkirk (0750) 20096/20054.* This row of 18th-century dwelling houses has recently been extensively renovated and now houses an attractive and lively museum dealing with Selkirk's long and rich history. The building's history and its long link with the ironmongery trade are thoughtfully re-created. The Robson Gallery has constantly changing exhibitions. Listening post in ironmongers shop, and video in upstairs gallery.

**Hawick Museum**

*In Wilton Lodge Park, on western outskirts of Hawick. Apr-Sep, Mon-Sat 1000-1200 and 1300-1700, Sun 1400-1700; Oct-Mar, Mon-Fri 1300-1600, closed Sat, Sun 1400-1600. (Roxburgh District Council). Tel: Hawick (0450) 73457.* In the ancestral home of the Langlands of that Ilk, an unrivalled collection of local and Scottish Border relics, natural history, art gallery, etc. Situated in 107-acre Wilton Lodge Park, open at all times: riverside walks, gardens, greenhouses, recreations and playing fields. Small cafe.

**Hermitage Castle:** *In Liddesdale, 5½m NE of Newcastleton. Opening standard. (AM). Tel: 031-244 3101.* This strikingly dramatic 13th-century castle was a stronghold of the de Soulis family and, after 1341, of the Douglases. It has had a vivid, sometimes cruel history; to here Mary, Queen of Scots made her exhausting ride from Jedburgh in 1566 to meet Bothwell, a journey which almost cost her her life. The building consists of four towers and connecting walls, outwardly almost perfect.

**The Hirsel, Homestead Museum, Craft Centre and Grounds:** *On A697, immediately W of Coldstream. All reasonable daylight hours every day of the year. Entrance by donation. Groups by arrangement. (Lord Home of the Hirsel, KT). Tel: Coldstream (0890) 2834.* Museum housed in old farmstead buildings (with integrated Craft Centre) with history of estate, old tools, natural history. Walks in Leet Valley, round the grounds of Hirsel House (not open to the public). Famous rhododendron wood.

Tearoom open Sun and bank holiday afternoons, and for groups by arrangement.

**Jedburgh Abbey:** *High Street, Jedburgh. Opening standard, except Oct-Mar closed Thu afternoon and Fri. (AM). Tel: 031-244 3101.* This Augustinian abbey is perhaps the most impressive of the four great border abbeys, founded by David I in 1138. The noble remains are extensive, the west front has a fine rose window, known as St. Catherine's Wheel, and there is a richly carved Norman doorway. Remains of other domestic buildings have been recovered recently.

**Kelso Abbey:** *Bridge Street, Kelso. Opening standard. Free. (AM). Tel: 031-244 3101.* This 12th-century Tironensian abbey, was one of the earliest completed by David I and was built on a plan unique to Scotland. It was one of the largest of the Border abbeys. When the Earl of Hertford entered Kelso in 1545 the abbey was garrisoned as a fortress and was taken only at the point of the sword; the garrison of 100 men, including 12 monks, was slaughtered, and the building was almost entirely razed. The tower is part of the original building.

**Manderston:** *Off A6105, 2m E of Duns. Mid May-Sep, Thu & Sun 1400-1730. Groups by arrangement. (Mr A Palmer). Tel: Duns (0361) 83450.* This

Edwardian country house is one of the last great classical houses to be built in Scotland. The house contains a silver staircase, thought to be unique. It also gives an insight into life 'below stairs'. It has extensive estate buildings and gardens particularly noted for their rhododendrons. Tearoom, shop, gardens, stables and marble dairy.

**Mary, Queen of Scots House:** *Queen Street, Jedburgh. Easter-Oct, daily 1000-1700. (Roxburgh District Council). Tel: Jedburgh (0835) 63331.* A 16th century bastel house in which Mary, Queen of Scots is reputed to have stayed in 1566 when attending the Court of Justice. Now a museum containing several relics associated with the Queen. Delightful gardens surround the house which also forms part of the Jedburgh Town Trail.

**Melrose Abbey:** *Main Square, Melrose. Opening standard. (AM). Tel: 031-244 3101.* This Cistercian Abbey is the finest and largest of the Border abbeys, founded in 1136 by David I. It is notable for its fine traceried stonework. It suffered the usual attacks of all the Border abbeys during English invasions, but parts of the nave and choir dating from a rebuilding of 1385 include some of the best and most elaborate work of the period in Scotland. In addition to the flamboyant stonework, note on the roof the figure of a pig playing bagpipes. There is an interesting museum in the Commendator's House, at the entrance.

**Neidpath Castle:** *A72, 1m W of Peebles. 31 Mar-4 Apr, 30 Apr-9 Oct, Mon-Sat 1000-1300, 1400-1700, Sun 1300-1700. (Lord Wemyss' Trust). Tel: Aberlady (087 57) 201.* In a beautiful valley among wooded hills, Neidpath Castle is dramatically situated high above the River Tweed. This mediaeval castle, with walls nearly 12 feet thick, contains a rock-hewn well and pit prison, and two of the three original vaults. It is also an interesting example of how such a fortress could be adapted to the more civilised living conditions of the 17th century. There are fine views from several levels, right up to the parapet. The castle was once besieged by Cromwell and cannon damage is still visible.

**Priorwood Gardens:** *In Melrose, by Abbey, on A6091. Open daily Apr-Oct 1000-1730, Winter 7 Nov-24 Dec daily 1000-1730. Closed Saun and lunch times. Admission by donation. (NTS). Tel: Melrose (089 682) 2965.* A garden which specialises in flowers suitable for drying, also apple trees in variety. There is an NTS Visitor Centre. Picnic tables, orchard walk, dry flower garden, NTS shop.

**Scottish Museum of Woollen Textiles:** *On main road (A72) at Walkerburn, 9m ESE of Peebles. All year, Mon-Sat 1000-1730. Easter-Christmas, Sun 1200-1630. Free. (Clan Royal of Scotland). Tel: Walkerburn (089 687) 281 or 283 (0900-1500).* This display features the development of the woollen industry from a cottage industry to a major occupation of the Borders. Many interesting exhibits. Group bookings by arrangement. Coffee and tea shop.

**Smailholm Tower:** *Off B6404, 6m NW of Kelso. Opening standard, closed in winter. (AM). Tel: 031-244 3101.* An outstanding example of a 16th-century Border peel tower built to give surveillance over a wide expanse of country. It is 57 feet high, in a good state of preservation and houses an exhibition of costumed dolls and tapestries on the theme of Sir Walter Scott's 'Minstrelsy of the Scottish Border'. At nearby Sandyknowe Farm, Scott spent some childhood years.

**Thirlestane Castle and Border Country Life Museum:** *Lauder, 28m S of Edinburgh on A68. All May, Jun, & Sep, Wed, Thu & Sun only; Jul & Aug, every day except Sat. (grounds) 1200-1800, (castle) 1400-1700. Tel: Lauder (05782) 430.* Fine castle steeped in Scottish history, still the home of the Maitland family after four centuries. Magnificent 17th-century state rooms. Tea room, gift shop, gardens, museum and castle. The Border Country Life Museum Trust was established in 1981 to set up a museum to depict country life in the Scottish Borders from prehistoric times to the present day. Displays reflect the traditions, folklore and land use of the Borders. Demonstrations of vintage tractors and traditional farming methods are organised periodically by the Border Vintage Agricultural Association.

**Traquair House:** *B709, off A72, 8m ESE of Peebles. Easter then daily 1 May-30 Sep 1330-1730. Also in Jul, Aug and 1st two weeks in Sep, 1030-1730. Grounds and restaurant only from Easter. (P Maxwell Stuart). Tel: Innerleithen (0896) 830323.* Dating back to the 10th century, this is said to be the oldest continuously inhabited house in Scotland. 27 Scottish and English monarchs have visited it, including Mary, Queen of Scots, of whom there are relics. It was once the home of William the Lion who held court here in 1209. The well-known Bear Gates were closed in 1745, not to be reopened until the Stuarts should ascend the throne. Ale is regularly produced at the 18th-century brewhouse, and there are woodland walks and four craft workshops. Exhibitions are held during the summer months and the annual Traquair Fair is held the first weekend in August. Material available on cassette by arrangement. Restaurant/tearoom, gift shop, gallery, brewery, woodland and River Tweed walks and newly planted maze.

**The Woodland Centre:** *At Monteviot, 3m N of Jedburgh at junction of A68 and B6400. Easter-end Oct, Sun, Wed & bank holiday Mons only; 1 June-30 Sept. Open daily 1030-1730 or by prior arrangement for parties. (Marquis of Lothian). Tel: Jedburgh (0835) 62201 (Lothian Estates Office).* An interpretation centre, based on the old home farm of a large country estate. The major theme is the use of woodlands and timber. Exhibitions, woodland walks, pinery, games and puzzles, shop, slide show, adventure play area, tea room, parking.

## EDINBURGH

**Brass Rubbing Centre:** *Canongate Tolbooth, Royal Mile. Jun-Sep, weekdays 1000-1800; Oct-May, weekdays 1000-1700; Suns during Festival 1400-1700. Free. A charge is made for every rubbing, which includes cost of materials and a royalty to the churches where applicable. Tel: 031-225 2424, ext 6638/6678.* Rubbings of the brass commemorating Robert the Bruce and the Burghead Bull, a Pictish incised stone c AD 700 are among the selection available. Instruction and materials supplied.

**Butterfly Farm:** *5m S of Edinburgh on A7 towards Dalkeith. 25 Mar-31 Oct, daily 1000-1730. (Dobbies Garden Centre) Tel: 031-663 4932.* The farm, housed in a large greenhouse with lush tropical plants, cascading waterfalls and lily ponds, provides the setting for butterflies from all over the world to fly freely around. Exotic insects, photographic displays, tearoom, garden centre, tropical fish shop, children's playground and picnic area. Free car parking.

**Calton Hill:** *Off Regent Road at E end of city centre. All times. Free. Monument: Apr-Sep, Tues, Sat 1000-1800, Mon 1300-1800; Oct-Mar 1000-1500. (Edinburgh District Council) Tel: 031-225 2424.* A city centre hill, 350 feet above sea level, with magnificent views over Edinburgh and the Firth of Forth. The monumental collection on top includes a part reproduction of the Parthenon, intended to commemorate the Scottish dead in the Napoleonic Wars; it was begun in 1824 but ran out of funds and was never completed. The 102 feet high Nelson Monument (completed 1815) improves the view from its high parapets. The buildings of the Royal Observatory (1744 and 1818) are open on application to: The Custodian, City Observatory, Calton Hill, Edinburgh.

**Canongate Kirk:** *On the Canongate, Royal Mile. If closed apply the Manse, Reid's Court, near the church. Tel: 031-556 3515.* The church, built by order of James VII in 1688, is the Parish Church of the Canongate and also the Kirk of Holyroodhouse and Edinburgh Castle. The church silver dates from 1611. Restored in 1951, the church contains much heraldry. The burial ground contains the graves of Adam Smith, the economist, 'Clarinda', friend of Robert Burns, and Robert Fergusson, the poet.

**Canongate Tolbooth:** *Canongate, Royal Mile. Tel: 031-225 2424, ext 6678.* Built in 1591 with outside stair and a turreted tower. Temporary exhibitions are held throughout the year. Edinburgh Brass Rubbing Centre at street level.

**Craigmillar Castle:** *A68, 3¹/₂m SE of city centre. Opening standard (closed Thu (pm) and Fri) in winter. (AM). Tel: 031-244 3101.* Imposing ruins of massive 14th-century keep enclosed in the early 15th century by an embattled curtain wall; within are the remains of the stately ranges of apartments dating from the 16th and 17th centuries. The castle was burnt by Hertford in 1544. There are strong connections with Mary, Queen of Scots, who frequently stayed here. While she was in residence in 1566 the plot to murder Darnley was forged.

**Crystal Visitor Centre:** *Eastfield, Penicuik, 10m S of Edinburgh. All year. Tours Mon-Fri 0900-1530. Shop, Restaurant and Audio-Visual, 0900-1700 Mon-Sat and Sun 1100-1700. Tour charge (except for disabled). Children under 10 years not admitted to factory tour.* Conducted tours are available, unveiling every aspect of the glassmaker's craft. Children under 10 years not admitted on factory tours. No photography.

Audio-visual presentations Mon-Sat, 0900-1630. Licensed cafeteria, children's play area and picnic facilities.

**Dean Village:** *Bell's Brae, off Queensferry Street, on Water of Leith.* There was grain milling in this notable village of Edinburgh for over 800 years. The view downstream through the high arches of Dean Bridge is among the most picturesque in the city. A walk along the waterside leads to St. Bernard's Well, an old mineral source (open by arrangement).

**Edinburgh Castle:** *Castle Rock, top of the Royal Mile. Apr-Sep, Mon-Sat 0930-1705, Sun 1100-1705; Oct-Mar Mon-Sat 0930-1620, Sun 1230-1535. (AM). Tel: 031-244 3101.* One of the most famous castles in the world, whose battlements overlook the Esplanade where the floodlit Military Tattoo is staged each year, late August to early September. The castle stands on a rock which has been a fortress from time immemorial. The oldest part of the buildings which make up the castle is the 12th-century chapel dedicated to St. Margaret. In addition to the Great Hall built by James IV, with fine timbered roof, and the Old Palace, which houses the Regalia of Scotland and the Military Museum; the castle also holds the Scottish National War Memorial, opened in 1927.

**Georgian House:** *No 7 Charlotte Square. 1 Apr-31 Oct, Mon-Sat 1000-1700, Sun 1400-1700; 1-30 Nov, Sat 1000-1630, Sun 1400-1630. Last admission ¹/₂ hour before closing. (NTS). Tel: 031-225 2160.* The lower floors have been furnished as they might have been by their first owners, showing the domestic surroundings and reflecting the social conditions of that age. Charlotte Square itself was built at the end of the 18th century and is one of the most outstanding examples of its period in Europe. Bute House is the official residence of the Secretary of State for Scotland. The West side of the square is dominated by the green dome of St. George's Church, now West Register House.

**Gladstone's Land:** *747B Lawnmarket, Royal Mile. 1 Apr-31 Oct, Mon-Sat 1000-1700, Sun 1400-1700; 1-30 Nov, Sat 1000-1630, Sun 1400-1630. Last admission ¹/₂ hour before closing. (NTS). Tel: 031-226 5856.* Completed in 1620, the six-storey tenement contains remarkable painted ceilings, and has been refurbished as a typical home of the period.

**Greyfriar's Bobby:** *Corner of George IV Bridge and Candlemaker Row. All time. Free.* Statue of Greyfriar's Bobby, the Skye terrier who, after his master's death in 1858, watched over his grave in the nearby Greyfriars Churchyard for 14 years.

**High Kirk of Edinburgh (St. Gile's Cathedral, The High Kirk of Edinburgh):** *On the Royal Mile. Mon-Sat 0900-1700 (1900 in summer), Sun (pm). Free. Tel: 031-225 4363.* There has been a church here since the 9th century. Of the present building, the tower is late 15th century. At one time, there were four churches here, and yet another served as a prison. See also the exquisite Thistle Chapel. In the street outside the west door is the Heart of Midlothian, a heart-shaped design in the cobblestones. It marks the site of the Old Tolbooth, built in 1466, which was stormed in the 1736 Porteous Riots and demolished in 1817. Restaurant.

**Hillend:** *Biggar Road, S outskirts of Edinburgh. Charge for chairlift and session tickets for skiers are also available. (Lothian Regional Council). Tel: 031-445 4433.* The largest artificial ski slope in Britain. Facilities include chairlift, drag lift, ski-hire, tuition, showers and changing rooms. Grass skiing available May to September. Fine views from top of chairlift (available to non-skiers) of the Pentland Hills, over Edinburgh and beyond. Refreshments and picnic area.

**Huntly House:** *Canongate, Royal Mile. Jun-Sep, weekdays 1000-1800; Oct-May, weekdays 1000-1700; Sun during Festival 1400-1700. Free. Tel: 031-225 2424, ext 6678.* Built in 1570, this fine house was later associated with members of the Huntly Family. It is now a city museum illustrating Edinburgh Life down the ages, and contains important collections of Edinburgh silver and glass and Scottish pottery.

**Kirk of the Greyfriars:** *Greyfriars Place, S end of George IV Bridge. Easter-Sep, Mon-Fri 1000-1600, Sat 1000-1200. Free. Guided tour of Kirk and Kirkyard last Sun each month, Apr-Sep 1430. Free. Tel: 031-225 1900.* The Kirk, dedicated on Christmas Day, 1620, was the scene of the adoption and Signing of the National Covenant on 28 February 1638. The Kirkyard, inaugurated in 1562, is on the site of a 15th century Franciscan Friary. In 1679, 1,400 Covenanters were imprisoned in the Kirkyard. Various literature available.

**John Knox House:** *45 High Street, Royal Mile. All year, Mon-Sat 1000-1700. Tel: 031-556 6961.* A picturesque house, said to be the only 15th century house in Scotland, having traditional connections with John Knox, the famous Scottish reformer. The recent restoration programme has revealed the original walls, fireplaces and painted ceiling. There is also a 10-minute video film of John Knox's life in Geneva and Scotland.

**Meadowbank Stadium:** *193 London Road. Tel: 031-661 5351.* Sports complex, opened in 1970, was the venue for the Commonwealth Games of that year, and is now used for a wide variety of major sporting events throughout the year, with facilities for over 30 sports. Temporary membership is available to visitors on application to the Sports Centre. The Centre was also host to the Commonwealth Games in 1986.

**Outlook Tower and Camera Obscura:** *Castle Hill, between the Castle and Lawnmarket. All year daily, Apr-Oct, Mon-Fri 0930-1730, Sat & Sun 1000-1800; Nov-Mar, Mon-Fri 0930-1700, Sat & Sun 1030-1630. Last admission 45 minutes before closing. (Landmark). Tel: 031-226 3709.* This unique Victorian optical device projects a spectacular live image of the surrounding city onto a viewing table high in the Outlook Tower. Also rooftop terrace, and related optical displays including 'Holography', a permanent public collection of 3D laser images; pin-hole photography; space photography.

**Palace of Holyroodhouse:** *Foot of the Royal Mile. Apr-Oct 0930-1715, Sun 1030-1630; Nov-Mar 0930-1545 (not Sun). The Palace is also closed during Royal and State Visits and for periods before and after visits; check dates in May to July. Tel: 031-556 7371.* The Palace of Holyroodhouse is the official residence of the Queen in Scotland. The oldest part is built against the monastic nave of

Holyrood Abbey, little of which remains. The rest of the palace was reconstructed by the architect Sir William Bruce for Charles II. Here Mary, Queen of Scots lived for six years; here she met John Knox; here Rizzio was murdered, and here Prince Charles Edward Stuart held court in 1745. State apartments, house tapestries and paintings; the picture gallery has portraits of over 70 Scottish kings, painted by De Wet in 1684-86.

**Parliament House:** *Parliament Square, behind the High Kirk of St. Giles, Royal Mile. All year, Tue-Fri 1000-1600. Free. Tel: 031-225 2595, ext 223.* Built 1632-39 this was the seat of Scottish government until 1707, when the governments of Scotland and England were united. Now the Supreme Law Courts of Scotland. See the Parliament Hall with fine hammer beam roof and portraits by Raeburn and other major Scottish artists. Access (free) to the splendid Signet Library on an upper floor is by prior written request only, to: The Librarian, Signet Library, Parliament House, Edinburgh. Outside is the mediaeval Mercat Cross, which was restored in 1885 by W E Gladstone. Royal proclamations are still read from its platform. Restaurant.

**Royal Botanic Garden:** *Inverleith Row, Arboretum Road (car parking). Daily 0900 (Sun 1100) to one hour before sunset, summer; 0900-dusk,*

*winter. Free. Plant houses 1000 (Sun 1100) to 1700, summer; 1000 (Sun 1100) to dusk, winter. During Festival, opens at 1000 on Sun. Free. Tel: 031-552 7171.* The Royal Botanic Garden has a world famous rock garden and probably the biggest collection of rhododendrons in the world. The unique exhibition plant houses show a great range of exotic plants displayed as indoor landscapes and a plant exhibition hall displays many aspects of botany and horticulture. Tearoom and publications counter.

**Royal Observatory:** *Blackford Hill. (Visitor Centre) all year, daily, Mon-Fri 1000-1600, Sat, Sun & public hols 1200-1700. Tel: 031-667 3321.* Situated at the home of the Royal Observatory and University Department of Astronomy, the Visitor Centre demonstrates the work of astronomers, especially with telescopes in Australia and Hawaii. Also on show is the largest telescope in Scotland. Wide ranging bookshop, fine views of Edinburgh from hill. Alternative entrance for wheelchairs.

**Scotland's Clan Tartan Centre:** *70-74 Bangor Road, Leith, Edinburgh. Daily 0900-1730. Free. Tel: 031-553 5100 (0900-1800).* Exhibition, reference library and audio-visual display. Computerised tracing of clan links, extensive range of tartan accessories and clan crests.

Full Highland dress. Restaurant, large free car park and free courtesy bus (phone for details).

**Scott Monument:** *In Princes Street. Apr-Sep, Mon-Fri 0900-1800; Oct-Mar, Mon-Fri 0900-1500. Tel: 031-225 2424, ext 6596/6689.* Completed in 1844, a statue of Sir Walter Scott and his dog Maida, under a canopy and spire 200 feet high, with 64 statuettes of Scott characters. Fine view of the city from the top.

**Scottish National Gallery of Modern Art:** *Belford Road. All year, Mon-Sat 1000-1700, Sun 1400-1700 (extended hours during Festival). Free. Tel: 031-556 8921.* Scotland's collection of 20th-century painting, sculpture and graphic art, with masterpieces by Derain, Matisse, Braque, Hepworth, Picasso and Giacometti; and work by Hockney, Caulfield and Sol Le Witt. Also Scottish School. Cafe.

**Scottish National Portrait Gallery:** *E end of Queen Street. Weekdays 1000-1700 (extended hours during Festival), Sun 1400-1700. Free. Tel: 031-556 8921.* Illustrates the history of Scotland through portraits of the famous men and women who contributed to it in all fields of activity from the 16th century to the present day, such as Mary, Queen of Scots, James VI and I, Flora MacDonald, Robert Burns, Sir Walter Scott, David Hume and Ramsay MacDonald. The artists include Raeburn, Ramsay, Reynolds and Gainsborough. Reference section of engravings and photographs including calotypes by Hill and Adamson.

**Zoo:** *Entrance from Corstorphine Road (A8), 4m W of city centre. All year, daily, summer 0900-1800, winter 0900-1700 (or dusk if earlier). Sun opening 0930. Tel: 031-334 9171.* Established in 1913 by the Royal Zoological Society of Scotland, this is one of Britain's leading zoos, with a large and varied collection of mammals, birds and reptiles in extensive grounds on Corstorphine Hill. Edinburgh Zoo is world famous for its large breeding colony of Antarctic Penguins. Restaurants, bars, adventure playground and shops.

## LOTHIAN

**Antonine Wall:** *From Bo'ness to Old Kilpatrick, best seen off A803 E of Bonnybridge, 12m S of Stirling. All reasonable times. Free. (AM). Tel: 031-244 3101.* This Roman fortification stretched from Bo'ness on the Forth to Old Kilpatrick on the Clyde. Built about AD 142-143, it consisted of a turf rampart behind a ditch, with forts about every two miles. It was probably abandoned about AD 163. Remains are probably best preserved in the Falkirk/Bonnybridge area, notably Rough Castle, and at Bearsden.

**Athelstaneford Church:** *Off B1343, 4m N of Haddington. All reasonable times. Free; donations. Tel: Athelstaneford (062088) 243 or (062088) 378.* The plaque by the church tells the story of the origins of St Andrews Cross (the Saltire), which was first adopted as the Scottish flag at this place. A floodlit flag flies permanently on the site.

**Barns Ness West of Dunbar:** Interesting coastal stretch with lighthouse and selection of outcropping limestones. Car park, nature trail, sea angling.

**Bass Rock:** *Off North Berwick. Boat trips from North Berwick go round the Bass Rock. Tel: North Berwick (0620) 2197 (Tourist Information Centre).* A massive 350-feet-high rock, 1 mile in circumference, 3.25 miles ENE of North Berwick whose many thousands of raucous seabirds include the third largest gannetry in the world. Once a Covenanters' prison. Accessible on SW side only.

**Beecraigs Country Park, Linlithgow:** 700 acre country park with nature trails, trout farm, deer farm, country crafts, trim course and plenty of opportunities for a variety of sporting pursuits.

**Blackness Castle:** *B903, 4m NE of Linlithgow. Opening standard, except Oct-Mar closed Mon afternoon and Tues. (AM). Tel: 031-244 3101.* Interesting 15th century castle built out of the shore of the Forth,

suggesting a fortified ship in appearance. Once it was one of the most important fortresses in Scotland and was one of the four castles which by the Articles of Union were to be left fortified. Since then it has been a state prison in Covenanting time, a powder magazine in the 1870's, and more recently, for a period, a youth hostel.

**Bo'ness & Kinneil Railway:** *Off Union Street, Bo'ness. All year, Sat and Sun. Tel: Bo'ness (0506) 822298.* Working steam railway system, with historic locomotive and rolling stock. Live steam and authentic station buildings. Refreshments and sales stand. Buffer Stop Cafe (snacks), picnic area, visitor trail and visitor centre. Free car parking. Steam trains run summer weekends from 1200 - 1700.

**Crichton Castle:** *B6367, 7m SE of Dalkeith, nr. Pathead, Midlothian. Opening standard, except Oct-Mar, Sat and Sun only. (AM). Tel: 031-244 3101.* The keep dates from the 14th century, although today's ruins are mostly 15th/17th century. This castle, elaborate in style, has an arcaded range and impressive Italianate facade, including piazza. The upper frontage of which is wrought with faceted stonework and was erected by the Earl of Bothwell in the 16th century. The little Collegiate Church, ½m north, dating from 1499 and still in use, is notable for its tower and barrel vaulting. Signposted walk to Borthwick.

**Dalmeny House:** *By South Queensferry, 7m W of Edinburgh, take A90 then B924. 1 May-29 Sep, daily 1400-1730. Closed Fri and Sat. (Earl of Rosebery). Tel: 031-331 1888.* The Primrose family, Earls of Rosebery, have lived here for over 300 years. The present house dates from 1815, in Tudor Gothic style, built by William Wilkins. Interior Gothic splendour of hammerbeamed hall, vaulted corridors and classical main rooms. Magnificent collection of 18th-century British portraits, French furniture, tapestries, porcelain from the Rothschild Mentmore collection, the Napoleon collection and other works of art. Lovely grounds and 4½-mile shore walk from Crammond to South Queensferry.

**Forth Bridges:** *Queensferry, 10m W of Edinburgh.* For over 800 years travellers were ferried across the Firth of Forth. Queensferry was named from Queen Margaret who regularly used this passage between Dunfermline and Edinburgh in the 11th century. The ferry ceased in 1964 when the Queen opened the Forth Road Bridge, a suspension bridge then the longest of its kind in Europe (1,993 yards). Also here is the rail bridge of 1883-90, one of the greatest engineering feats of its time. It is 2,765 yards long.

**Hailes Castle:** *Off A1, 5m E of Haddington. Opening standard, except Oct-Mar*

closed Wed pm & Thu. *(AM). Tel: 031-244 3101.* 13th/15th century stronghold in oddly low-lying situation. Here Bothwell brought Mary, Queen of Scots on their flight from Borthwick Castle in 1567. There is a fine 16th-century chapel.

**The Heritage of Golf:** *West Links Road, Gullane, 14m ENE of Edinburgh. Open by appointment. Free. Tel: Aberlady (087 57) 277.* The exhibition shows how the game of golf developed after it arrived in Scotland from Holland in the 15th century. The visitor can see the simple origins, the natural materials and the skill of the early makers; and the development of golf from early days to the present.

**Hopetoun House:** *W of South Queensferry, May-Sep, daily 1100-1730 (last admission 1700). (Marquess of Linlithgow). Tel: 031-331 2451 (0900-1700).* This great Adam mansion is the home of the Hope family, Earls of Hopetoun and later Marquesses of Linlithgow. Started in 1699 to the designs of Sir William Bruce, it was enlarged between 1721-54 by William Adam and his son, Robert. The mansion still contains much of the original furniture from the 1760's and many portraits, which include, Rubens, Rembrandt and Canaletto. The extensive grounds include deer parks with fallow and red deer and St Kilda sheep. Also sea walk, formal rose gardens, educational day centre and stables museum featuring 'Horse and Man in

Lowland Scotland'. Nature trail, licensed restaurant. Family museum, rooftop viewing platform. Free parking.

**John Muir Country Park:** *Near Dunbar.* Extensive country park, extending 8.5 miles along from Dunbar Castle westwards, with sandy and rocky beaches, woodland walks and picnic areas. Easy parking from Belhaven.

**Linlithgow Palace:** *S shore of loch, Linlithgow. Opening standard. (AM). Tel: 031-244 3101.* The splendid ruined Palace overlooking the loch is the successor to an older building which was burned down in 1424. The Chapel and Great Hall are late 15th-century and the fine quadrangle has a richly-carved 16th-century fountain. In 1542 Mary, Queen of Scots was born here while her father, James V, lay dying at Falkland Palace. In 1746 the palace was burned, probably by accident, when occupied by General Hawley's troops. George V held a court in the Lyon Chamber here in 1914. This now roofless palace still represents one of the most remarkable achievements in Scottish mediaeval architecture.

**Museum of Flight:** *By East Fortune Airfield, off B1347, 4½m S of North Berwick. Jul-Aug, daily 1000-1600, and several open days. Free. (National Museums of Scotland). Tel: Athelstaneford (062 088) 308.* Aircraft on display at this World War II former RAF airfield range from a supersonic Lightening fighter to the last Comet 4 which was in airline service. The varied collection also includes a Spitfire, a 1930 Puss Moth and a 'Blue Streak' rocket. Special exhibitions relate to the development of fighter aircraft from 1914 to 1940 and to the airship R34 which flew from East Fortune to New York in 1919. Toilets, picnic area. Free car and coach park.

**Rosslyn Chapel:** *At Roslin, off A703, 7½m S of Edinburgh. 1 Apr-31 Oct. Mon-Sat 1000-1700, Sun 1200-1645. Tel: 031-440 2159.* This 15th century chapel is one of Scotland's lovliest and most historic churches, renowned for its magnificent sculpture and Prentice Pillar. It is situated in a beautiful wooded setting near the village of Roslin. Coffee shop and craft shop.

**Scottish Mining Museum:** *At Morrisons' Haven, on B1348, 8m E of Edinburgh, on the E.Lothian coast at Prestonpans. Summer closed Mon. Tue-Fri 1000-1630, Sat & Sun 1200-1700. Winter closed Mon. Tue-Fri 1000-1530, Sat & Sun 1200-1630. Guided tours. No refreshments. Free. (Scottish Mining Museum Trust). Tel: 031-663 7519.* A former colliery site with 800 years of mining history. Visitor Centre provides audio-visual programme plus walk-through exhibition and displays concerning mining and related industries at site. Cornish Beam Pumping Engine House

and Exhibition Hall containing mining artefacts. Self-drive Coal Heritage Trail to Lady Victoria Colliery. Also on view are three steam locomotives, a steam navvy, a colliery winding engine and remains of a Hoffman Kiln. Special 'Steam Days' on first Sunday of each month Apr-Oct. Organised parties must book. Refreshments, free car parking, picnic area, free leaflets.

**Stevenson House:** *Near Haddington, East Lothian. House and garden: 7 Jul-14 Aug, Thu, Sat & Sun; other times by arrangement. Groups welcome. (Mrs J C H Dunlop). Tel: Haddington (062 082) 3376.* Although the mansion house dates from the 13th century, the present house dates mainly from the 16th century. It was altered both structurally and in decoration during the 18th century. The guided tour includes details of the history, furniture, pictures and china. Well landscaped gardens (both House Garden and Walled Kitchen Garden).

**Tantallon Castle:** *A198, 3m E of North Berwick. Opening standard, except Oct-Mar closed Wed and Thu am. (AM). Tel: 031-244 3101.* Very impressive fortification in magnificent clifftop setting. Earliest parts date from 14th century. Associated with the Earls of Douglas. Although the castle withstood a regular siege by James V in 1528, it was eventually destroyed by General Monk in 1651.

**The House of the Binns:** *Off A904, 4m E of Linlithgow. Easter and 1 May-Sep, daily (except Fri) 1400-1700 (last tour 1630). Parties to book beforehand. (Park) 1000-1900. (NTS). Tel: Linlithgow (050683) 4255.* Occupied for more than 350 years, The Binns dates largely from the time of General Tam Dalyell, 1615-1685, and his father. It reflects the early 17th-century transition in Scottish architecture from fortified stronghold to gracious mansion. There are magnificent plaster ceilings, fine views across the Forth and a visitor trail.

## FIFE

**Aberdour Castle:** *At Aberdour, A92, 10m E of Dunfermline. Opening standard, except closed Thu am and Fri in winter. (AM). Tel: 031-244 3101.* Overlooking the harbour at Aberdour, the oldest part is the tower, which dates back to the 14th century. To this other buildings were added in succeeding centuries. A fine circular doocot stands nearby, and here also is St. Fillan's Parish Church, part Norman, part 16th century.

**Balbirnie Park and Craft Centre:** *In Balbirnie Estate, Markinch, on eastern outskirts of Glenrothes New Town. (Craft Centre) all year, Tue-Sat 1000-1730, Sun 1330-1730. Free. Tel: Glenrothes (0592) 755975.* Glenrothes Landscaped parkland

*Falkland Palace*

round early 19th century mansion (now Glenrothes Development Corporation headquarters). Interesting tree species and spectacular rhododendron collection. Craft Centre has seven workshops of potter, leatherworker, jeweller and silversmith, modern furniture maker, stained glass artist, fashion designer and reproduction furniture maker. Glenrothes itself has fine examples of modern sculpture.

**Balmerino Abbey:** *On S shore of River Tay on unclassified road 5m W of Newport. View from outside only. Free. (NTS). Tel: Gauldry (082 624) 733.* Cistercian abbey founded in 1229 by Queen Ermingade, second wife of William Lyon. Ruined during period of reformation. Set in particularly peaceful gardens.

**Botanic Gardens:** *St. Andrews.* Often overlooked amid the town's many other attractions, the diversity of the world-wide collection of plants is not to be missed.

**Culross Abbey:** *7¹/²m W of Dunfermline. All reasonable times. Free. Tel: 031–244 3101.* The remains of a 13th-century Cistercian Monastery. The choir of the Abbey Church is the present Parish Church.

**Culross Palace:** *Culross, 7¹/²m W of Dunfermline. Opening standard. (AM). Tel: 031-244 3101.* Culross, on the north shore of the

River Forth, is a most remarkable example of a small town of the 16th and 17th centuries which has changed little in 300 years. The small 'palace' was built between 1597 and 1611 by Sir George Bruce, who developed the sea-going trade in salt and coal from Culross. With crow-stepped gables and pantiled roofs, the 'palace' also has outstanding painted ceilings. Other buildings which must be seen include the Study, the Town House, the Ark and the Nunnery.

**Douglas Bader Garden for the Disabled:** *Duffus Park, Cupar.* The garden has raised beds, rock gardens, shrub border, fountains, waterfalls and sheltered seating.

**Dunfermline Abbey and Palace:** *Monastery Street, Dunfermline. Apr-Sep, Mon-Sat 0930-1200, 1300-1700, Sun 1400-1700; Oct-Mar, Mon-Sat 0930-1200, 1300-1600, Sun 1400-1600. Free. Tel: 031-244 3101.* This great Benedictine house owes its foundation to Queen Margaret, wife of Malcolm Canmore (1057-93) and the foundations of her modest church remain beneath the present nave, a splendid piece of late Norman work. At the east end are the remains of St. Margaret's shrine, dating from the 13th century. Robert the Bruce is buried in the choir, his grave marked by a modern brass. Of the monastic buildings, the ruins of the refectory, pend and guest-house still remain. The guest-house was later reconstructed as

a royal palace, and here Charles I was born.

**Earlshall Castle:** *1m E of Leuchars, 6 miles from St. Andrews. Open Easter, Sat, Sun, Mon, thereafter Thu-Sun 1400-1800, closes last Sun in Sep. Tel: Leuchars (033 483) 205.* Built in 1546 by Sir William Bruce, ancestor of present owners – private family home. Jacobite relics, military trophies and special exhibitions.

**Fife Folk Museum:** *At Ceres, 3m SE of Cupar. Apr-Oct, Mon-Sat (except Tue) 1400-1700, Sun 1430-1730. (Central & North Fife Preservation Society). Tel: Ceres (033 482) 380 (outwith office hours).* Situated in the 17th-century Weigh House, near an old bridge in an attractive village, this museum is a growing collection in a unique setting, showing the agricultural and rural life of Fife in bygone times. Countryside annexe opened in 1983. Nearby is the attractive Ceres Church (1806) with a horse-shoe gallery. Alternative wheelchair entrance.

**Hill of Tarvit House:** *A916, 2m S of Cupar. House: open weekends during Easter weekend, Apr & Oct, Sat & Sun 1400-1800; 1 May-30 Sep, daily 1400-1800 (last admission 1730). Garden: grounds open all year, 1000-sunset. (NTS). Tel: Cupar (0334) 53127.* An Edwardian country house of 1696, designed by Sir Robert Lorimer for Mr. Frederick Boner Sharp, an art collector of note. Fine collection of furniture, portraits, paintings, tapestries, chinese porcelain and bronzes. Tearoom (weekends only, Apr, May, Jun, Sep, Oct and daily July, Aug). Lovely gardens, woodland walk to hilltop viewpoint.

**Isle of May:** Sailings from Anstruther to this Firth of Forth island with ruined 12th-century chapel. The island is a nature reserve with a bird observatory.

**Kellie Castle and Gardens:** *On B9171, 3m NNW of Pittenweem, 10m S of St. Andrews. (Castle) Easter weekend, Apr and Oct, Sat, Sun 1400-1800; 1 May-30 Sep, daily 1400-1800 (last admission 1730). (Gardens) all y$·r, daily, 1000-dusk. (NTS). Tel: Arncroach (033 38) 271.* Fine architecture of the 16th/17th centuries, though the earliest parts date from the 14th century. Owned by the Oliphants for over 250 years, then by the Earls of Mar and Kellie, it was restored nearly a century ago by Professor James Lorimer. His grandson, the sculptor Hew Lorimer, is resident custodian. Notable plaster work and painted panelling. 4 acres of fine Victorian gardens.

**Largo:** Birthplace of Alexander Selkirk 'Robinson Crusoe'. Statue of Crusoe at Lower Largo.

**Royal Palace of Falkland:** *A912, 11m N of Kirkcaldy. Easter-30 Sep, Mon-Sat 1000-1800, Sun 1400-1800; 1-31 Oct, Sat 1000-1800,* *Sun 1400-1800, last admission 1700. (NTS). Tel: Falkland (033 757) 397.* A lovely Royal Palace in a picturesque little town. The buildings of the Palace, in Renaissance style, date from 1501-41. This was a favourite seat of James V, who died here in 1542, and of his daughter Mary, Queen of Scots. The Royal Tennis Court of 1539 is still played on. The gardens are small but charming.

**St. Andrew's Castle:** *Shore at St. Andrews. Opening standard. (AM). Tel: 031-244 3101.* This ruined castle, which has been rebuilt at several periods, overlooks the sea and was founded in 1200 as a fortress and principal residence of the Bishop of St. Andrews. Here Cardinal Beaton was murdered in 1546, and the first round of the Reformation struggle was fought out in the siege that followed. The impressive bottle dungeon and secret passage – a mine and counter-mine – are notable features.

**St. Andrew's Cathedral:** *Beside the castle at St. Andrews. Charge for museum and St. Rule's (Regulus') Tower. Opening standard. (AM). Tel: 031-244 3101.* Founded in 1160 and consecrated in 1318, St. Andrew's Cathedral was once the largest church in the country. Its design is said to have exceeded the capacity of the builders of the day to construct it. The remains include parts of the east and west gables, the south wall of the nave, and portions of the choir and south transept. There is a fascinating museum and St. Rule's Tower, dating from 1127, gives a magnificent view of the town.

**St Andrews University:** *St Andrews town centre. Tel: St Andrews (0334) 76161.* The oldest university in Scotland, founded in 1412. See the 15th-century Church of St Salvator, now the chapel for the united colleges of St Salvator (1455) and St Leonard (1512); St Mary's College (1537) with its quadrangle; and the 16th-century St Leonard's Chapel. Also in the town are St Mary's House built in 1523 and now St Leonard's School Library, and Holy Trinity Church with a 16th century tower and interesting interior features. Guided tours operate twice daily through the summer.

**St. Fillan's Cave:** *Cove Wynd, Pittenweem, near harbour, 9m SSE of St. Andrews. All year, 1000-1300, 1430-1730. (St. John's Episcopal Church). Tel: (0333) 311495.* St Fillan's Cave gave Pittenweem (Pictish for The Place of The Cave) its name. Situated behind the harbour and now surrounded by houses, with tiny well and stone staircase. Augustinian monks from the Isle of May established the Priory, the Great House and the Prior's lodging above the cave, cutting through the rock from the garden to the holy cave-shrine below. Restored and rededicated in 1935.

**Scottish Fisheries Museum:** *At Anstruther harbour, 10m SSE of St. Andrews. All year, daily Apr-Oct, 1000-1730, Nov-Mar, daily 1000-1700, Sun 1000-1700. Tel: Anstruther (0333) 310628.* 16th to 19th century buildings housing marine aquarium, fishing and ships' gear, model and actual fishing boats (including 'Fifie' and 'Zulu' in harbour). Well presented museum documenting the life of the east coast fisher folk. Reference library, tearoom.

**The Study:** *In Culross. All year by arrangement: Apr, Jun, Jul, Aug and Oct, Sat & Sun 1400-1600. (The Study, Town House and audio-visual). (NTS). Tel: Newmills (0383) 880359.* Built in 1633, the tower contains a turnpike stair and a large room on the first floor houses a museum. Fine views of the Forth. Tearoom.

**Vane Farm Nature Reserve:** *On the S shore of Loch Leven, on B9097, off M90 and B996, 4½m S of Kinross. Apr-Oct, daily 1000-1700, Nov-Mar, daily 1000-1600, except Christmas/New Year. (RSPB). Tel: Kinross (0577) 62355.* The Nature Centre is a converted farm building equipped with displays designed to interpret the surrounding countryside and the loch. Between the last week of September and April, the area is a favourite feeding and resting place for vast numbers of wild geese and duck, and binoculars and telescopes are provided for observation. Also observation hide and nature trail. Shop selling wide range of RSPB gifts. Car park with picnic space. Path up Vane Hill through birchwoods with impressive views.

## PERTH

**Achray Forest Drive:** *Off A821, 4m N of Aberfoyle. Easter-end Sep, daily 1000-1800. Tel: Aberfoyle (087 72) 383.* Scenic drive on Forestry Commission roads with fine views of the Trossachs. Walks, picnic places, play area and toilets.

**Atholl Country Collection:** *Blair Atholl. Open every afternoon 1330-1730 during the summer season, also weekday mornings from 0930 during Jul and Aug, or by arrangement. Group rates on application to John Cameron. Tel: Blair Atholl (079681) 232.* Folk museum with blacksmith's 'smiddy' and crofter's stable and byre. Emphasis on the importance of flax growing and spinning to the economy of the district. Road, rail and postal services, the school, the kirk, the vet and gamekeeper are all featured. Picnic area and adjacent to Blair Castle Craft Centre.

**Beech Hedge:** *A93, just S of Meikleour, 12m NNE of Perth.* Listed as the highest of its kind in the world the Beech Hedge was planted in 1746 and is now 600 yards long and 85 feet high. Information board.

**Ben Lawers Visitor Centre:** *Off A827, 14m WSW of Aberfeldy. Visitor Centre open Easter-May and 1-30 Sep, 1100-1600; 1 Jun-31 Aug, 1000-1700; daily. (NTS). Tel: Killin (056 72) 397.* Visitor Centre has information on botany, geology, history of the Ben Lawers, Perthshire's highest mountain (3,984 feet) noted for its variety of alpine flowers. There is a Nature Trail and a variety of guided walks in summer.

**Blair Castle:** *Near A9, 6m NNW of Pitlochry. Easter-mid Oct, Mon-Sat 1000-1700, Sun 1400-1700. (Duke of Atholl). Tel: Blair Atholl (079 681) 207.* A white turreted baronial castle, seat of the Duke of Atholl, chief of Clan Murray. The oldest part is Cumming's Tower, 1269. Mary, Queen of Scots, Prince Charles Edward Stuart and Queen Victoria stayed here. When the castle was in Hanoverian hands in 1746, General Lord Murray laid siege to it on the Prince's behalf, making it the last castle in Britain to be besieged. The Duke is the only British subject allowed to maintain a private army, the Atholl Highlanders. There are fine collections of furniture, portraits, lace, china, arms, armour, Jacobite relics and masonic regalia. Licensed restaurant, gift shop, deer park, pony-trekking, nature trails, picnic areas and caravan park. Free car and coach parks.

**Branklyn Garden:** *Dundee Road (A85) Perth. 1 Mar-31 Oct, daily 0930-sunset. (NTS). Tel: Perth (0738) 25535.* Described as the finest two acres of private garden in the country, this outstanding collection of plants, particularly rhododendrons, alpines, azaleas, herbaceous and peat garden plants, attracts gardeners and botanists from all over the world. Worth visiting for the Meconopsis blue poppies alone!

**Caithness Glass (Perth):** *Inveralmond, Perth. On A9 north of the town. All year. Free. Factory shop: Mon-Sat 0900-1700, Sun 1300-1700, Sun 1100-1700 (Easter-end Sep). Factory viewing: Mon-Fri 0900-1630. (Caithness Glass plc.). Tel: Perth (0738) 37373.* Visitors are welcome at the factory to see the fascinating process of glass-making. Factory shop, paperweight museum and gallery, and licensed restaurant. Ample car/coach parking.

**David Marshall Lodge:** *Off A821, 1m N of Aberfoyle. Mid Mar-mid Oct, daily 1000-1800. (FC).* Visitor Centre and starting point for walks in the Queen Elizabeth Forest Park. It commands wide views over the upper Forth Valley to the Menteith Hills, Campsie Fells and Ben Lomond.

**John Dewar & Sons:** *Dunkeld Road, Inveralmond, Perth. All year except holidays. Tours: Mon-Wed 1015 & 1415, Thu & Fri 1015 & 1400. Free. (Mr R Keiller, visits organiser). Tel: Perth (0738) 21231.* During a conducted tour of 1½ hours visitors see the casks of matured whisky arriving for blending and follow the process through to bottling and despatch. Gift shop.

**Dunkeld Bridge:** *Over the River Tay at Dunkeld. All times. Free.* One of Thomas Telford's finest bridges, built in 1809. An attractive riverside path leads from here downstream to the famous *Birnam Oak,* last relic of Macbeth's Birnam Wood, and then around the village of Birnam. Best view is from riverside garden. Wheelchair users should approach from the square through the archway. Hotel and tearoom adjacent.

**Dunkeld Cathedral:** *High Street, Dunkeld, 15m NNW of Perth. Opening standard. Free. (AM). Tel: 031-244 3101.* Refounded in the early 12th century on an ancient ecclesiastical site, this cathedral has a beautiful setting by the Tay. The choir has been restored and is in use as the parish church. The nave and the great north-west tower date from the 15th century.

**Dunkeld Little Houses:** *Dunkeld, A9 15m NNW of Perth. Tourist Information Centre with audio-visual presentation. Open Easter-31 May, 1 Sep-23 Dec, Mon-Sat 1000-1300, 1400-1630. 1 Jun-31 Aug, Mon-Sat 1000-1800, Sun 1400-1700. Ell Shop: 1 Apr-31 May & 1 Sep-23 Dec, Mon-Sat 1000-1300, 1400-1630. 1 Jun-31 Aug, Mon-Sat 1000-1800, Sun 1400-1700. Free.* *(NTS). Tel: Dunkeld (03502) 460.* The houses date from the rebuilding of the town after the Battle of Dunkeld, 1689. Charmingly restored by NTS and Perth County Council, they are not open to the public but may been seen from the outside and information on them gained from the Visitor Centre or from the National Trust for Scotland's representative at the Ell shop.

**Fair Maid's House Gallery:** *North Port, Perth. All year, Mon-Fri 1100-1600, Sat 1100-1700. Gallery closed Jan. Craft Shop open all year. Free. Tel: Perth (0738) 25976.* One of the oldest buildings in Perth, now housing contemporary Scottish crafts and a gallery. Exhibition changes each month, covering painting, embroidery, tapestry, sculpture, etching and print-making.

**Fortingall Yew:** *Fortingall, 9m W of Aberfeldy.* The great yew in an enclosure in the churchyard is over 3,000 years old, perhaps the oldest tree in Britain. The attractive village, which was rebuilt in 1900 with many thatched cottages is claimed to be the birthplace of Pontius Pilate.

**Glengoulandie Deer Park:** *9m from Aberfeldy on B846 to Kinloch Rannoch. Daily, 0900-one hour before sunset. Tel: Kenmore (08873) 509.* Native animals housed in a natural environment. Many endangered species are kept, and there are fine herds of red deer and Highland cattle. No guide dogs.

**Glenturret Distillery:** *From Crieff take A85 to Comrie for 1m, then turn right at crossroads for ¼m. Mar-Dec, Mon-Fri 0930-1730, last tour 1630; Apr-Oct, Sat 1000-1700 last tour 1600. Tel: Crieff (0764) 2424.* Scotland's oldest distillery, with guided tour and free taste. Award-winning heritage centre, audio-visual and 3-D exhibition museum. Good facilites for blind visitors.

**Inchmahome Priory:** *On an island in the Lake of Menteith, A81, 4m E of Aberfoyle. Access by boat from lakeside, Port of Menteith. Opening standard, except closed Oct-Mar. Admission free. (AM). Tel: 031-226 2570.* The ruins of an Augustinian house, founded in 1238, where the infant Mary, Queen of Scots was sent for refuge in 1547.

**Loch of the Lowes:** *Off A923, 2m NE of Dunkeld (SWT). Tel: Dunkeld (035 02) 337.* This Scottish Wildlife Trust reserve is famous for its breeding osprey pair; visitors can watch these birds on the nest from a special hide. Visitor centre, staff ranger and observation hill. Wide range of provision for visitors with special needs.

**Museum of Scottish Tartans:** *Drummond Street, Comrie, 6m W of Crieff. Apr-Oct, Mon-Sat 1000-1700, Sun 1400-1700; Nov-Mar, Mon-Fri 1100-1500, Sat 1000-1300, Sun by arrangement. (Scottish Tartans Society). Tel: Comrie (0764) 70779.* The Scottish Tartans Society is the custodian of the largest collection in existence of material relating to tartans and Highland dress, historic costumes and artefacts; weavers cottage; dye plant garden. There is a research service on surnames, clans and tartans, and an archive of every known tartan.

**Pass of Killiecrankie:** *Off A9, 3m N of Pitlochry. NTS Visitor Centre: Easter, 31 May and 30 Oct, daily 1000-1700. Jun-Aug, daily 0930-1800. Site open all day. (NTS). Tel: Pitlochry (0796) 3233.* A famous wooded gorge where in 1689 the Government troops were routed by Jacobite forces led by 'Bonnie Dundee'. Soldier's Leap. NTS centre features the battle, natural history and ranger services. The Pass is on the network of Garry-Tummel walks, which extend for 20 miles in the area. Snack bar.

**Pitlochry Festival Theatre:** *Off A9 bypass at Pitlochry local access. May-Oct, open all day for refreshments and art exhibitions. (Box Office) Tel: Pitlochry (0796) 2680.* Scotland's 'Theatre in the Hills' is now rehoused in a magnificent new building by the River Tummel. Opened by Prince Charles in 1981, it is a must for all holidaymakers. A repertoire of five or six different plays are presented each season, with concerts on most Sundays. Catering and bar

facilities. Coffee shop open from 1000; lunch 1200-1400; restaurant 1830-2000. Magnificent view from foyer and restaurant.

**Pitlochry Power Station and Dam:** *Off A9 at Pitlochry. Easter-end Oct, daily 0940-1730. (North of Scotland Hydro Electric Board). Tel: Pitlochry (0796) 3152.* One of nine hydro stations in the Tummel Valley. The dam created Loch Faskally where boating and fishing are available. Salmon can be seen through windows in the fish ladder. Exhibition and film inside power station.

**Queen Elizabeth Forest Park:** *Between the E shore of Loch Lomond and the Trossachs. (FC).* In this 45,000 acres of forest, moor and mountainside there are many walks. On A821 is the David Marshall Lodge, a picnic pavilion and information centre. 'Duke's Road' from Aberfoyle to the Trossachs has fine views.

**Rumbling Bridge:** *A823 at Rumbling Bridge. Free. All reasonable times.* The River Devon is spanned here by two bridges, the lower one dating from 1713, the upper one from 1816. A footpath from the north side gives good access to spectacular and picturesque gorges and falls, one of which is known as the Devil's Mill. Another, Cauldron Linn, is a mile downstream, whilst Vicar's Bridge is a beauty spot a mile beyond this.

**Scone Palace:** *Off A93 (Braemar Road), 2m NE of Perth. Easter-Oct, Mon-Sat 0930-1700; Sun 1330-1700 (Jul & Aug 1000-1700), other times by arrangement. (Earl of Mansfield). Tel: Perth (0738) 52300.* The present castellated palace, enlarged and embellished in 1803, incorporates the 16th-century and earlier palaces. It has notable grounds and a pinetum and is still a family home. The Moot Hill at Scone, known in the 8th century and earlier, was the site of the famous coronation Stone of Scone, brought there in the 9th century by Kenneth MacAlpine, King of Scots. In 1296 the Stone was seized by the English and taken to Westminster Abbey. The ancient Abbey of Scone was destroyed by followers of John Knox. Magnificent collection of porcelain, furniture, ivories, 18th-century clocks and 16th-century needlework. Full catering facilites. Coffee shop, restaurant, produce and gift shop, gardens, playground, banqueting, pinetum. Parties of disabled visitors welcome.

### ANGUS

**Aberlemno Sculptured Stones:** *At Aberlemno, B9134, 6m NE of Forfar. All times. Free. (AM). Tel: 031-244 3101.* In the churchyard is a splendid upright cross-slab with Pictish symbols; three other stones stand beside the road.

**Arbroath Abbey:** *In Arbroath. Opening standard. (AM). Tel: 031-244 3101.* Founded in 1178 by William the Lion and dedicated to St Thomas of Canterbury, it was from here that the famous Declaration of Arbroath asserting Robert the Bruce as King was issued in 1320. Important remains of the church survive; these include one of the most complete examples of an abbot's residence.

**Arbroath Cliffs Nature Trail:** Starts from north east end of promenade. 3 miles of cliff scenery, well-defined footpath. Descriptive booklets from local tourist information centre.

**Arbroath Signal Tower Museum:** Part of Scotland's Fishing Heritage Trail, this museum is housed in a tower formerly used to communicate with the Bell Rock lighthouse offshore.

**Ardestie and Carlungie Earth-Houses:** *N of A92, Ardestie: about 6m E of Dundee, at junction with B962. Carlungie: 1m N on unclassified road to Carlungie. All times. Free. (AM). Tel: 031-244 3101.* Two examples of large earth-houses attached to surface dwellings. At Ardestie the gallery is curved and 80 feet in length: the Carlungie earth-house is 150 feet long, and is most complex; used in first centuries AD.

**Barrie's Birthplace:** *9 Brechin Road, Kirriemuir. Easter weekend, 1 May-30 Sep, Mon-Sat 1100-1730, Sun 1400-1730, last admission 30 mins before closing. (Mrs. Elizabeth M Drainer, Tel: Kirriemuir (0575) 72538 (Home). (NTS). Tel: Kirriemuir (0575) 72646.* Here in this white-washed cottage playwright, Sir John M Barrie was born in 1860. Manuscripts, personal possessions and mementoes of actors and producers associated with his plays are shown in the museum.

**Braes of Angus:** Forest walks, picnic areas etc, at Glen Doll, 18 miles NW of Kirriemuir, N to Clova, then unclassified road.

**Brechin Cathedral and Round Tower:** *At Brechin. Viewed from the churchyard. All reasonable times. (AM). Tel: 031-244 3101.* 12th century cathedral, partially demolished in 1807, restored 1900-02. Attached to the cathedral are one of the two remaining round towers of the Irish type in Scotland, dating back to the 11th or 12th century.

**Broughty Castle Museum, Dundee:** *Broughty Ferry, 4m E of city centre. Mon-Thu & Sat 1000-1300 and 1400-1700 (closed Fri). Sun, (Jul-Sep only) 1400-1700. Free. Booking essential for large groups. (City of Dundee District Council). Tel: Dundee (0382) 23141 or 76121.* Former estuary fort, now museum. Local history gallery includes sections on fishing, lifeboat, ferries and growth of town. Important collection of relics from Dundee's former whaling industry including harpoons, knives and scrimshaw. Wildlife of sea-shore. Display of arms and armour, and military history of castle. Small shop.

**The Caledonian Railway:** Preserved at Brechin, this fine Caledonian terminus is open to visitors. Part of the former Caledonian main line is in the process of restoration.

**Howff Burial Ground, Dundee:** *Meadowside. Daily, closes 1700. Tel: Dundee (0382) 23141.* Formerly the gardens of the Greyfriars' Monastery, the Howff was granted to Dundee as a burial ground by Mary, Queen of Scots. Used as a burial ground between the 16th and 19th centuries, it contains many finely carved tombstones. It was also used as a meeting place by Dundee's Incorporated Trades until 1778, hence the name 'howff'.

**McManus Galleries, Dundee:** *Albert Square, city centre. All year, Mon-Sat 1000-1700. Free. (Prior notice of groups preferred). (City of Dundee District Council). Tel: Dundee (0382) 23141.* Dundee's principal museum and art gallery. Local history displays including major new galleries on trade and industry, social and civic history. Archaeology gallery under redevelopment. Art galleries contain important collection of Scottish and Victorian paintings; and silver, glass, ceramics, furniture. Regular touring exhibitions. Shop.

**Mills Observatory, Dundee:** *Balgay Hill, north side of the city. Apr-Sep, Mon-Fri 1000-1700, Sat 1400-1700; Oct-Mar, Mon-Fri 1500-2200, Sat 1400-1700. Free. (Booking essential for large groups). (City of Dundee District Council). Tel: Dundee (0382) 67138.* A public astronomical observatory with telescopes, displays on astronomy and space exploration, lecture room with projection equipment, and small planetarium. Viewing of sky subject to weather conditions. Balcony with fine views over River Tay. Audio-visual programme. Small shop and toilets.

**Montrose Basin:** Important wildfowl refuge and nature reserve holding high populations of wintering birds. Estuary of the River Esk.

**RRS Discovery:** *On Waterfront, Victoria Dock. pr-May, Sep, daily 1400-1700, Sat, Sun, Bank Holidays 1100-1700. Jun 1000-1700. Tel: Dundee (0382) 201175/25282.* Royal Research Ship Discovery is Captain Scott's famous antarctic exploration vessel, built in Dundee in 1901. The ship's crew welcomes visitors aboard. Final restoration by Dundee Heritage Trust.

**Unicorn, Dundee:** *Victoria Dock, just E of Tay Road Bridge. 1 Apr-mid Oct, every day. Sun-Fri 1000-1700, Sat 1000-1600. (The Unicorn Preservation Society). Tel: Dundee (0382) 200900.* The

*Unicorn* is a 46-gun wooden frigate now in the course of restoration. She was launched at Chatham in 1824 and is Britain's oldest ship afloat. Displays on board of the history of the *Unicorn,* ship-building and the Royal Navy.

## ABERDEEN

**Aberdeen Art Gallery and Museums:** *Schoolhill. All year. Mon-Sat 1000-1700 (Thu 1000-2000), Sun 1400-1700. Free. Parking available. (City of Aberdeen District Council). Tel: Aberdeen (0224) 646333. Artline: 24-hour recorded information service, Tel: Aberdeen (0224) 632133.* Permanent collection of 18th, 19th and 20th century art with the emphasis on contemporary works. A full programme of special exhibitions. Music, dance poetry, events, film, coffee shop, gallery shop, reference library, print room. Disabled access: A lift is available in the Gallery for disabled visitors which takes them to the first floor galleries and also gives access to the McBey print room and reference library. Guide dogs permitted.

**Aberdeen Fishmarket:** *Off Market Street.* Aberdeen is one of the major fishing ports of Britain, landing hundreds of tons of fish daily. Every morning (Mon-Fri) the fishing fleets unload their catches, which are auctioned off amid tense bustle. Best visited 0730-0930.

**Aberdeen Maritime Museum:** *Provost Ross's House, Shiprow. All year, Mon-Sat 1000-1700. Free. Tel: Aberdeen (0224) 585788.* Situated in one of Aberdeen's oldest buildings (1593), the museum uses models, paintings and audio-visual displays to tell the story of local shipbuilding, the fishing industry, the North Sea oil and gas developments. Museum shop.

**Bridge of Dee:** Built in 1500 by Bishop Gavin Dunbar in James V's reign. Its seven arches span 400 feet and it formerly carried the main road south. The mediaeval solidity of the structure is enlivened by heraldic carvings.

**Brig O'Balgownie:** Also known as the 'Auld Brig o' Don', this massive arch, 62 feet wide, spans a deep pool of the river and is backed by fine woods. It was completed c. 1320 and repaired in 1607. In 1605 Sir Alexander Hay endowed the bridge with a small property, which has so increased in value that it built the New Bridge of Don (1830), a little lower down, at a cost of £26,000, bore most of the cost of the Victoria Bridge, and contributed to many other public works. Now closed to motor vehicles.

**Cruickshank Botanic Gardens:** *Chanonry. All year, Mon-Fri 0900-1630, also May-Sep, Sat and Sun 1400-1700. Free. (University of Aberdeen). Tel: Aberdeen (0224) 272704, ext 5247.* Extensive collection of shrubs, herbaceous and Alpine plants, heather and succulents. Rock and water gardens.

**James Dun's House:** *Schoolhill. All year. Mon-Sat 1000-1700. Free. Tel: Aberdeen (0224) 646333.* This former residence of James Dun, master and rector of Aberdeen Grammar School, is now a museum featuring special temporary exhibitions of particular interest to families. Museum shop.

**Duthie Park and Winter Gardens:** *Polmuir Road/ Riverside Drive. All year, daily, 1000-dusk. Free. Tel: Aberdeen (0224) 583155.* One of Aberdeen's many parks – and one of the favourites with the residents. It features an all-year round display of colour in the Winter Gardens, as well as the unique 'rose hill' where the city's enthusiasm for roses is best seen. Westburn, Seaton, Hazlehead also well worth a visit.

**Kings College/Marischal College:** Contrasting colleges of the University of Aberdeen founded 1495. Kings's Buildings date from 16th century, interesting chapel and crown spire. Marischal spectacular granite frontage built in 1906.

**St. Machar's Cathedral:** *Chanonry. All year, 0900-1700. Free. Tel: Aberdeen (0224) 485988.* This granite cathedral was founded in 1131 on an earlier site, though the main part of the building dates from the mid-15th century. The west front with its twin towers is notable, and the painted wooden heraldic nave ceiling is dated 1520. The nave is in use as a parish church.

## NORTH EAST

**Anderson's Story Book Glen:** *At Maryculter, off Lower Deeside Road, 5m WSW of Aberdeen. 1 Apr-31 Oct, 1000-1800. Tel: Aberdeen (0224) 732941.* The Glen is the result of 11 years work by the Anderson family. Storybook characters and places come to life in a colourful outdoor setting of flowers, streams and waterfalls. There are seating areas and a restaurant seating 250 which serves snacks and 3-course meals.

**Balmoral Castle:** *On A93, 8m W of Ballater. Grounds and exhibition of paintings and works of art in the Ballroom of the castle. May-Jun-Jul daily except Sun 1000-1700 (may be closed when members of the Royal Family are in residence). Tel: Crathie (03384) 334.* The family holiday home of the Royal Family for over a century. The earliest reference to it, as Bouchmorale, was in 1484. Queen Victoria visited the earlier castle in 1848; Prince Albert bought the estate in 1852; the castle was rebuilt by William Smith of Aberdeen with modifications by Prince Albert and was first occupied in 1855. Souvenir shops, refreshment room, country walks and pony-trekking.

**Baxter's Visitor Centre:** ½m W of Fochabers on main Aberdeen-Inverness road (A96). 1 Apr-28 Oct (Guided tours), Mon-Fri 1000-1200 and 1300-1600 (Fri-last tour 1400). Weekends 14 May-11 Sep (no tours). No Factory Tours during staff holidays. Free. Tel: Fochabers (0343) 820 393. Slide show with commentary, Old Baxter Shop, replica of the original George Baxter and Sons establishment where Baxters of Speyside were formed. George Baxter cellar, shop and tearoom. Highland cattle nearby.

**Bennachie Forest:** Don View Visitor Centre. 4 miles north of Monymusk on minor road from Kemnay to Keig. Exhibits, picnic place, walks.

**Braemar Castle:** A93, at Braemar. May-early Oct, daily (ex Fridays) 1000-1800. (Farquharson of Invercauld). Tel: Braemar (033 83) 219. This turreted stronghold, built in 1628 by the Earl of Mar, was burnt by Farquharson of Inverey in 1689. It was rebuilt about 1748 and garrisoned by Hanoverian troops. There is a round central tower, a spiral stair, barrel-vaulted ceilings and an underground pit prison. Fully furnished family residence. Interesting historical relics. Free car and bus park.

**Brodie Castle:** Off A96, 4½m W of Forres. Easter and 1 Apr-31 Sep. Mon-Sat 1100-1800, Sun 1400-1800. Last admission 1715. (NTS). Tel: Brodie (030 94) 371. The castle, associated with the Brodie family for 500 years, was largely rebuilt after the earlier structure was burned in 1645; it is based on a 16th century 'Z' plan, with additions made in the 17th and 19th centuries. The house contains fine French furniture, English, Continental and Chinese porcelain, and a major collection of paintings. A woodland walk has been laid out in the gardens by the edge of a 4-acre pond. Picnic area, adventure playground, car park, shop and small tearoom.

**Bullars of Buchan:** Off A975, 7m S of Peterhead. A vast chasm in the cliffs, 200 feet deep, which no man can see with indifference said Dr Johnson in 1773. A haunt of innumerable seabirds.

**Burns Family Tombstones and Cairn:** Off A94, 8m SW of Stonehaven at Glenbervie Church. All times. Free. The Burnes (Burns) family tombstones in the churchyard were restored in 1968 and a Burns memorial cairn is nearby.

**Castle Fraser:** 3m S of Kemnay off B993. Castle: 1 May-30 Sep, daily 1400-1800 (last tour 1715). Gardens and Grounds: all year, daily 0930-sunset. (NTS). Tel: (033 03) 463. Castle Fraser begun about 1575. It belongs to the same great period of native architectural achievements as Crathes and Craigievar Castles, and is the largest and grandest of the Castles of Mar. Two notable families of master masons, Bel and Leiper, were involved in its

construction, completed in 1636. Noted for its great hall. Garden and picnic area and tearoom.

**Craigievar Castle:** On A980, 6m S of Alford, 26m W of Aberdeen. Castle: 1 May-30 Sep, daily 1400-1800 (last tour 1715). Grounds: open all year 0930-sunset. (NTS). Tel: Lumphanan (033 983) 635. This masterpiece of Scottish baronial architecture stands on the Braes of Leochel-Cushnie in the midst of 100 acres of farm and parkland. Completed in 1626 for William Forbes (Willie the Merchant or Danzig Willie), it stands today virtually as the builders left it – a fairytale castle of turrets, chimney stacks, corbelling and gables. Famous for magnificent original plaster ceilings, carved panelling and all family contents. Picnic area, woodland walks.

**Drum Castle:** Off A93, 10m WSW of Aberdeen. 1 May-30 Sep, daily 1400-1800 (last admission 1715). Grounds open all year, 0930-sunset. (NTS). Tel: (03308) 204. A massive granite tower built towards the end of the 13th century adjoins a mansion of 1619. The Royal Forest of Drum was conferred in 1323 by Robert the Bruce on his armour-bearer and clerk-register, William de Irwin. The family connection remained unbroken until the death of Mr H Q Forbes Irvine in 1975. The house stands on a 400 acre estate with lawns, rare trees and shrubs, and inside are antique furniture and silver, family portraits and relics. Coffee room, adventure playground and wayfaring course.

**Dunnottar Castle:** *Off A92, S of Stonehaven. All year. Mon-Sat 0900-1800, Sun 1400-1700. Closed Fri, Oct-Apr. Tel: Stonehaven (0569) 62173.* An impressive ruined fortress on a rocky cliff 160 feet above the sea, a stronghold of the Earls Marischal of Scotland from the 14th century. Montrose besieged it in 1645. During the Commonwealth wars, the Scottish regalia were hidden here for safety. Cromwell's troops occupied the castle but in 1652 this treasure was smuggled out by the wife of the minister at Kinneff, 7 miles south, and hidden under the pulpit in his church.

**Elgin Cathedral:** *North College Street, Elgin. Opening standard. (AM). Tel: 031–244 3101.* When entire, this was perhaps the most beautiful of Scottish cathedrals, known as the lantern of the North. It was founded in 1224, but in 1390 it was burned by the Wolf of Badenoch. It did not fall into ruin until after the reformation. Much 13th-century work still remains; the nave and chapter house are 15th-century. There is a 6th-century Pictish slab in the choir.

**Fyvie Castle:** *Off A947, 8m SE of Turriff and 25m NW of Aberdeen. 1 May-30 Sep, daily 1100-1800 (last admission 1715). (National Trust for Scotland). Tel: Fyvie (065 16) 266.* The five towers of Fyvie Castle enshrine five centuries of Scottish history, each being built by the five families who owned the castle. The oldest part dates from the 13th century and it is now one of the grandest examples of Scottish baronial architecture. Apart from the great wheel stair, the finest in Scotland, and the 17th century morning room, with its contemporary panelling and plaster ceiling, the interior as created by the 1st Lord Leith of Fyvie reflects the opulence of the Edwardian era. There is an exceptionally important collection of portraits including works by Batoni, Raeburn, Ramsay, Gainsborough, Opie and Hoppner. In addition, there are arms and armour and 16th century tapestries. Tearoom, grounds including loch.

**Glendronach Distillery:** *On B9001, between Huntly and Aberchirder, 19m N of Inverurie. All year, Mon-Fri 1000 or 1400 (by arrangement only). Free. Tel: Forgue (046682) 202 (0830-1630).* Visitor Centre and guided tour around malt whisky distillery dating from 1826.

**Glenfarclas Distillery:** *Off A95, 17m WSW of Keith and 17m NE of Grantown-on-Spey. All year. Mon-Fri 0900-1630; Jul, Aug, Sep, Sat 1000-1600. Closed Xmas, New Year. Free. Groups by arrangement. Tel: Ballindalloch (08072) 257.* Tours of a well-known malt whisky distillery,

visual exhibition and museum of old illicit distilling equipment in Reception Centre.

**Glenfiddich Distillery:** *Just N of Dufftown on A941, 16m S of Elgin. All year (except between Xmas and New Year) Mon-Fri 0930-1630; mid May-mid Oct, Sat 0930-1630, Sun 1200-1630. Free. Tel: Dufftown (0340) 20373.* After an audio-visual programme available in six languages, visitors are shown around the distillery and bottling hall and are then offered a complimentary dram. Picnic area, gift shop at car park.

**The Glenlivet Distillery Visitor Centre:** *B9008, 10m N of Tomintoul. Easter-end Oct, Mon-Sat 1000-1600. Free. Coach parties by arrangement. Tel: Glenlivet (08073) 427 (during season) and Keith (05422) 6294 (during winter).* Guided tours of distillery. Exhibits of ancient whisky tools and artefacts and life-size reproduction of Landseer's painting 'The Highland Whisky Still'. Free whisky sample. Children under 8 not admitted to production areas but welcome to Reception Centre.

**Glenshee Chairlift:** *Off A93, 10m S of Braemar. Daily, 0900-1700. Charge for chairlift. Tel: Braemar (033 83) 320.* Ascends the Cairnwell mountain (3,059 feet) from the summit of the highest main road pass in Britain (2,199 feet). Restaurant.

**Grampian Transport Museum:** *At Alford, 27m W of Aberdeen on A944. 1 Apr-30 Sep, daily 1030-1700 also first two weekends in Oct. Tel: Alford (0336) 2292.* A large independent transport museum, opened in April 1983. Extensive collection of road vehicles, including horse drawn, steam, commercial and vintage motor cars. Pedal cycles and motorcycles also well represented. Highland rail transport is described in the railway museum in Alford's former railway station.

**Haddo House:** *Off B999, 4m N of Pitmedden, 19m N of Aberdeen. (House) 1 May–30 Sep, daily 1400-1800 (last tour 1715).* Designed in 1731 by William Adam, a pupil of Sir William Bruce and father of the Adam brothers, for William, second Earl of Aberdeen, Haddo House replaced the old House of Kellie, home of the Gordons of Methlick for centuries. Much of the interior is 'Adam Revival' carried out about 1880 for John, seventh Earl and first Marquess of Aberdeen and his Countess, Ishbel. Garden, Trust shop and tearoom.

**Huntly Castle:** *Castle Street, Huntly. Opening standard. (AM). Tel: 031-244 3101.* An imposing ruin which replaced mediaeval Strathbogie Castle which, until 1544, was the seat of the Gay Gordons, the Marquesses of Huntly, the most powerful family in the north until the mid-16th

century. There are elaborate heraldic adornments on the castle walls. The castle, now stands in a wooded park, was destroyed by Moray in 1452, rebuilt, then rebuilt again in 1551-54, burned 40 years later and again rebuilt in 1602.

**Kildrummy Castle:** *A97, 10m W of Alford. Opening standard. (AM). Tel: 031-244 3101.* The most extensive example in Scotland of a 13th century castle. The four round towers, hall and chapel remains belong in substance to the original. The great gatehouse and other work is later, to the 16th century. It was the seat of the Earls of Mar, and played an important part in Scottish history until 1715 when it was dismantled.

**Lecht Ski Tow:** *Off A939, 7m SE of Tomintoul. During ski-ing season only. (Lecht Ski Co Ltd.). Tel: (09754) 240.* Ski tows operating to slopes on both sides of the Lecht Road which here is a section of the military road built in the mid-18th century from Perth to the Moray Firth. Famous for its snowfalls. Licensed cafeteria, ski hire, ski school. Free car park.

**Leith Hall:** *B9002, 7m S of Huntly. (House) 1 May-30 Sep, daily 1400-1800. (last tour 1715). (Garden) all year, daily 0930-sunset. (NTS). Tel: (04643) 216.* The mansion house of Leith Hall is at the centre of a 263-acre estate which was the home of the head of the Leith and Leith-Hay

family from 1650. The house contains personal possessions of successive lairds, most of whom followed a tradition of military service. The grounds contain varied farm and woodlands. There are two ponds, a bird observation hide and three countryside walks, one leading to a hilltop viewpoint. Unique 18th century stables; Soay sheep; ice house. Extensive and interesting informal garden of borders, shrubs and rock garden. Picnic area and tearoom.

**Loanhead Stone Circle:** *¼m NW of Daviot, 5m NW of Inverurie, off B9001. All reasonable times. Free. (AM). Tel: 031-244 3101.* The best known example of a widespread group of recumbent stone circles in east Scotland.

**Pennan:** *10m E of MacDuff on B9031.* Coastal fishing village which provided location for film Local Hero.

**Pitmedden Garden and Museum of Farming Life:** *Outskirts of Pitmedden village on A920, 14m N of Aberdeen, off B999. (Garden) All year, daily 0930-sunset. (Museum) 1 May-30 Sep, daily 1100-1800. (NTS). Tel: Udny (065 13) 2352.* The highlight is the 17th century Great Garden originally laid out by Sir Alexander Seton, with elaborate floral designs, pavilions, fountains and sundials. The 'thunder houses' at either end of the west belvedere are rare in Scotland. The Museum of Farming Life contains a collection of agricultural and domestic implements. On the 100-acre estate is a woodland and farmland walk. Visitor Centre, tearoom, exhibition on formal gardens, picnic area.

**Pluscarden Abbey:** *From B9010 at Elgin take unclassified road to Pluscarden, 6m SW. All year daily 0500-2030. Free. Tel: (034 389) 257 (0900-1100 and 1430-1700).* Originally a Valliscaulian house, the monastery was founded in 1230. In 1390 the Church was burned, probably by the Wolf of Badenoch who burned Elgin about the same time. It became a dependent priory of the Benedictines' Abbey of Dunfermline in 1454 until the suppression of monastic life in Scotland in 1560. Thereafter the buildings fell into ruins until 1948 when a group of Benedictine monks from Prinknash Abbey, Gloucester, returned to restore it. Monastic church services open to the public.

**Rob Roy's Statue:** *Peterculter by A93. All times. Free.* Statue of Rob Roy standing above the Leuchar Burn can be seen from the bridge on the main road.

**Stonehaven Tolbooth Museum:** *At quay at Stonehaven. Jun-Sep, daily (except Tue) 1400-1700, plus Mon, Thu, Fri and Sat 1000-1200. Free. (North-East of Scotland Museums Service). Tel: Peterhead (0779) 77778.* This 16th-century former storehouse of the Earls Marischal was later used as a prison. In

1748-49 Episcopal ministers lodged inside and baptised children through the windows. The museum displays local history, archaeology and particularly fishing.

**Tomintoul Museum:** *The Square, Tomintoul. Easter-end Oct, Mon-Sat 0930-1300, 1400-1730; Sun 1400-1530; Jul, Aug, Mon-Sat 0900-1900, Sun 1100-1900. Free. Tel: Forres (0309) 73701.* At 1160 feet Tomintoul is the highest village in the Highlands. Museum has displays on local history, folklife, a reconstructed farm kitchen, wildlife, climate, landscape and geology. Tourist Information Centre.

## THE NORTHERN HIGHLANDS

**Ardessie Fisheries:** *On A832, by Little Loch Broom, between Gairloch and Ullapool. Easter-15 Oct, Mon-Sat 1000-1900. Tel: Dundonnell (085 483) 252 (any time).* A fish farm with many facilities under cover. Rainbow trout reared for the table, and local restocking service with rainbow trout, brown trout and salmon. Visitors can see the fish at all stages of growth and feed the larger fish. Fresh trout always available. Locally caught wild salmon on sale in season (June-August); smoked salmon and smoked trout also available.

**Ardvreck Castle:** *A837, 11m E of Lochinver, on Loch Assynt. All reasonable times. Free.* Built in 1490 by the

MacLeods, who in the mid-13th century obtained Assynt by marriage; the three-storeyed ruins stand on the shores of Loch Assynt. After his defeat at ulrain, near Bonar Bridge, in 1650, the Marquess of Montrose fled to Assynt but was soon captured and confined here before being sent to Edinburgh and executed.

**Balnakeil Craft Village:** *1m W of Durness. 1 Apr-30 Sep, 1000-1800. Free. Tel: Durness (097 181) 342.* Twelve independently-owned businesses operated by craft workers, specialising in pottery, woodwork, tapestry, jewellery, bookbinding, candlemaking and many other crafts. The village was originally a Ministry of Defence early warning station, restored for crafts in 1964. Coffee shop, exhibition.

**Beauly Priory:** *At Beauly, A9, 12m W of Inverness. Apr-Sep standard opening, closed Oct-Mar. (AM). Tel: 031-244 3101.* Ruins of a Valliscaulian Priory founded in about 1230. Notable windows and window-arcading.

**Caithness Glass:** *Harrowhill, Wick. All year. Free. Factory shop: Mon-Fri 0900-1700, Sat 0900-1300 (all year), Sat 0900-1600 (summer only). Factory viewing: Mon-Fri 0900-1630 (all year). (Caithness Glass plc). Tel: Wick (0955) 2286.* See hand-made glass blowing from the raw materials stage through all the processes to the finished article. Cafe and factory shop. Ample car/coach parking.

**Cape Wrath:** *12m NW of Durness.* The most northerly point of Scotland's north-west seaboard. A passenger ferry (summer only) connects with a minibus service to the cape.

**Castle of Old Wick:** *Off A9, 1½m S of Wick.* On a headland above the sea, over a deep cleft in the rocks, this almost windowless square tower of the Cheynes dates back to the 14th century.

**Cawdor Castle:** *At Cawdor on B9090, 5m SW of Nairn. May-Sep, 1000-1700 (Rt Hon The Earl of Cawdor). Tel: Cawdor (06677) 615.* The old central tower of 1372, fortified in 1454 (a family home for over 600 years), is surrounded by 16th-century buildings, remodelled during the following century. Notable gardens surround the castle. Shakespeare's Macbeth was Thane of Cawdor, and the castle is one of the traditional settings for the murder of Duncan. Licensed restaurant, snack bar and picnic area in grounds; beautiful gardens and extensive nature trails; 9-hole pitch and putt golf course and putting green.

**Dornoch Cathedral:** *In Dornoch. All year. 0900-dusk. Free.* Founded in 1224 by Gilbert, Archdeacon of Moray and Bishop of Caithness. This little cathedral was partially destroyed by fire in 1570, restored in the 17th century, in 1835-37, and again in 1924. The fine 13th-century stonework is still to be seen.

**Dornoch Craft Centre:** *Town Jail. All year. Summer, Mon-Sat 0930-1700, Sun 1200-1700; Winter, Mon-Fri 0930-1700. Free. Tel: Dornoch (0862) 810555.* Weaving of tartans on Saurgr power looms, kilt making and soft toy making. Small exhibition in Jail cells. Coffee room (Apr-Sep).

**Dounreay Nuclear Power Development Establishment:** *Dounreay, 10m W of Thurso. Easter-Sep, daily 0900-1630. Free. No dogs. Tours (free) by arrangement through the exhibition, Tel: Thurso (0847) 62121, ext 656. (United Kingdom Atomic Energy Authority).* An interesting exhibition giving visitors a general conception of nuclear power and of the activities and work taking place at the establishment. Conducted tours of the prototype Fast Reactor every afternoon (over 14's only). Picnic area.

**Dun Dornaieil Broch:** *20m N of Lairg. A836, then on Loch Hope road. All times. Free. (AM). Tel: 031-244 3101.* Notable example of a prehistoric broch.

**Dunrobin Castle:** *Off A9, 12½m NNE of Dornoch. 1 Jun-15 Sep, Mon-Sat 1030-1730, Sun 1300-1730. Open to groups all year by prior arrangement. (Countess of Sutherland). Tel: Golspie (04083) 3177.* Magnificently set in a great park and formal gardens, overlooking the sea. Dunrobin Castle was originally a square keep built about 1275 by Robert, Earl of Sutherland, from whom it got its name Dun Robin. For centuries this has been the seat of the Earls and Dukes of Sutherland. The present outward appearance results from extensive changes made 1845-50. Fine paintings, furniture and a steam-powered fire engine are among the miscellany of items to be seen. Beach and tearoom.

**Durness Old Church:** *At Balnakeil, ½m W of Durness, near Craft Village. All reasonable times. Free.* Built in 1619, now a ruin.

**Eas Coul Aulin:** *At the head of Loch Glencoul, 3m W of A894.* The tallest waterfall in Britain, dropping 658 feet (200 metres). There are occasional cruises to the waterfall.

**Falls of Shin:** *A836, 5m N of Bonar Bridge.* Spectacular falls through rocky gorge; famous for salmon leap.

**Fortrose Cathedral:** *At Fortrose, 8m SSW of Cromarty. Opening standard. Free. (AM). Tel: 031-244 3101.* The surviving portions of this 14th-century cathedral include the south aisle with its vaulting and much fine detail.

**Gairloch Heritage Museum:** *In Gairloch, on A832. Easter-end Sep, Mon-Sat 1000-1700. Tel: Badachro (044 583) 243.* Award-winning museum with displays of all aspects of the past life in the West Highland area from prehistoric times to the present day. Licensed restaurant attached.

**Girnigoe and Sinclair Castles:** *3m N of Wick.* Two adjacent castles on a cliff edge above Sinclair Bay. Girnigoe dates from the end of the 15th century while Sinclair was built in the early 17th.

**Grey Cairns of Camster:** *6m N of Lybster on Watten Road, off A9. All reasonable times. Free. (AM). Tel: 031-244 3101.* Two megalithic cairns: a round cairn and a long cairn containing chambers, probably 4th millenium BC.

**Handa Island Nature Reserve:** *Handa Island, 3m NW of Scourie. Access: day visits by local boatmen from Tarbet. Apr-mid Sep, Mon-Sat 1000-1700. Accommodation is well equipped, bothy available to members of RSPB only (contact RSPB, 17 Regent Terrace, Edinburgh). Warden on island. (RSPB). Tel: 031-556 5624.* An island seabird sanctuary with vast numbers of fulmars, shags, gulls, kittiwakes and auks. Arctic and great skuas on moorland. Shelter for visitors with displays.

**The Indian Temple:** *Above Evanton on Fyrish Hill off A9.* Erected by General Sir Hector Munro (1726-1805) and said to represent the gates of Seringapatan, the town he captured in the Indian campaign of 1781.

**Inverewe Gardens:** *On A832, 6m NE of Gairloch. (Gardens) all year, daily 0930-sunset. (Visitor Centre and Shop) 1 Apr-4 May, Mon-Sat 1000-1700, 5 Sep-23 Oct. Mon-Sat 1000-1700, Sun 1200-1700; 5 May-4 Sep, Mon-Sat 1000-1830, Sun 1200-1830. Restaurant. (NTS). Tel: Poolewe (044 586) 200.* Plants from many countries flourish in this garden created by Osgood MacKenzie over 120 years ago, giving an almost continuous display of colour throughout the year. Eucalyptus, rhododendrons, and many Chilean and South American plants are represented in great variety, together with Himalayan lilies and giant forget-me-nots from the South Pacific. Garden for disabled, shop, restaurant, caravan and camp site, petrol, plants sales. Groups of disabled visitors welcome.

**Lhaidhay Caithness Croft Museum:** *On A9, 1m N of Dunbeath. Easter-30 Sep, daily 0900-1700. Tel: Dunbeath (05933) 244.* An early 18th-century croft complex with stable, dwelling house and byre under one thatched roof with adjoining barn. Completely furnished in the fashion of its time. The barn has a notable crux roof. Picnic area.

**Lyth Arts Centre:** *Signposted 4 miles off A9 between Wick and John O'Groats. 26 Jun-6 Sep, daily 1000-1800. (Mr W Wilson). Tel: Lyth (0955 84) 270.* Travelling exhibitions including Scottish fine art, crafts and tapestry. Snack bar, gardens.

**MacDonald Tower:** *Mitchell Hill, Dingwall.* Impressive monument to General Sir Hector MacDonald who was born near Dingwall. There is a special exhibit recalling his military career in the museum at Town House.

**Sir John MacDonald Monument:** *Rogart.* Birth place of the first Prime Minister of Canada. Unveiled by John Diefenbaker in 1963.

**Hugh Miller's Cottage:** *Church Street, Cromarty, 22m NE of Inverness via Kessock Bridge. Easter-30 Sep, Mon-Sat 1000-1200, 1300-1700 (June-4 Sep only, also Sun 1400-1700). (NTS). Tel: Cromarty (03817) 245.* The birthplace of Hugh Miller (1802—56) – stonemason – became eminent geologist, naturalist, theologian and writer. The furnished thatched cottage, built c 1711 by his great grandfather, contains an exhibition and video programme on his life and work.

**St. Andrew's Church, Golspie:** Early 18th century. Built on the site of an ancient chapel to St. Andrew.

**St. Duthus Chapel and Collegiate Church:** *Tain. Chapel: All reasonable times. Free. Church: Open daily, enquire locally. Free. Tel: Tain (0862) 2140.* The chapel was built between 1065 and 1256. St. Duthus died in 1065 and was buried in Ireland, but 200 years later his remains were transferred to Tain. The chapel was destroyed by fire in 1427. St. Duthus Church was built c 1360 by William, Earl and Bishop of Ross, in Decorated style, and became a notable place of pilgrimage. Folk museum and Clan Ross Centre in grounds.

**St. Mary's Chapel, Crosskirk:** *Off A836, 6m W of Thurso. All reasonable times. Free. (AM). Tel: 031-244 3101.* A rudely-constructed chapel with very low doors narrowing at the top in Irish style. Probably 12th century.

**St. Peter's Church:** *Near the Harbour at Thurso. All reasonable times. Free.* Ruins situated in the attractively restored old part of Thurso. Of mediaeval or earlier origin; much of the present church dates from the 17th century.

**Smoo Cave:** *A838, 1½m E of Durness. All reasonable times. Free.* Three vast caves at the end of a deep cleft in the limestone cliffs. The entrance to the first resembles a Gothic arch. The second cavern, access difficult, has a waterfall. The third is inaccessible.

**Strathnaver Museum:** *Off A836, at Farr, near Bettyhill. Summer, Mon-Sat, 1400-1700. Donations (J and R McKay). Tel: Mrs. Rudie, Bettyhill (06412) 330.* The former Farr Church (18th century) now houses this museum of local history. This is historic Clan MacKay country and is associated with the Sutherland Clearances.

**Struie Hill:** *6m SE of Bonar Bridge on A836.* Viewpoint with magnificent panoramas east and west of Dornoch Firth.

**Thurso Heritage Museum:** *Town Hall, Jun-Sep, Mon-Sat 1000-1300, 1400-1700. Tel: Thurso (0847) 62459.* Exhibition of agricultural and domestic life, local trades and crafts with a room of an old Caithness cottage.

**Whiten Head:** *5m N of A838 and 6m E of Durness. No road access; boat trips from Durness in summer.* A splendid perpendicular cliff with a fine series of caves.

**Wick Heritage Centre:** *Bank Row, Wick. Jun-Sep, Mon-Sat 1000-1230, 1400-1700, or by arrangement for groups. (Wick Society). Tel: Wick (0955) 3385.* Prize-winning exhibition of the herring fishing industry; also displays of domestic and farming life. Gardens and tearoom.

# WESTERN AND CENTRAL HIGHLANDS

**Appin Wildlife Museum:** *On A828 at Appin Home Farm, 25m N of Oban. All year, daily 1000-1800. Donations. Tel: Appin (063 173) 308.* The Forest Ranger (John Scorgie) has over the years collected specimens of the local wildlife, to let visitors know what to look for in the area.

**Ardanaiseig Gardens:** *E of B845, 22m E of Oban. 31 Mar-31 Oct, daily 1000-dusk. Tel: Kilchrenan (08663) 333.* Rhododendrons, azaleas, rare shrubs and trees. Magnificent views across Loch Awe and of Ben Cruchan. The hotel restaurant is open for morning tea, luncheon and afternoon tea.

**Ardchattan Priory:** *On the N side of Lower Loch Etive, 6½m NE of Oban. Open all times. Free. (AM). Tel: 031-244 3101.* One of the Valliscaulian houses founded in Scotland in 1230, and the meeting place in 1308 of one of Bruce's Parliaments, among the last at which business was conducted in Gaelic. Burned by Cromwell's soldiers in 1654, the remains include some carved stones. The gardens of Ardchattan House, adjoining the Priory, are open Apr-Sep; admission charge. Achnaba Church, near Connel, has notable central communion pews.

**Aviemore Centre:** *Off A9, 32m S of Inverness. All year, daily 1000 onwards. Admission free (charge for facilities). Group rates on request from Sales Dept. Stakis plc. Tel: (03552) 47177. Tel: Aviemore (0479) 810624.* Leisure, sport and conference centre with wide range of recreational and entertainment facilities, including: cinema/theatre, swimming pool, ice rink, saunas, artificial ski slope, go-karts, discos, restaurants, and many more.

**Ballachulish Interpretative Centre:** *In Ballachulish.* Opened in 1981. Displays and information about immediate area, including the 200 year history of the local slate industry.

**Ben Nevis:** *Near Fort William.* Britain's highest mountain (4,406 ft/ 1,344 m) and most popular mountain for both rock-climber and hillwalker. It is best seen from the north approach to Fort William, or from the Gairlochy Road, across the Caledonian Canal.

**Bernera Barracks:** *At Glenelg, on unclassified road W of A87 at Shiel Bridge. All times. Free.* The remains of Bernera Barracks, erected c 1722 and used continuously until after 1790.

**Bonawe Iron Furnace:** *At Bonawe, 12m E of Oban, off A85. Opening standard, Apr-Sep only. Tel: 031-244 3101.* The restored remains of a charcoal furnace for iron-smelting, established in 1753, which worked until 1876. The furnace and ancillary buildings are in a more complete state of preservation than any other comparable site.

**Cairngorm Chairlift:** *A951 from A9 at Aviemore, then by Loch Morlich to car park at 2,000 feet. All year, daily 0900-1630, depending on weather. (Cairngorm Chairlift Company Limited). Tel: Cairngorm (047 986) 261.* At the car park is a large Day Lodge containing restaurant, bar, shop and snack bar. At the top of the chairlift is the Ptarmigan snack bar, the highest observation building in Great Britain at 3,600 feet with magnificent views to west and north-east. Also alpine garden.

**Clan MacPherson Museum:** *In Newtonmore on A9/A86, 15m S of Aviemore. May-Sep, Mon-Sat 1000-1730, Sun 1430-1730. Free. Tel: Newtonmore (054 03) 332.* Relics and memorials of Clan Chiefs and other MacPherson families. Exhibits include a letter to Prince Charles Edward Stuart from his father, a massive silver epergne depicting an incident in the life of Cluny of the '45 after the Battle of Culloden, green banner of the clan, Victorian royal warrants, crests, James MacPherson's fiddle and other historical relics.

**Clava Cairns:** *Near Culloden, off B9006, 6m E of Inverness. All reasonable times. Free. (AM). Tel: 031-244 3101.* Late Neolithic or Early Bronze Age chambered cairns with standing stone circles.

**Commando Memorial:** *Off A82, 11m NE of Fort William.* An impressive sculpture by Scott Sutherland, erected in 1952 to commemorate the Commandos of World War II who trained in this area. Fine views of Ben Nevis and Lochaber.

**Darnaway Farm Visitor Centre:** *Off A96, 3m W of Forres. 1 Jun-20 Sep, daily 1000-1700. (Monay Estates). Also available tours to Darnaway Castle (Jun-Aug, Wed & Sun). Tour of estate with countryside ranger (Tue & Thu, begins at 1415). Tel: Monay Estates – Forres (0309) 72213.* At the Visitor Centre, an exhibition of the farms and forest of Moray Estates, with audio-visual programme. Viewing platform to watch cows being milked. Nature trails and woodland walks, picnic areas, tearoom and play area.

**Eilean Donan Castle:** *Off A87, 9m E of Kyle of Lochalsh. Easter-Sep, daily 1000-1230, 1400-1800. (Mr J D H MacRae). Tel: Kyle (0599) 85 202.* On an islet (now connected by a causeway) in Loch Duich, this picturesque castle dates back to 1220. It passed into the hands of the MacKenzies of Kintail who became Earls of Seaforth. In 1719 it was garrisoned by Spanish Jacobite troops and was blown up by an English man o'war. Now completely restored, it incorporates a war memorial to the Clan MacRae, who held it as hereditary Constables on behalf of the MacKenzies. Gift Shop.

**Falls of Foyers:** *Foyers 17m SW of Inverness B852.* Upper fall is 30 feet and lower 90 feet.

**Farigaig Forest Centre:** *Off B862 at Inverfarigaig, 17m S of Inverness. Easter-mid Oct 0930-1900. Free. (FC). Tel: Gorthleck (04563) 249.* A Forestry Commission interpretation centre in a converted stone stable, showing the development of the forest environment in the Great Glen. Forest walks.

**Fort George:** *B9039, off A96 W of Nairn. Opening standard. (AM). Tel: 031-244 3101.* Begun in 1748 as a result of the Jacobite rebellion, this is one of the finest late artillery fortifications in Europe, which is still in use. There is also the Regimental Museum of the Queen's Own Highlanders.

**Garvamore Bridge:** *6m W of Laggan Bridge, on unclassified road, 17m SW of Newtonmore. All times. Free.* This two-arched bridge at the south side of the Corrieyarick Pass was built by General Wade in 1735.

**Glencoe and Dalness:** *A82, 3m E of Glencoe Cross, runs through the glen. (Visitor Centre) Easter-31 May, 5 Sep-23 Oct, daily 1000-1730; 1 Jun-4 Sep, daily 0900-1830. (NTS). Tel: Ballachulish (085 52) 307.* The finest and perhaps the most famous glen in Scotland through which a main road runs. Scene of the Massacre of Glencoe, 1692, and centre for some of the best mountaineering in the

country (not to be attempted by the unskilled). Noted for wildlife which includes red deer, wildcat, golden eagle, ptarmigan. NTS owns 14,200 acres of Glencoe and Dalness. Ski centre, chairlift and ski tows (weekends and New Year and Easter holiday periods only, other times by charter arrangement) at White Corries. Visitor Centre gives general information, particularly on walks. Visitor Centre, special presentation, Ranger Service, walks and trails, shop, picnic area and tea bar.

**Glencoe and North Lorn Folk Museum:** *In Glencoe Village, off A82, on S shore of Loch Leven. May-Sep, Mon-Sat 1000-1730.* Clan and Jacobite relics, also domestic implements, weapons, costumes, photographs, dolls' houses and dolls, agricultural tools, dairy and slate quarrying equipment are included in this museum housed in a number of thatched cottages.

**Glencoe Chairlift:** *Off A82 by Kingshouse. Jan-Apr, weekends and Easter 0900-1730; Jun-Sep, daily 1000-1700. Tel: Kingshouse (08556) 226.* Chairlift to 2,100 feet offers magnificent views of the areas around Glencoe and Rannoch Moor. Summer: access chairlift, snack bar, car park, toilets. Winter: two chairlifts and three tows for ski-ing, car park, toilets and snack bars.

**Glenelg Brochs:** *Unclassified road from Eilanreach, 12m W of Shiel Bridge. All times. Free. (AM).*

*Tel: 031-244 3101.* Two Iron Age brochs, Dun Telve and Dun Troddan, have walls still over 30 feet high.

**Glenfinnan Monument:** *A830, 18½m W of Fort William. Easter-31 May, 5 Sep-23 Oct, 1000-1730; 1 Jun-4 Sep, 0930-1830. (NTS). Tel: (039783) 250.* The monument commemorates the raising of Prince Charles Edward Stuart's standard at Glenfinnan on 19 August 1745. It was erected by MacDonald of Glenaladale in 1815; a figure of a Highlander surmounts the tower. The Visitor Centre tells of the Prince's campaign from Glenfinnan to Derby and back to the final defeat at Culloden. Audio-visual programme, snack bar and viewpoint.

**Glengarry Forest:** *Off A82 2m W of Glengarry Village.* Picnic Place, walks. Also picnic place on shore of Loch Oich, on A82 at south end of loch.

**Glen Grant Distillery:** *Rothes. Late Apr-end Sep, Mon-Fri 1000-1600. Free. Tel: Rothes (034 03) 413 (during season) and Keith (05422) 8924 (during winter).* Tours of the distillery, with Reception Centre and whisky sample. Children under 8 not admitted to production areas but welcome in Reception Centre.

**Glenmore Forest Park:** *7m E of Aviemore, off A9152. Open all year. (FC). Tel: Kincraig (05404) 223 or Cairngorm (047986) 271.* Over 12,000 acres of pine and spruce woods and mountainside on the north-west slopes of the Cairngorms, with Loch Morlich as its centre. This is probably the finest area in Britain for wildlife, including red deer, reindeer, wildcat, golden eagle, ptarmigan, capercailzie, etc. Remnants of old Caledonian pinewoods. Well-equipped caravan sites and hostels open all year, canoeing, sailing, fishing, swimming, forest trails and hillwalking, and an Information Centre. Campsite, forest walks, toilets, picnic area, shop, cafe and wayfaring trail.

**Great Glen (Highland Heritage) Exhibition:** *Centre of Fort Augustus beside the canal. Apr-Oct, daily 0930-1700. Free, but donations welcome. Tel: Fort Augustus (0320) 6341.* Visitor Centre for those wishing to take in the atmosphere of the history of Scotland's 'Great Glen'. All aspects of Highland Heritage are covered with further exhibits planned for the future. Garden area with picnic tables.

**Highland Folk Museum:** *A9 at Kingussie, 12m SW of Aviemore. All year, Apr-Oct, Mon-Sat 1000-1800, Sun 1400-1800; Nov-Mar, Mon-Fri 1000-1500. (Highland Regional Council). Tel: Kingussie (054 02) 307.* The open air museum includes an 18th century shooting lodge, a 'Black House' from Lewis, a Clack Mill, a turf-walled house from the Central Highlands and exhibits of farming equipment. Indoors, the farming

museum has fine displays of a barn, dairy, stable and an exhibition of Highland tinkers; and there are special features on weapons, costume, musical instruments and Highland furniture. Picnic garden. Special events Easter-September.

**Highland Wildlife Park:** *Off A9 (B9152), 7m S of Aviemore. Open daily 1000-1700 (closing times vary during spring and autumn); Jul-Aug 1000-1800, closed winter season. Tel: Kincraig (054 04) 270. Office open 0900-1700.* This notable wildlife park features breeding groups of Highland animals and birds in a beautiful natural setting. Drive-through section has red deer herd, bison, Highland cattle, etc. Aviaries display capercailzie, eagles; also wolves, wildcats and nearly 60 other species. There is an exhibition on 'Man and Fauna in the Highlands', and a children's animal park. Also souvenir shop, cafeteria and picnic area.

**Inveraray Bell Tower:** *In Inveraray. Late May-late Sep, Mon-Sat 1000-1300, 1400-1700; Sun 1500-1800. (Scottish Episcopal Church of All Saints). Tel: Inveraray (0499) 2433.* The 126-feet high granite tower houses Scotland's finest ring of bells and the world's third-heaviest ring of ten bells, which are rung regularly. Excellent views, pleasant grounds.

**Inveraray Castle:** *½m N of Inveraray. Apr-Jun, Sep-mid Oct, Mon-Sat (not Fri) 1000-1230, 1400-1730, Sun 1300-1730; Jul-Aug, Mon-*

*Sat 1000-1730, Sun 1300-1730. (Argyll Estates). Tel: Inveraray (0499) 2203.* Inveraray has been the seat of the chiefs of Clan Campbell, Dukes of Argyll, for centuries. The present castle was started in 1743 when the third Duke engaged Roger Morris to build it. Subsequently the Adam family, father and sons, were also involved. The magnificent interior decoration was commissioned by the fifth Duke from Robert Mylne. In addition to many historic relics, there are portraits by Gainsborough, Ramsay and Raeburn. Tearoom and craft shop. Gardens open on selected weekends.

**Inverliever Forest:** *B845 Lochawe.* Forest trail, walks, picnic places, camp site.

**Kintail:** *N of A87 between Lochs Cluanie and Duich, 16m E of Kyle of Lochalsh. (NTS). Tel: (059 981) 219.* Magnificent Highland scenery including the Five Sisters of Kintail, peaks rising to 3,500 feet. Red deer and wild goats. Visitor Centre at Morvich open 1 Jun to end Sep Mon-Sat 0900-1800, Sun 1300-1800.

**Ladycroft Agricultural Museum:** *At Archiestown, by Aberlour, on the B9102 Grantown Scenic route whisky trail. All year, 1000-dusk. (Mr & Mrs C W Spence). Tel: Carron (034 06) 274.* A museum of the time when all the farm implements were worked by horses. There are life-size models of men and horses.

**Landmark Visitor Centre:** *Carrbridge, 6m N of Aviemore on old A9. All year. Open 0930-1730 in winter, 0930-2130 in summer. Tel: Carrbridge (047 984) 613.* This 'Landmark' Visitor Centre was the first of its kind in Europe. Ten thousand years of Highland history are shown in the triple-screen audio-visual theatre and a dramatic exhibition interprets the history of Strathspey. Now has sculpture park, tree-top trail and woodland maze. Adventure playground with giant slides and aerial net walkways. Also new pine forest nature centre. Craft and bookshop, restaurant, bar, snack bar, picnic area and plant centre. Free parking.

**Lochalsh Woodland Garden:** *Off A87, 3m E of Kyle of Lochalsh. All year, daily. (NTS). Tel: Balmacara (059 986) 207.* A wide variety of native trees and shrubs and more exotic plants from Tasmania, New Zealand, the Himalayas, Chile, Japan and China in the grounds of Lochalsh House (not open to the public). There are pleasant walks and an ecology display in the coach house.

**Loch-an-Eilean Visitor Centre:** *B970, 2½m S of Aviemore. May-Sep. Free. (Rothiemurclus Estate) Tel: Aviemore (0479) 810 647.* This exhibition which is held in a cottage by the loch and a beautiful ruined castle, traces the history of the native Scots Pine forest from the Ice Age until

today, its management and conservation. Good local interest for birdwatchers.

**Loch Garten Nature Reserve:** *Off B970, 8m NE of Aviemore. If Ospreys present, daily mid Apr-Aug 1000-2000 along signposted track to Observation Post. Other access into bird sanctuary strictly forbidden Apr-Aug but elsewhere on the reserve access unrestricted throughout the year. Free. (RSPB). Tel: Aviemore (0479) 83694.* Ospreys, extinct in Scotland for many years, returned here to breed in 1959. Their treetop eyrie may be viewed through fixed binoculars from the Observation Hut. Other local specialities include creasted tits, crossbills and capercailzies. The surrounding area owned by the RSPB, includes extensive stretches of old Caledonian Pine forest with rich and varied wildlife.

**Loch Morar:** *SE of Mallaig.* Said to be the deepest loch in Scotland and the home of Morag, a monster with a strong resemblance to the Loch Ness Monster.

**Loch Nan Uamh Cairn:** *Off A830, S of Arisaig.* The loch is famous for its association with Bonnie Prince Charlie. The memorial cairn on the shore marks the spot from which Prince Charles Edward Stuart sailed for France on 20 September, 1746 after having wandered round the Highlands as a fugitive with a price of £30,000 on his head.

**Loch Ness:** *SW of Inverness.* This striking 24-mile long loch in the Great Glen forms part of the Caledonian Canal which links Inverness with Fort William. For much of its length it is over 700 feet deep. The loch contains the largest volume of fresh water of any lake in the British Isles. Famous world wide for its mysterious inhabitant, the Loch Ness Monster. It is also ideal for cruising and sailing.

**Loch Ness Monster Exhibition:** *At Drumnadrochit on A82, 14m SW of Inverness. Peak season daily 0900-2130, off season times vary, please check. Tel: Drumnadrochit (04562) 573.* A revised and greatly extended exhibition presents evidence of the existence of unknown creatures in Loch Ness. Also explains some dubious early pictures. Sales counter.

**Neptune's Staircase:** *3m NW of Fort William off A830 at Banavie.* A series of 8 locks, built between 1805 and 1822, which raises Telford's Caledonian Canal 64 feet.

**Parallel Roads:** *Glen Roy, unclassified road off A86, 18m NE of Fort William.* Unusual parallel lines conspicuous on both sides of picturesque glen north of Fort William. These 'parallel roads' are hillside terraces marking levels of lakes dammed by glaciers during the Ice Age.

**Roderick MacKenzie Memorial:** *1m E of Ceannacroc on A887, 13m*

*W of Invermoriston. All times. Free.* A cairn on the south of the road commemorates the heroic action of Roderick MacKenzie, a supporter of Prince Charles Edward Stuart who drew off pursuit by pretending to be his leader. He was shot dead by pursuing soldiers and in the resulting confusion of identity, the real Prince Charlie was able to flee from the area.

**St. Benedict's Abbey:** *Fort Augustus, A82.* Former fort takes its name from William Augustus, Duke of Cumberland, who made it his headquarters after the Battle of Culloden in 1746. Abbey built in 19th-century. Now houses a boys' school run by Benedictine monks.

**Scot II Cruises:** *Departure point: top of Muirton Locks, Inverness. Signposted with thistle. Afternoon Cruise: 1415 (18 Apr-23 Sep), Mon-Sat. Morning Cruise: 1015 (25 Apr-2 Sep), Mon-Sat. Evening Cruise: 1900 (30 May-5 Aug), Mon-Fri. (British Waterways Board). Tel: Inverness (0463) 233140.* Scot II was built in 1932 originally as a Canal Tug. She now cruises on the Caledonian Canal and Loch Ness, offering an interest-packed voyage past Tomnahurich Hill through swing bridges and locks, past a lighthouse and out on to the beautiful Loch Ness to historic Urquhart Castle. Licensed bar, snack bar, toilets.

**Sea Life Centre:** *Barcaldine, on A828, 11m N of Oban. 1 Apr-31 Oct, daily. Tel: (063 172) 386.* Centre houses a large and exciting display of native marine life. Visitors can experience the feeling of being on the sea-bed without getting wet and come face to face with octopus, catfish and seals. Both the aquarium and restaurant have a beautiful lochside setting.

**James Stewart Tablet:** *2m SW of Ballachulish on shores of Loch Linnhe.* Commemorates James Stewart who was tried and unjustly hanged for the Appin murder in 1752 and made famous in R L Stevenson's 'Kidnapped'.

**Strathspey Railway:** *Aviemore (Speyside) to Boat of Garten. Access at Aviemore: cars in Dalfaber Road, pedestrians take underpass from Main Road at Bank of Scotland. Train Services Easter weekend – mid May Sun only. Weekends mid-May to mid-Oct; Jul-Aug, Mon-Thu; Jun, Mon 1200-1700 approx. (Strathspey Railway Co Ltd). Tel: Aviemore (0479 83) 692.* The line is part of the former Highland Railway (Aviemore-Forres section) closed in 1965 and reopened 1978 after restoration work begun in 1972. Passenger steam train service run entirely by volunteers. Station buildings at Aviemore (Speyside) were brought from Dalnaspidal and the footbridge from Longmorn. Timetables

available. Museum of small relics and other static rolling stock on display at Boat of Garten.

**Urquhart Castle:** *2m SE of Drumnadrochit, on W shore of Loch Ness. Opening standard. (AM). Tel: 031-244 3101.* Once one of the largest castles in Scotland, the castle is situated on a promontory on the banks of Loch Ness, from where sitings of the 'monster' are most frequently reported. The extensive ruins are on the site of a vitrified fort, rebuilt with stone in the 14th century. The castle was gifted by James IV, in 1509, to John Grant of Freuchie, whose family built much of the existing fabric and held the site for four centuries. The castle was blown up in 1692 to prevent its being occupied by Jacobites.

**West Highland Museum:** *Cameron Square, Fort William. All year, Mon-Sat 1000-1300, 1400-1700 (Jun and Sep 0930-1730, Jul and Aug 0930-2100). Tel: Fort William (0397) 2169.* Historical, natural history and folk exhibits, local interest and a tartan section. Jacobite relics including a secret portrait of 'Bonnie Prince Charlie'.

**White Corries Chairlift:** *Off A82 by Kinghouse.* Chairlift to 2,100 feet offers magnificent views of Glencoe and Rannoch Moor.

# SCOTLAND'S ISLANDS

## ARRAN

**Brodick Castle Garden and Country Park:** *1¹/₂m N of Brodick pier, Isle of Arran. Castle: 1-30 Apr, 1-15 Oct, Mon, Wed and Sat. May-Sep, daily 1300-1700 (last admission 1640). Goatfell, park and gardens: all year, daily 1000-1700. Tearoom: (dates as Castle) Mon-Sat 1000-1700, Sun 1200-1700. Last admission 20 minutes before closing. (NTS). Tel: Brodick (0770) 2202.* This ancient seat of the Dukes of Hamilton dates in part from the 13th century, with extensions of 1652 and 1844. The contents include silver, porcelain and fine paintings, sporting pictures and trophies. There are two gardens: the woodland garden (1923) is now one of the finest rhododendron gardens in Britain; the formal garden dates from 1710. In 1980 the gardens became a country park, supported by the Countryside Commission for Scotland, with a ranger service. Nature trail specially designed for wheelchair users. Tearoom, shop, nature trail and adventure playground.

**Goatfell:** *3¹/₂m NNW of Brodick, Arran.* At 2,866 feet this is the highest peak on Arran. NTS property includes Glen Rosa and Cir Mhor, with grand walking and climbing. The golden eagle may occasionally be seen, along with hawks, harriers, etc.

**Isle of Arran Heritage Museum:** *Rosaburn, Brodick, Isle of Arran.*

*Early May to end Sep, Mon-Fri 1000-1300 and 1400-1630. Tel: Brodick (0770) 2636.* A group of old buildings which were originally an 18th-century croft farm on the edge of the village. Smithy, cottage furnished in late 19th-century style, stable block with displays of local history, archaeology and geology. Demonstrations of spinning and other hand crafts arranged periodically. Picnic area and tearoom.

## BUTE

**Rothesay Castle:** *At Rothesay, Isle of Bute. Opening standard, except Oct–Mar closed Thu am and Fri. (AM). Tel: 031-244 3101.* One of the most important mediaeval castles in Scotland. Rothesay was stormed by Norsemen in 1240; their breach can still be detected. The walls, heightened and provided with four round towers in the late 13th century, enclose a circular courtyard unique in Scotland.

**St. Blane's Chapel:** *8¹/₂m S of Rothesay, Isle of Bute. All reasonable times. Free. (AM). Tel: 031-244 3101.* Ruins of a chapel built c 1100. Nearby are the foundations of a monastery founded by St Blane in the 6th century.

## COLONSAY

**Kiloran Gardens:** *Kiloran, Isle of Colonsay. Daily, all reasonable times. Free. Tel: Colonsay (095 12) 312.*

*(Mrs E McNeill).* An island garden noted for its rhododendrons and shrubs, including embothriums and magnolias. Self-catering accommodation.

## GIGHA

**Achamore House Gardens:** *Isle of Gigha, off the Mull of Kintyre. All year, daily, 1000-dusk. (Gardens only - house not open to the public). Car and passenger ferry from Tayinloan. (D W N Landale). Tel: Gigha (058 35) 254.* Rhododendrons, camellias and many semi-tropical shrubs and plants may be seen at these gardens developed over the past 30 years. Elsewhere on this fertile island, see the ruined church at Kilchattan, which dates back to the 13th century. Boathouse bar, visitor reception centre and Gigha Hotel 1/2 mile away.

## HARRIS

**St. Clement's Church:** *At Rodel, S end of Harris, Western Isles. All reasonable times. Free; apply key-keeper. (AM). Tel: 031-244 3101.* A cruciform church of c 1500 with rich decoration and sculptured slabs. Restored in 1873.

## IONA

**Iona:** *Off the SW tip of Mull; take A849 to Fionnphort, then ferry. Also steamer trips from Oban. Tel: Iona (06817) 404.* In 563 St Columba with 12 followers came to this little island to found a monastery from which his monks travelled over much of Scotland preaching Christianity to the Picts. The monastery, often attacked up to the 9th century by Norse raiders, was replaced in 1203 but, along with the cathedral, fell into decay. Restoration started early this century. The monastery is the home of the Iona Community, founded by Dr George MacLeod in 1938, who have done much restoration of the Cathedral, which has a beautiful interior and interesting carvings. For centuries Iona was the burial place of Scottish kings and chiefs. The oldest surviving building is St Oran's Chapel, c 1080 (restored). The remains of the 13th century nunnery can be seen and outside the Cathedral is 10th-century St Martin's Cross, 14 feet high and elaborately carved. Abbey gift and bookshop open 1000-1630 daily. Abbey coffee house open 1000-1630 daily except Sundays.

## ISLAY

**Kildalton Crosses:** *Isle of Islay. All reasonable times. Free. (AM). Tel: 031-226 2570.* Two of the finest Celtic crosses in Scotland, and sculptured slabs, are in Kildalton churchyard.

## LEWIS

**Black House:** *Arnol. A857 NW from Stornoway then A858.* Old croft house kept in original condition. Now a museum.

**Callanish Standing Stones:** *Callanish, off A858, 12m W of Stornoway, Lewis. All times. Free. (AM). Tel: 031-244 3101.* A unique cruciform setting of megaliths second in importance only to Stonehenge. It was probably carried out in a series of additions between 3000 and 1500 BC. An avenue of 19 monoliths leads north from a circle of 13 stones, with rows of more stones fanning out to south, east and west. Inside the circle is a small chambered tomb.

**Church of St Moulag:** *N end of the Isle of Lewis. Open all reasonable times. (Scottish Episcopal Church). Tel: (0859) 3609.* Known in the Gaelic as Teampull mhor (big temple) this chapel was probably built in the 12th century. Now restored; occasional services held.

**Dun Carloway Broch:** *A858, 16m WNW of Stornoway, Isle of Lewis. Opening standard. Free. (AM). Tel: 031-244 3101.* One of the best presented Iron Age broch towers. Still standing about 30 feet high.

**Lewis Castle Grounds:** *W of Harbour, Stornoway, Isle of Lewis. All reasonable times. Free. (Grounds only).* The modern castle, now a technical college (not open to the public), stands in the wooded grounds given to the town by Lord Leverhulme. Noted for their rhododendrons. Castle ground gardens and public park.

## MULL

**Mull Little Theatre:** *Dervaig, Isle of Mull. Open Spring-Autumn. Tel: Dervaig (06884) 267.* Officially the smallest professional theatre in the country, according to the Guinness Book of Records, providing a variety of performances in summer.

**Mull and West Highland Narrow Gauge Railway:** *Easter, 30 Apr-1 Oct, Mon-Sat. Sun operates only when Caledonian MacBrayne are running a Sun service. (Mull and West Highland Narrow Gauge Railway Co Ltd). Tel: Craignure (06802) 494.* 101/4" gauge railway operating a scheduled service to Torosay Castle and Gardens from Craignure (Old Pier) Station. Steam and diesel-hauled trains, superb sea and mountain panorama and woodland journey. Distance 1¼ miles, journey time 20 minutes, Souvenir shop at booking office at Craignure. Tearoom at Torosay Castle. Disabled must be able to get in and out of wheelchairs.

**Torosay Castle:** *A849, 1½m SSE of Craignure, Isle of Mid Apr-mid Oct, daily 1030-1700. Gardens open sunrise to sunset. Tel: Craignure (06802) 421.* The gardens and much of the house are open to the public. The Victorian castle is of Scottish Baronial architecture in a magnificent setting; its features include reception rooms and a variety of exhibition rooms. The 11 acres of Italian terraced gardens by Lorimer contain a statue walk and water garden. Served by a 10 1/4-inch gauge steam railway from Craignure Old Pier. Tearoom.

## ORKNEY

**Churchill Barriers:** *A961 S of Kirkwall. B9056 from Aith.* Four causeways built on the orders of Winston Churchill during the Second World War to seal the eastern approaches to Scapa Flow naval base.

**Italian Chapel:** *Lambholm, Orkney. All times. Free. (POW Chapel Preservation Committee).* Using a Nissen hut, Italian prisoners-of-war in 1943 created this beautiful little chapel out of scrap metal, concrete and other materials. All the painting was done free hand.

**Knap of Howar:** *W side of island of Papa Westray, 800 metres W of Holland House, Orkney. All reasonable times. Free. (AM). Tel: 031-244 3101.* Only recently recognised as one of the oldest sites in Europe, these two 5000-year-old dwellings have also yielded many unusual artefacts – whalebone mallets and a spatula and unique stone borers and grinders.

**Maes Howe Chambered Cairn:** *Off A965, 9m W of Kirkwall, Orkney. Opening standard. (AM). Tel: 031-244 3101.* An enormous burial mound, 115 feet in diameter, dating back to c 2500 BC, and containing a burial chamber which is

unsurpassed in Western Europe. In the 12th century Viking marauders broke into it in search of treasures and Norse crusaders sheltered from a storm in the Howe. They engraved a rich collection of Runic inscriptions upon the walls.

**Ring of Brodgar:** *Between Loch of Harray and Loch of Stenness, 5m NE of Stromness, Mainland, Orkney. All times. Free. (AM). Tel: 031-244 3101.* Magnificent stone circle of 36 stones (originally 60) surrounded by a deep ditch cut into solid bedrock. Nearby are large mounds and other standing stones, notably the Comet Stone.

**St. Magnus Cathedral:** *Kirkwall, Orkney. Mon-Sat 0900-1300, 1400-1700. Closed Sun (except for services). Free.* The most northerly cathedral in Britain, founded by Jarl Rognvald in 1137 and dedicated to his uncle St. Magnus. The remains of both men are in the massive central piers. The original building dates from 1137 to 1200 but additional work went on for a further 300 years. It is still in regular use as a Church, and contains some of the finest examples of Norman architecture in Scotland, with small additions in transitional styles and very early Gothic.

**Skara Brae:** *19m NW of Kirkwall, Mainland, Orkney. Opening standard. (AM). Tel: 031-244 3101.* A Neolithic village occupied from about 3000

BC to perhaps 2700 BC. The main period of settlement included eight or so houses joined by covered passages. Stone beds, fire places, cupboards and dressers survive. The inhabitants were farmers and herds who burned their dead in tombs like Quoyness. The amazing preservation of the village is due to its inundation by sand which buried it for 4500 years until it was revealed by a storm in 1850.

**Standing Stones of Stenness:** *Between Loch of Harray and Loch of Stenness, 5m NE of Stromness, Mainland, Orkney. All times. Free. (AM). Tel: 031-244 3101.* Four large upright stones are the dramatic remains of a stone circle, c 3000 BC, encircled by a ditch and bank. The area around Stenness is particularly rich in such remains.

## RHUM

**Kinloch Castle:** *Isle of Rhum, access by boat from Mallaig. Mar–Oct, as a hotel and hostel. Tours by arrangement with The Castle staff. (NCC). Tel: Mallaig (0687) 2026.* Extraordinary and magnificent residence built at the turn of the century for Sir George Bullough, still containing many of its sumptuous fittings. The island itself is a mountainous nature reserve where the Nature Conservancy Council have for some years conducted experiments in deer and forestry management.

## SHETLAND

**Hermaness:** *Unst, Shetland.* Nature reserve noted for the breeding of the great skua; also gannets, puffins and guillemots.

**Jarlshof:** *Sumburgh Head, Approx. 22m S of Lerwick, Shetland. Opening standard, except closed Tue and Wed afternoon in winter. (AM). Tel: 031-244 3101.* One of the most remarkable archaeological sites in Europe with the remains of three extensive village settlements occupied from Bronze Age to Viking times, together with a mediaeval farmstead and the 16th-century house of the Earls Robert and Patrick Stewart.

**Mousa Broch:** *On the island of Mousa, accessible by boat from Sandwick, Shetland. Daily bus service between Lerwick and Sandwick. Boat for hire; May-Sep afternoons; also Sat and Sun mornings, and some evenings. Opening standard. Free. (AM). Tel: 031-244 3101.* The best preserved example of the remarkable Iron Age broch towers peculiar to Scotland. The tower stands over 40 feet high. Its outer and inner walls contain a rough staircase which can be climbed to the parapet.

**Scalloway Castle:** *6m W of Lerwick, Shetland. Opening standard. Free. (AM). Tel: 031-244 3101.* Built in 1600 by Earl Patrick Stewart, in mediaeval style. When the Earl, a notoriously cruel character, was executed in 1615, the castle fell into disuse.

## SKYE

**Clan Donald Centre:** *At Armadale on A851, 1/2m N of Armadale Pier. Apr-Oct, every day of the week 1000-1730 (last entry 1700). Tel: Ardvasar (047 14) 227/305.* Skye's Award-winning Visitor Centre, located in a rebuilt section of Armadale Castle, once home of Lord Macdonald. The Museum of the Isles has an audio-visual display telling the history of the great Gaelic Kingdom of the Lords of the Isles. The Stables houses a licensed Restaurant serving fresh local produce, particularly fish and home-baking. Shop well stocked with gifts and books. There are 46 acres of Sheltered Woodland Gardens and several miles of Nature Trails. A Countryside Ranger Service offers guided walks and talks. Also a Children's Skyelark Scheme and evening Theatre and Music events. Quality self-catering cottages available. Toilets. Car-park, suitable for disabled. Contact the Visitor Services Manager.

**Dunvegan Castle:** *Dunvegan, Isle of Skye. Easter-mid Oct 1400-1700 (mid-May to Sep 1030-1700). Closed Sun. (J MacLeod of MacLeod). Tel: Dunvegan (047 022) 206.* Historic stronghold of the Clan MacLeod, set on the sea loch of Dunvegan, still the home after 700 years of the chiefs of MacLeod. Possessions on view, books, pictures, arms and treasured relics, trace the history of the family and clan from the days of their Norse ancestry

through thirty generations to the present day. Boat trips from the castle jetty to the seal colony. Restaurant and shops.

**Kilmuir:** *N of Uig, A855.* Burial place of Flora MacDonald.

**Kilt Rock:** *Off A855, 17m N of Portree, Skye. Seen from the road. Care should be taken not to go too near the edge of the cliff.* The top rock is composed of columnar basalt, the lower portion of horizontal beds, giving the impression of the pleats in a kilt. There is also a waterfall nearby.

**Talisker Distillery:** *Dyrnoch, A863 W from Sligachan.* Visitors can enjoy conducted tours throughout the tourist season.

## STAFFA

**Fingal's Cave:** *On the uninhabited island of Staffa, 8m off the W coast of Mull. Seen by steamer and boat trips from Oban and Mull. Tel: 041-552 8391.* A huge cave, 227 feet long and some 66 feet high from sea level, flanked by black pillared walls and columns. The basaltic rock formations of Staffa, where there are other curious caves, are famous. Fingal's Cave inspired Mendelssohn's *The Hebrides* overture. Catering/bar facilities on Caledonian MacBrayne steamer; depending on tour taken, there is access to refreshments en route.

# CENTRAL AND SOUTH WEST SCOTLAND

**Alloway:** *Southern suburb of Ayr.* Birth place of Robert Burns. Location of Burns Interpretation Centre. Burns Cottage and other sites associated with the poet.

**Alloway Kirk:** *In Alloway. 2¹ʲ²m S of Ayr. All reasonable times. Free. Tel: Alloway (0292) 41252 (mornings).* Ancient church, a ruin in Burns' day, where his father William Burns is buried. Through its window, Tam saw the dancing witches and warlocks in the poem *Tam o'Shanter.* Adjacent to Burns Centre, Burns Monument Hotel and 1/2 mile from Burns Cottage/ Tearoom.

**Arbigland Gardens:** *By Kirkbean, off A710, 12m S of Dumfries. May-end Sep: Tue, Thu, Sun 1400-1800. House open afternoons Whit Week and Aug holiday week. (Captain J B Blackett). Tel: Kirkbean (038788) 28.* These extensive woodlands, formal and water gardens are arranged round a sandy bay which is ideal for children. John Paul Jones' birthplace is nearby, and his father was the gardener at Arbigland. Tearoom.

**Bachelors' Club:** *Tarbolton, B744, 7¹ʲ₂m NE of Ayr off A758. Easter-31 Oct, daily 1200-1700; other times by arrangement.* A 17th-century house where in 1780 Robert Burns and his friends founded a literary and debating society, the Bachelors' Club. In 1779, Burns

attended dancing lessions here, and in 1781 he was initiated as a Freemason. Period furnishings, with reminders of Burns' life at Lochlea Farm. Small coffee shop.

**Bannockburn Heritage Centre:** *Off M80, 2m S of Stirling. 1 Apr–Oct, daily 1000-1800. Audio-visual presentation (last showing 1730). (NTS). Tel: Bannockburn (0786) 812664.* The audio-visual presentation tells the story of the events leading up to the significant victory in Scottish history (1314). In June 1964 the Queen inaugurated the Rotunda and unveiled the equestrian statue of Robert the Bruce. Information available on cassette.

**Boswell Museum and Mausoleum:** *In Auchinleck. A76, 17m E of Ayr. Seen from outside at all times. For entry and guided tour, contact Mr. G P Hoyle, 131 Main Street, Auchinleck; prior notice appreciated. Free: donations welcome. (Auchinleck Boswell Society). Tel: Cumnock (0290) 20757.* The ancient Parish Church, formerly a Celtic well, was enlarged by Walter fitz Alan in 1145-65, and again by David Boswell in 1641-43. It is now a museum of the Boswell family, and also contains a memorial to William Murdoch (1745-1839), a pioneer of lighting and heating by gas. The Boswell Mausoleum, attached, built by Alexander Boswell (Lord Auchinleck) in 1754, is the burial place of five known generations, including

James Boswell, Dr Johnson's famous biographer. (Tour 1½ hrs). Small car park. 2 miles away at Lugar a walking tour on Murdoch, including his birthplace at Belo Mill, opened in 1984.

**Bothwell Castle:** *At Uddingston on A74, 7m SE of Glasgow. Opening standard, except Oct–Mar closed. Thu afternoon and Fri. (AM). Tel: 031-244 3101.* Once the largest and finest stone castle in Scotland, dating from the 13th century and reconstructed by the Douglases in the 15th century. In a picturesque setting above the Clyde Valley.

**Bruce's Stone:** *6m W of New Galloway by A712. All reasonable times. Free. (NTS). Tel: 041-552 8391.* This granite boulder on Moss Raploch records a victory by Robert the Bruce over the English in March 1307, during the fight for Scotland's independence.

**Bruce's Stone:** *N side of Loch Trool, unclassified road off A714, 13m N of Newton Stewart. All reasonable times. Free. Tel: Newton Stewart (0671) 2431.* A massive granite memorial to Robert the Bruce's first victory over the English leading to his subsequent success at Bannockburn. Fine views of Loch Trool and the hills of Galloway.

**Burns Cottage and Museum:** *B7024, at Alloway, 2m S of Ayr. All year. Jun-Aug 0900-1900,*

*Apr, May, Sep, Oct 1000-1700 (Sun 1400-1700); Nov-Mar 1000-1600 (not Sun). (Trustees of Burns Monument). Tel: Ayr (0292) 41215.* In this thatched cottage built by his father, Robert Burns was born, 25 January 1759, and this was his home until 1766. Adjoining the cottage is a leading museum of Burnsiana. This is the start of the Burns Heritage Trail which can be followed to trace the places linked with Scotland's greatest poet. Tearoom, gift shop, museum and gardens. Information available on cassette.

**Burns House, Dumfries:** *Burns Street. All year. Mon-Sat 1000-1300, 1400-1700, Sun 1400-1700. Closed Sun and Mon Oct-Mar. Tel: Dumfries (0387) 55297.* In November 1791 Robert Burns moved to Dumfries as an Exciseman and rented a three-room flat (not open to public) in the Wee Vennel (now Bank Street). In May 1793 he moved to a better house in Mill Vennel (now Burns Street) and here he died on 21 July 1796, though his wife Jean Armour stayed in the house until her death in 1834. The house has been completely refurbished and many relics of the poet are on show.

**Burns House Museum, Mauchline:** *Castle Street, Mauchline, 11m ENE of Ayr. Easter-31 Oct, Mon-Sat 1100-1230, 1330-1730, Sun 1400-1700 (or by arrangement). Tel: Mauchline (0290) 50045.* On the upper floor is the

room which Robert Burns took for Jean Armour in 1788. It has been kept intact and is furnished in the style of that period. The remainder of the museum contains Burnsiana and a collection of folk objects. There is a large collection of Mauchline boxware and an exhibition devoted to curling and curling stones which are made in the village. Nearby is Mauchline Kirkyard (scene of *the Holy Fair*) in which are buried four of Burns' daughters and a number of his friends and contemporaries. Other places of interest nearby are 15th-century Mauchline Castle and Poosie Nansie's Tavern.

**Burns Mausoleum:** *St Michael's Churchyard, Dumfries. All reasonable times. Free. Tel: Dumfries (0387) 53862.* Burns was buried in St Michael's Churchyard near to the house in Mill Vennel where he died in 1796. In 1819 his remains were moved into the present elaborate mausoleum.

**Burns Monument, Alloway:** *B7024 at Alloway, 2m S of Ayr. Apr-mid Oct, daily 0900-1900. (Trustees of Burns Monument). Tel: Ayr (0292) 41321.* Grecian monument (1823) to the poet with relics dating back to the 1820's. Nearby is the attractive River Doon, spanned by the famous Brig o' Doon, a single arch (possibly 13th century), central to Burns' poem *Tam o' Shanter*. Museum, gift shop, gardens.

**Burns Monument and Museum, Kilmarnock:** *Kay Park. Closed till further notice. Admission by arrangement. Tel: Kilmarnock (0563) 26401.* The Monument is a statue by W G Stevenson, offering fine views over the surrounding countryside. The Kay Park Museum houses displays on the life and works of Burns, and has an extensive Burns Library.

**Caerlaverock Castle:** *Off B725, 9m S of Dumfries. Opening standard. (AM). Tel: 031-244 3101.* This seat of the Maxwell family dates back to 1270. In 1330, Edward I laid siege to it and in 1638 it capitulated to the Covenanters after a siege lasting 13 weeks. The castle is triangular with round towers. The heavy machicolation is 15th century and over the gateway between two splendid towers can be seen the Maxwell crest and motto. The interior was reconstructed in the 17th century as a Renaissance mansion, with fine carving.

**Caerlaverock National Nature Reserve:** *B725, S of Dumfries by Caerlaverock Castle. All year. Free. (NCC). Tel: Glencaple (038 777) 275.* 13,594 acres of salt marsh and intertidal mud and sand flats between the River Nith and the Lochar Water. A noted winter haunt of wildfowl, including barnacle geese. Access unrestricted, except in sanctuary area (600 acres), but intending visitors should contact the warden for advice on safety. Care must be taken relating to tides and quicksand.

**Cameronians (Scottish Rifles) Regimental Museum:** *Mote Hill, off Muir Street, Hamilton. All year. Mon-Sat 1000-1300, 1400-1700, closed all day Thursday. Free. Tel: Hamilton (0698) 428 688.* Display of uniforms, medals, banners, silver and documents, relating to the regiment and also to Covenanting times.

**Carfin Grotto:** *Carfin Village, 2m N of Motherwell. Daily. Outdoor devotions only on Sun (May-Oct) at 1500. Free. Tel: Motherwell (0698) 63308.* Grotto of Our Lady of Lourdes and a place of pilgrimage. Hall open for teas during the summer (Sunday only).

**Carrick Castle:** *On W bank of Loch Goil, 5m S of Lochgoilhead. All reasonable times. Free. Tel: (0698) 66111, ext. 2245.* Built in the 14th century and first recorded in 1511, the walls of this great rectangular keep are entire though roofless. The Argylls kept their writs and charters here, and used it as a prison. Fortified in 1651 in expectation of a siege by Commonwealth forces, it was burned by the Earl of Atholl's troops in 1685.

**Castle Kennedy Gardens:** *N of A75, 3m E of Stranraer. Apr-Sep, daily 1000-1700. Tel: Stranraer (0776) 2024.* The Earl and Countess of Stair live at the adjoining Castle. These are nationally famous

gardens particularly well known for their rhododendrons, azaleas, magnolias and embothriums. The notable pinetum was the first in Scotland. Tearoom and plant centre.

**Castle Sween:** *On E shore of Loch Sween, 15m SW of Lochgilphead. All reasonable times. Free. (AM). Tel: 031-244 3101.* This is probably the oldest stone castle on the Scottish mainland, built in the mid-12th century. It was destroyed by Sir Alexander MacDonald in 1647.

**Coats Observatory:** *Coats Observatory, Oakshaw Street, Paisley. Mon-Fri 1400-1700, Sat 1000-1300 and 1400-1700. Free. Groups by prior arrangement. (Renfrew District Council). Tel: 041-889 3151.* There has been a continuous tradition of astronomical observation and meteorological recording since the observatory was built in 1882. The recent updating of seismic equipment and the installation of a satellite weather picture receiver has made it one of the best equipped observatories in the country.

**'Countess Fiona':** *Cruising on Loch Lomond from Balloch pier. Easter to end Sep daily 1015; also July & August 1545. (Alloa Brewery Co Ltd). Tel: 041-226 4271.* The only traditional type cruise ship now on Loch Lomond. Covered observation lounge, ample seated deck area. Full 5-hour (approx) cruise from Balloch calls at

Luss, Rowardennan, Tarbet and Inversnaid. Licensed bar and self-service snack bar.

**Crarae Glen Garden:** *A83, 10m SW of Inveraray. All year, daily 0900-1800. (Crarae Garden Charitable Trust). Tel: Minard (0546) 86633.* Among the lovliest open to the public in Scotland, these gardens of Crarae Lodge, beside Loch Fyne and set in a Highland Glen, are note for rhododendrons, azaleas, conifers and ornamental shrubs.

**Crossraguel Abbey:** *A77, 2m SW of Maybole. Opening standard, except Oct-Mar Thu and Fri. (AM). Tel: 031-244 3101.* A Cluniac monastery built in 1244 by the Earl of Carrick during the reign of Alexander II. The Abbey was inhabited by Benedictine monks from 1244 until the end of the 16th century, and the extensive remains are of high architectural distinction. The gatehouse and dovecot are specially illuminating.

**Culzean Castle and Country Park:** *A719, 12m SSW of Ayr. Castle: open 1–10 Apr, 1 May-31 Aug daily 1000-1800; 11-30 April, 1 Sep-31 Oct daily 1200-1700 (last tour ½ hour before closing), other times throughout the year by appointment. Country Park, all year, daily 9-sunset. Visitor Centre, shop, etc. open 1-30 Apr, 1 Sep-31 Oct, daily 1000-1700; 1 May-31 Aug, daily 1000-1800. Best seen Apr-Sep. (NTS; Strathclyde Regional Council; Kyle and*

Carrick, Cunninghame, Cumnock and Doon Valley District Councils). Tel: Kirkoswald (065 56) 274. The splendid castle, one of Robert Adam's most notable creations, although built around an ancient tower of the Kennedy's dates mainly from 1777. Special features are the Round Drawing Room, the fine plaster ceilings and magnificent oval staircase. The Eisenhower Presentation explains the General's associaion with Culzean.

In 1970 Culzean became the first country park in Scotland; in 1973 a Reception and Interpretation Centre with exhibition etc was opened in the farm buildings designed by Robert Adam. The 565-acre grounds include a walled garden established in 1783, aviary, swan pond, camelia house and orangery. Ranger naturalist service with guided walks, talks and films in summer. Licensed self-service restaurant.

**Darvel:** *Under 10m E of Kilmarnock on A71.* Birth place of Sir Alexander Fleming, discoverer of penicillin; a garden commemorates him and his work.

**Doune Castle:** *Off A84 at Doune, 8m NW of Stirling. Opening standard except Oct-Mar closed, Fri and alternate Sat. (AM). Tel: 031-244 3101.* Splendid ruins of one of the best preserved mediaeval castles in Scotland, built late 14th or early 15th century by the Regent Albany. After his

execution in 1424 it came into the hands of the Stuarts of Doune, Earls of Moray, in the 16th century, and the 'Bonnie Earl of Moray' lived here before his murder in 1592. The bridge in the village was built in 1535 by Robert Spittal, James IV's tailor, to spite the ferryman who had refused him a passage.

**Doune Motor Museum:** *At Doune on A84, 8m NW of Stirling. Apr-Oct, daily 1000-1700. (Earl of Moray). Tel: Doune (0786) 841 203.* The Earl of Moray's collection of vintage and post-vintage cars, including examples of Hispano Suiza, Bentley, Jaguar, Aston Martin, Lagonda and the second oldest Rolls Royce in the world. Cafeteria.

**Drumlanrig Castle:** *Off A76, 3m N of Thornhill, Dumfriesshire and 16m off A74 by A702. Tel: Thornhill (0848) 30248.* Unique example of late 17th century Renaissance architecture in pink sandstone, built on the site of earlier Douglas strongholds. Set in parkland ringed by the wild Dumfriesshire hills. Louis XIV furniture, and paintings by Rembrandt, Holbein, Murillo, Ruysdael. Adventure woodland play area, nature trail, gift shop and tearoom. Guide dogs by prior arrangement. Lift available but unaccompanied.

**Dunblane Cathedral:** *In Dunblane, A9, 6m N of Stirling. Opening standard, except summer when 1400-*

1700 on Sunday. Free. (AM). Tel: 031-244 3101. The existing building dates mainly from the 13th century but incorporates a 12th-century tower. The nave was unroofed after the Reformation but the whole building was restored in 1829-95.

**Dundonald Castle:** $4^{1/2}m$ *SW of Kilmarnock.* Both Robert II and Robert III of Scotland died here. On isolated hill, most of the tower survives.

**Electric Brae:** *A719 9m S of Ayr (also known as Croy Brae). All times. Free.* An optical illusion is created so that a car appears to be going down the hill when it is in fact going up.

**Ellisland Farm:** *Off A76, $6^{1/2}m$ NNW of Dumfries. All reasonable times, but intending visitors are advised to phone in advance. Free. (Ellisland Trust). Tel: Dumfries (0387) 74 426.* Robert Burns took over this farm in June 1788, built the farmhouse, and tried to introduce new farming methods. Unsuccessful, he became an Exciseman in September 1789; in August 1791 the stock was auctioned, and he moved to Dumfries in November 1791. Some of the poet's most famous works were written at Ellisland, including *Tam o'Shanter* and *Auld Lang Syne*. The Granary houses a display showing Burns as a farmer. Farmhouse with museum room; granary building with Burns display; riverside walk.

**Finlarig Castle:** *S point of Loch Tay near Killin.* One time seat of the Breadalbanes these ruins have a beheading pit thought to be the only one left in Scotland.

**Finlaystone:** *By A8 W of Langbank, 17m W of Glasgow. Mon-Sat 0900-1700, Sun 1400-1700 (Woods and Gardens). (House) Apr-Aug, Sun afternoon, or by arrangement. (Mr George MacMillan). Tel: Langbank (047 554) 285 (1230-1300 or evenings).* Country estate with woodland walks, nursery gardens, formal gardens, adventure playgrounds and pony trekking. Countryside Ranger Service. The house has some fine rooms, Victorian relics, flower prints and an international collection of dolls shown in the billiard room. Historical connections with John Knox and Robert Burns. Afternoon teas (Apr-Sep).

**Galloway Deer Museum:** *On A712, by Clatteringshaws Loch, 6m W of New Galloway. Apr-Sep, daily 1000-1800. Free. (FC). Tel: New Galloway (064 42) 285.* The museum, in a converted farm steading, has a live trout exhibit as well as many features on deer and other aspects of Galloway wildlife, Geology and history. Bruce's Stone on Raploch Moss is a short walk away.

**Galloway Forest Park:** *Off A714, 10m NW of Newton Stewart. Free. (FC). Tel:* *Newton Stewart (0671) 2420.* 250 square miles of magnificent countryside in Central Galloway, including Merrick (2,765 feet) the highest hill in southern Scotland. The land is owned by the Forestry Commission and there is a wide variety of leisure facilities including forest trails, fishing, a red deer range, a wild goat park, a forest drive and a deer museum. Murray's monument dominates a hillside off the A712. It was erected to commemorate the son of a local shepherd who became a professor at Edinburgh University.

**Galloway House Gardens:** *At Garlieston, 8m S of Wigtown. All year, daily, all reasonable times. Admission by collection box, in aid of Scotland's Garden Scheme and Sorbie Church Organ Fund. Tel: Garlieston (098 86) 225.* Galloway House was built in 1740 by Lord Garlies, eldest son of the 7th Earl of Galloway, and later enlarged by Burn, and the hall decorated by Lorimer. Not open to the public.
The grounds cover some 30 acres and go down to the sea and sandy beach. There are fine old trees, and as a speciality in May/June there is a well-grown handkerchief tree. In season there are many snowdrops, pretty old-fashioned daffodils and a good collection of rhododendrons and azaleas. Also a walled garden with greenhouses and a camellia house. Home-baked teas are available in Garlieston village.

**Girvan:** *23m S of Ayr on A77.* Small fishing port from which boat trips to the 114 foot high Ailsa Craig take place. Also the location of Grant's Whisky distillery.

**Glenkiln:** *10m NNW of Dumfries, unclassified road by the reservoir.* Around the reservoir stand sculptures by Henry Moore, Epstein, Rodin and others.

**Glenluce Abbey:** *Off A75, 2m N of Glenluce. Opening standard. (AM). Tel: 031-244 3101.* Founded in 1192 by Roland, Earl of Galloway, for the Cistercian order. A fine vaulted chapter house is of architectural interest.

**Greenhill Covenanter's House:** *In Biggar on A702, 26m from Edinburgh, A74 (South) 12m. Easter, then mid May-mid Oct, daily 1400-1700. (Biggar Museum Trust). Tel: Biggar (0899) 21050.* Burn Braes Farmhouse, rescued in ruinous condition and rebuilt at Biggar, ten miles from the original site. Exhibits include relics of local Covenanters, Donald Cargill's bed (1681), 17th century furnishings, costume dolls rare breeds of animals and poultry. Reduced price for joint admission to Gladstone Court Street Museum. Audio-visual programme.

**Kilberry Sculptured Stones:** *Off B8024, 20m SSW of Lochgilphead. All reasonable times. Free. (AM). Tel: 031-244 3101.* A fine collection of late mediaeval sculptured stones.

**Kilmarnock:** *13m N of Ayr on A77.* The first collection of poems by Robert Burns was published here in 1786; a copy and other original mss are held at the Burns museum. Dean Castle has outstanding collection of mediaeval musical instruments and is within the Dean Castle Country Park. The Johnnie Walker distillery is open for visitor's tours.

**Kirkoswald:** *15m S of Ayr on A77.* Souter Johnnie's cottage a thatched 18th century house, was once the home of John Davidson, the souter or cobbler of Burn's Tam o'Shanter.

**Land O'Burns Centre:** *Opposite Alloway Kirk, 2m S of Ayr. All year, daily, spring and autumn 1000-1730, Jun 1000-1730, Jul-Aug 1000-1800, winter 1000-1700. Admission free, small charge for audio-visual display (Kyle and Carrick District Council). Tel: Ayr (0292) 43700.* This visitor centre has an exhibition area and an audio-visual display on the life and times of Robert Burns. Landscaped gardens.

**Livingstone National Memorial:** *At Blantyre, A724, 3m NW of Hamilton. All year, daily 1000-1800, Sun 1400-1800. Tel: Blantyre (0698) 823140.* Shuttle Row is an 18th-century block of mill tenements where David Livingstone, the famous explorer/missionary was born in 1813, went to school and worked while studying to become a doctor. The National Memorial, containing very many interesting relics of the Industrial Revolution and of Africa, is in this building, now surrounded by parkland. The Africa Pavilion illustrates modern Africa and a Social History museum deals with agriculture, cotton spinning and mining in Blantyre and district. Tearoom, gardens, picnic area, play equipment and paddling pool.

**Loch Doon Castle:** *From A713, 10:m S of Dalmellington, take road to Loch Doon. All reasonable times. Free. (AM). Tel: 031-244 3101.* This early 14th-century castle was devised to fit the island on which it was originally built. When the waters of the loch were raised in connection with a hydro-electric scheme the castle was dismantled and re-erected on the shores of the loch. The walls of this massive building, once known as Castle Balliol, vary from 7-9 feet thick and stand about 26 feet high.

**Lochore Meadows Country Park:** *Between Lochgelly and Ballingry on B920. (Country Park) At all times. (Park Centre) Summer 0800-2000, winter 0900-1700. (Fishery) 15 Mar-6 Oct. (Country Park facilities: rates on application). Tel: Ballingry (0592) 860086.* Green, pleasant countryside around large loch reclaimed from coal mining waste in the 1960s. Reclamation makes fascinating story told in slide show, displays and ranger guided walks.

# TURN TO
# PAGES 2-5
# FOR
# COLOUR
# ROAD MAPS

Plenty of scope for birdwatching, wildlife study, walks, picnics. Many ancient historical remains. Cafe and information in park centre. Activities include boat and bank fishing, sailing, windsurfing, canoeing, golf, horse riding, trim trail, wayfaring, self-guided trails, picnic areas and cafeteria. Wide range of provisions for visitors with special needs. Groups welcome.

**Lochwinnoch Nature Reserve:** *Largs Road, Lochwinnoch, 9m SW of Paisley. All year, daily 1000-1715. School parties by arrangement. (RSPB). Tel: Lochwinnoch (0505) 842663.* Purpose built Nature Centre with observation tower, displays and shop. Two observation hides overlooking marsh reached by walk through woods. Third hide overlooking Barr Loch. Shop.

**Logan Botanic Gardens:** *Off B7065, 14m S of Stranraer. Daily Apr-Sep 1000-1700. Tel: Stranraer (0776) 86231.* Here a profusion of plants from the warm and temperate regions of the world flourish in some of the mildest conditions in Scotland. There are cabbage palms, tree ferns and many other Southern Hemisphere species. Salad bar, meals served all day.

**Logan Fish Pond:** *Off B7065, 14m S of Stranraer. Easter-Sep, Mon, Wed-Fri and Sun 1000-1200, 1400-1730. (Sir Ninian Buchan-Hepburn, Bt). Tel: Ayr (0292) 268181.* This tidal pool in the rocks, 30 feet deep and 53 feet round, was completed in 1800 as a fresh-fish larder for Logan House. Damaged by a mine in 1942, it was reopened in 1955. It holds some 30 fish, mainly cod, so tame that they come to be fed by hand.

**McLean Museum and Art Gallery:** *Greenock. All year, Mon-Sat 1000-1200, 1300-1700. Free. (Inverclyde District Council). Tel: Greenock (0475) 23741.* A local museum with art collection, natural history, shipping exhibits, ethnographic material and items relating to James Watt, who was born in Greenock. Small shop. Wheelchair access at rear of building.

**Mar's Wark:** *At the top of Castle Wynd, Stirling. All times. Free. (AM). Tel: 031-226 2570.* Mar's Wark is one of a number of fine old buildings on the approach to Stirling Castle. Built c 1570 by the first Earl of Mar, Regent of Scotland, it was a residence of the Earls of Mar until the 6th Earl had to flee the country after leading the 1715 Jacobite Rebellion.

**Maxwelton House:** *13m NW of Dumfries on B729, near Moniaive. (Garden): Apr-Sep, Mon-Thu 1400-1700. (Chapel): Apr-Sep, daily 1000-1800. (House & Museum): Jul-Aug, Mon-Thu 1400-1700. House at other times by appointment only. Admission charge. (Mr Paul Stenhouse). Tel: Moniaive (084 82) 385.* The house dates back to the 14th/15th centuries. Originally it was a stronghold of the Earls of Glencairn and later the birthplace of Annie Laurie, to whom William Douglas of Fingland wrote the famous poem. Museum of early kitchen, dairy and small farming implements.

**Maybole:** *10m S of Ayr on A77.* Stronghold of the Earls of Cassilis, the chiefs of the Kennedy's. A 17th century mansion used by them has been restored.

**Muirshiel Country Park:** *Off B786, N of Lochwinnoch, 9m SW of Paisley. Free. (Strathclyde Regional Council). Tel: Lochwinnoch (0505) 842803.* Attractive countryside featuring trails and walks in a high valley above moorland, with picnic sites and an information centre.

**Museum of the Scottish Lead Mining Industry:** *Goldscaur Road, Wanlockhead, on B797, 8m ENE of Sanquhar. Easter-Sep, daily 1100-1600. (Wanlockhead Museum Trust). Tel: Wanlockhead (065974) 387.* Indoor museum with mining and social relics. Visitor lead mine. Open air museum with beam engines, mines, smelt mill, but-and-ben cottages. Miners' Reading Society Library, founded 1756. Local gold, silver and minerals collection. Situated near Scotland's highest village.

**Old Blacksmith's Shop Visitor Centre:** *Gretna Green, just off A74 at Scottish/English border. Daily, all year. Tel: Gretna (0461) 38363/38224.* The old Blacksmith's Shop, famous for runaway marriages, has a museum with anvil marriage room and coach house. Gretna was once a haven for runaway couples seeking to take advantage of Scotland's then laxer marriage laws, when couples could be married by a declaration before witnesses; this was made illegal in 1940. Elopers can still, however, take advantage of Scots law permitting marriage without parental consent at 16. Among places where marriages took place were the Old Toll Bar (now bypassed) when the road opened in 1830, and the Smithy. Restaurant, bar and souvenir shop.

**Orchardton Tower:** *Off A711, 6m SE of Castle Douglas. Opening standard. Free. Apply custodian at nearby cottage. (AM). Tel: 031-244 3101.* An example, unique in Scotland, of a circular tower house, built by John Cairns about the middle of the 15th century.

**Paisley Abbey:** *In Paisley, 7m W of Glasgow. Outwith the hours of divine worship, open all year, Mon-Sat 1000-1500. Closed 1230-1330. Free. Group visits by arrangement. Tel: 041-889 7654 (0930-1230).* A fine Cluniac Abbey Church founded in 1163. Almost completely destroyed by order of Edward I of England in 1307. Rebuilt and restored after Bannockburn and in the century following. In 1553 the tower collapsed, wrecking N-transept, crossing the choir; they lay open to the sky for 350 years while the nave alone

was the parish church; but they were rebuilt and rejoined to the nave this century (1898-1907 and 1922-28). The choir contains a fine stone-vaulted roof, stained glass and the tombs of Princess Marjory Bruce and King Robert III. See the St. Mirin Chapel with St. Mirin carvings (1499). Note outside the Norman doorway, cloisters and Place of Paisley. The Barochan Cross, a weathered Celtic cross, 11 feet high and attributed to the 10th century, is also in the Abbey.

**Queen Elizabeth Forest Park:** *Between the E shore of Loch Lomond and the Trossachs. (FC).* In this 45,000 acres of forest, moor and mountainside there are many walks. On A821 is the David Marshall Lodge, a picnic pavilion and information centre. 'Duke's Road' from Aberfoyle to the Trossachs has fine views.

**Raiders Road:** *From A712 near Clatteringshaws Dam, or A762 at Bennan near Mossdale. Jun-Sep daily 0900-2100. (FC).* A 10-mile forest drive through the fine scenery of the Galloway Forest Park.

**Rob Roy's Grave:** *Balquhidder Churchyard, off A84, 14m NNW of Callander. All reasonable times. Free.* Three flat gravestones enclosed by railings are the graves of Rob Roy, his wife and two of his sons. The church itself contains St Angus' Stone (8th century), a 17th century bell from the old church and old Gaelic Bibles.

**Scotland's Safari Park:** *At Blair Drummond on A84 between Stirling and Doune (exit 10 off M9). 26 Mar-3 Oct (approx), daily from 1000. Admission charge for car and per head; includes several attractions; alternatively, safari bus available for visitors without own transport. Admission charge includes attractions inside. Last admission 1630. Group rates. For details of times and charges Tel: Doune (0786) 841456.* The collection includes lions, zebras, camels, a monkey jungle, giraffes, tigers, antelopes, bison, Ankole cattle and Pere David deer. There is a Pets Corner, aquatic mammal shows, Boat Safari round chimp island and an adventure playground. Self-service restaurant and bar, ice cream kiosks. Drive through wild animal reserves. Cinema (180). Giant astraglide, amusements, picnic and barbecue areas, shops. Kennels for dogs and special arrangements for groups of disabled visitors.

**Skelmorlie Aisle:** *Bellman's Close, off main street, Largs. Opening standard, closed in winter. Free. (AM). Tel: 031-244 3101.* A splendid mausoleum of 1636, with painted roof, interesting tombs and monuments.

**SS 'Sir Walter Scott':** *From Trossachs Pier, E end of Loch Katrine, 9m W of Callander. Early May-late Sep, Mon-Fri 1100, 1345 and 1515, Sat & Sun 1400 and 1530. (Strathclyde Regional Council Water Dept). Tel: 041-336 5333.*

Regular sailings in summer from the pier to Stronachlachar in this fine old steamer. Views include Ben Lomond. Cafeteria, shop, visitor centre.

**Stirling Bridge:** *By A9 off Stirling town centre. All times. Free.* The Old Bridge built c 1400, was for centuries of great strategic importance as the 'gateway to the north' and the lowest bridging point of the River Forth.

**Stirling Castle:** *In central Stirling. Apr-Sep, Mon-Fri 0930-1715, Sun 1030-1645; Oct-Mar, Mon-Sat 0930-1620, Sun 1230-1535, (AM). Tel: 031-244 3101.* Stirling Castle on its 250-feet great rock has dominated much of Scotland's vivid history. Wallace recaptured it from the English in 1297; Edward I retook it in 1304, until Bruce won at nearby Bannockburn in 1314. Later it was a favourite Royal residence: James II was born here in 1430 and Mary, Queen of Scots and James VI both spent some years here. Long used as a barracks, and frequently rebuilt, the old towers built by James IV remain, as do the fine 16th-century hall, the splendid Renaissance palace of James V, the Chapel Royal of 1594 and other buildings. On castle hill there is a visitor centre (same hours as castle; NTS) which has an audio-visual display as an introduction to the castle.

**Strathclyde Country Park:** *On both sides of M74 between Hamilton and Bothwell interchanges (A723 and A725). All year.* Free (charges for facilities). Tel: Motherwell (0698) 66155. A countryside park with man-made loch, nature reserve (permit only), sandy beach and a wide variety of sporting facilities. Within the park is Hamilton Mausoleum, created in the 1840's by the 10th Duke of Hamilton, which has a remarkable echo and huge bronze doors. Tours start: Summer daily at 1500, also Sat and Sun at 1900; winter Sat and Sun at 1400 (groups by arrangement, tel: Motherwell (0698) 66155).

**Threave Castle:** *N of A75, 3m W of Castle Douglas. Opening standard. Admission free. (AM). Tel: 031-244 3101.* Early stronghold of the Black Douglases, on an island in the Dee. The four-storeyed tower was bult between 1639 and 1690 by Archibald the Grim, Lord of Galloway. In 1455 it was the last Douglas stronghold to surrender to James II.

**Threave House Gardens and Wildfowl Refuge:** *S of A75, 1m W of Castle Douglas. Gardens: all year, daily 0900-sunset. Walled garden and glasshouses all year 0900-1700. Visitor Centre: Easter weekend-31 Oct. Wildfowl refuge: access Nov-Mar. Tel: (0556) 2575.* The gardens of this Victorian mansion display acres of naturalised daffodils in April and May. There are peat, rock and water gardens and a visitor centre. The garden is of 60 acres and is at its best in June to August with good autumn colours in November. Threave Wildfowl refuge nearby is a roosting and feeding place for many species of wild geese and ducks on and near the River Dee, access during November to March, to selected points only to avoid disturbance. Tearoom.

**Torhouse Stone Circle:** *Off B733, 4m W of Wigtown. All reasonable times. Free. (AM). Tel: 031-244 3101.* A circle of 19 boulders standing on the edge of a low mound. Probably Bronze Age.

**Wallace Memorial:** *On A737, 2m W of Paisley at Elderslie. All times. Free.* The town is the traditional birthplace of William Wallace. A modern memorial has been erected near an old house, perhaps on the site of the patriot's former home.

**Wallace Monument:** *Off A997 (Hillfoots Road), 1½m NNE of Stirling. Daily. Feb, Mar, Oct, 1000-1630, closed Wed & Thu; Apr-Sep, 1000-1730; May, Jun, Jul, Aug, 1000-1830. (Stirling District Council). Tel: Stirling (0786) 72140.* Commemorates William Wallace, who defeated the English at the Battle of Stirling Bridge in 1297. Built in 1870, with a statue of Wallace on the side of the tower. There are two audio-visual displays, a cafe, woodland walks and the Wallace Sword.

**Weaver's Cottage:** *At Kilbarchan, off A737, 5m W of Paisley. Easter-29 May, 1 Sep-end Oct, Tue, Thu, Sat and Sun 1400-1700; 1 Jun-31 Aug, daily 1400-1700, last admission*

*1630. (NTS). Tel: Kilbarchan (050 57) 5588.* In the 18th century Kilbarchan was a thriving centre of handloom weaving. The cottage is preserved as a typical weaver's home of the period, with looms, weaving equipment and domestic utensils. Attractive cottage garden.

**Whithorn Priory and Museum:** *Main Street, Whithorn, 10m S of Wigtown. Opening standard except Oct-Mar closed, Mon-Fri. (AM). Tel: 031-244 3101.* Here St Ninian founded the first Christian Church in Scotland in 397. The present priory ruins date from the 12th century. Early Christian crosses, some carved in the rock, others now displayed in the museum attached to the priory are notable.

**Wigtown Museum:** *County Buildings, Wigtown. May-end Sep, Mon, Wed, Fri, 1400-1600. Free Tel: Stranraer (0776) 5088.* Town Museum telling the story of Wigtown martyrs. New signposts to points of interest in Wigtown. Shop. Information on town trail which can be followed by wheelchair users.

**TURN TO PAGES 2-5 FOR COLOUR ROAD MAPS**

**GLASGOW:** The tourist attractions of Edinburgh are long established and well-known, but Scotland's great commercial centre in the west has only in recent years begun to attract attention from the tourist. But it is definitely worth exploring while on a visit to Scotland. Fine Victorian architecture, more than seventy parks, splendid Botanic Gardens, a comprehensive range of museums, a cathedral described as the most complete early-Gothic church anywhere in the country, the Kelvingrove Galleries with an outstanding civic collection of paintings – these are some of the attractions for the visitor.

**Art Gallery and Museum:** *In Kelvingrove Park. All year, weekdays 1000-1700, Sun 1400-1700. Free. (Glasgow Museums and Art Galleries). Tel: 041-357 3929.* This fine municipal art collection has outstanding Flemish, Dutch and Italian canvases, including magnificent works by Giorgione and Rembrandt, as well as a wide range of French Impressionist and British pictures. Other areas include sculpture, furniture designed by Charles Rennie Mackintosh and his contemporaries, silver, pottery, glass and porcelain, an important collection of European arms and armour and displays of archaeological, historical and ethnographic material.
The natural history displays illustrate geology, with minerals, dinosaurs

and other fossils. There is a comprehensive collection of British birds. The natural history of Scotland is treated in depth in a developing new gallery. Alternative entrance for wheelchairs.

**The Barras:** *¼m E of Glasgow Cross. All year, Sat and Sun 0900-1700. Free. Tel: 041-552 7258 (Wed-Sun 1000-1600).* Glasgow's world famous weekend market, with an amazing variety of stalls and shops. Founded one hundred years ago, the Barras is now home to over 800 traders each weekend. Look out for the Barras archways, children's creche and buskers. Numerous licensed premises and cafes. All markets are covered.

**Botanic Gardens:** *Entrance from Great Western Road (A82). Gardens 0700-dusk; Kibble Palace 1000-1645; Main Range 1300 (Sun 1200)-1645. Closes 1615 Oct-Mar. Free. Tel: 041-334 2422.* The glasshouses contain a wide range of tropical plants including an internationally recognised collection of orchids and the 'National Collection' of begonias. The Kibble Palace, an outstanding Victorian glasshouse, has a unique collection of tree ferns and other plants from temperate areas of the world. Outside features include a Systematic Garden, a Herb Garden and a Chronological Border.

**The Burrell Collection:** *Pollok Country Park. All year, Weekdays 1000-1700, Sun 1400-1700. Free. (Glasgow Museums and*

*Art Galleries). Tel: 041-649 7151.* Housed in a building opened in 1983, a world famous collection of textiles, furniture, ceramics, stained glass, art objects and pictures (especially 19th century French) gifted to Glasgow by Sir William and Lady Burrell. Restaurant and bar, parking and facilities for handicapped.

**Glasgow Cathedral:** *At E end of Cathedral Street. Opening standard. Free. (AM). Tel: 031-244 3101.* The Cathedral, dedicated to St. Mungo, is the most complete survivor of the great Gothic churches of south Scotland. A fragment dates from the late 12th century, though several periods (mainly 13th century) are represented in its architecture. The splendid crypt of the mid-13th century is the chief glory of the cathedral, which is now the Parish Church of Glasgow.

**City Chambers:** *George Square, Mon-Fri, guided tours at 1030 and 1430 or by arrangement. Sometimes restricted owing to Council functions. Free. Tel: 041-227 4017/8 (0830-1700).* Built in Italian Renaissance style, and opened in 1888 by Queen Victoria. The interiors, particularly the function suites and the staircases, reflect all the opulence of Victorian Glasgow.

**Custom House Quay:** *N shore of the Clyde, between Glasgow Bridge and Victoria Bridge. Tel: 041-649 0331.* The Quay is part of the Clyde Walkway, an ambitious project to give new life to the riverside. By Victoria Bridge is moored the *Carrick* (1864) and there is a fine view of Carlton Place on the opposite bank.

**George Square:** The heart of Glasgow with the City Chambers and statues of Sir Walter Scott, Queen Victoria, Prince Albert, Robert Burns, Sir John Moore, Lord Clyde, Thomas Campbell, Dr Thomas Graham, James Oswald, James Watt, William Gladstone and Sir Robert Peel.

**Hunterian Art Gallery:** *Glasgow University, Hillhead Street, 2m NW of city centre. All year, Mon-Fri 0930-1700, Sat 0930-1300. Free. Tel: 041-330 5431.* Unrivalled collections of work by Charles Rennie Mackintosh, including reconstructed interiors of the architect's house, and by J M Whistler. Works by Rembrandt, Chardin, Stubbs, Reynolds, Pissarro, Sisley, Rodin, plus Scottish painting from the 18th century to the present. Sculpture Courtyard. Varied programme of temporary exhibitions from 16th century to present. Sales point, university refectory nearby. Alternative wheelchair entrance.

**Hunterian Museum:** *Glasgow University, 2m NW of city centre. All year, Mon-Fri 0930-1700, Sat 0930-1300. Free. Tel: 041-330 4221.* Glasgow's oldest museum, opened in 1807. Exhibits include geological, archaeological and ethnological material; new coin gallery and exhibition on history of Glasgow University. Scottish Museum of the Year Award 1983 and 1984. Temporary exhibitions of scientific instruments are exhibited in the Natural Philosophy Building. The anatomical and zoological collections, and manuscripts and early printed books, can be seen on application. Bookstall and small coffee house in 18th-century style. Alternative wheelchair entrance (via lift), please telephone.

**Charles Rennie MacKintosh Society:** *Queens Cross, 870 Garscube Road (enter by Springbank Street). All year, Tue, Thu, Fri 1200-1730, Sun 1430-1700, and by arrangement. Free. Tel: 041-946 6600.* Queens Cross, a MacKintosh church, and now the international headquarters of the Charles Rennie MacKintosh Society. Reference library and small exhibition area, bookstall and tearoom.

**Merchants' House:** *W side of George Square. May-Sep, Mon-Fri 1400-1600. Free. The hall and ante-rooms may be seen by arrangement. (The Merchants' House of Glasgow). Tel: 041-221 8272.* This handsome building occupies one of the best sites in the city. Built in 1874 by John Burnet, it contains the Glasgow Chamber of Commerce, the oldest in Britain, the fine Merchants' Hall with ancient relics and good stained-glass windows, and the House's own offices. Tour and commentary on history of Merchants' House.

## The Mitchell Library:
*North Street. Mon-Fri 0930-2100, Sat 0930-1700. Free. (Glasgow District Council). Tel: 041-221 7030.* Founded in 1874, this is the largest public reference library in Scotland, with stock of over one million volumes. Its many collections include probably the largest on Robert Burns in the world. Coffee room (1030-1630).

## Museum of Transport:
*Kelvin Hall, 1 Bunhouse Road. Free. Weekdays 1000-1700; Sun 1400-1700. All year. (Glasgow Museums and Art Galleries). Tel: 041-357 3929.* Opened Spring 1988. A new and considerably enlarged museum of the history of transport, including a reproduction of a typical 1938 Glasgow street. Other new features are a larger display of the ship models and a walk-in Motor Car Showroom with cars from the 1930s up to modern times. Other displays include Glasgow trams and buses, Scottish-built cars, fire engines, horse-drawn vehicles, commercial vehicles, cycles and motorcycles, railway locomotives and a Glasgow Subway station. Restaurant, fast food and bar facilities will be shared with the adjacent indoor Sports Centre Shop.

## People's Palace:
*In Glasgow Green. All year, weekdays 1000-1700, Sun 1400-1700. Free. (Glasgow Museums and Art Galleries). Tel: 041-554 0223.* Opened in 1898, contains important collections relating to the tobacco and other industries, Glasgow stained glass, ceramics, and political and social movements including temperance, co-operation, women's suffrage and socialism. Wholefood snack bar/tearoom in Winter Gardens and shop. Alternative wheelchair entrance at west door (Winter Gardens).

## Pollok House:
*2060 Pollokshaws Road (A736). All year, weekdays 1000-1700, Sun 1400-1700. Free. (Glasgow Museums and Art Galleries). Tel: 041-632 0274.* Built c 1750, with additions 1890-1908 designed by Sir Robert Rowand Anderson. It houses the Stirling Maxwell collection of Spanish and other European paintings. Also displays of furniture, ceramics, glass and silver (mostly 18th century). Tearoom, gardens and shop. Alternative wheelchair entrance to tearoom.

## Victoria Park and Fossil Grove:
*Victoria Park Drive North, facing Airthrey Avenue. Mon-Sat 0800-dusk; Sun 1000-dusk. Fossil Grove open by arrangement. Free. Tel: 041-959 2128.* Cornish elms, lime trees, formal flower garden and arboretum. Within the park is the famous Fossil Grove, with fossil stumps and roots of trees which grew here 230 million years ago.

## Zoo:
*6m SE of city centre on M74 (Glasgow/Carlisle). All year, daily 1000-1800. Tel: 041-771 1185/6.* A medium sized but developing open plan colllection, taking in 25 hectares, with another 25 more being developed. Many rare animals, most of them breeding. Speciality cats, reptiles; also education department. Long walks, picnic areas, children's showground and car park.